# What Your Colleagues Are

Maria Walther speaks and writes from the lens of a practi[...] ...[...] knowledge and respect for the classroom. This power-packed instructional resource spotlights enticing examples of high-quality children's literature, provides engaging read-aloud experiences, and offers *one hundred* aligned "bursts" of shared reading. There is a consistent emphasis on supporting students through human-centered lessons that balance social-emotional learning alongside literacy learning. Moreover, this invaluable resource seamlessly integrates phonemic awareness, phonics, vocabulary, and oral language with reading and writing. I have no doubt that this professional text will guide educators in all settings as they build community, cultivate classroom conversation, and support learners in a variety of joyful literacy learning experiences.

—**Pamela Koutrakos**, Instructional Coach and Author
*Word Study That Sticks, The Word Study That Sticks Companion,*
and *Mentor Texts That Multitask*

*Shake Up Shared Reading* is truly a multipurpose literacy resource and a gift to the teaching community. With tremendous respect for limited instructional minutes and competing priorities, Maria Walther shares her wisdom, knowledge, and commitment to learning, combining research and authentic experiences with practicality, flexibility, and responsiveness. Walther is an incredible curator of important picture books, and you are guaranteed to find the book and the lesson you need right now; you will also build your own capacity to tap into the power of books for students' development of empathy, citizenship, and literacy.

—**Melanie Meehan**, Author
*Every Child Can Write*, and Coauthor, *The Responsive Writing Teacher*

*Shake Up Shared Reading* is the professional book we keep on our shelves and reach for as a forever reminder for what matters in the elementary classroom: purposeful and joyful reading experiences. Maria Walther brings that joy to life in practical application with clear learning targets connected to 100 shared-reading texts and connected lessons that grow student learning, in addition to blueprints for how to do it ourselves. Perhaps more than anything, I respect Maria's exaltation of varied voices in children's literature in order to ensure for students a more accurate, robust, and truthful understanding of the world. This is a cornerstone text for now.

—**Nawal Qarooni Casiano**
Educator, Author, Literacy Coach, and Staff Developer

Maria Walther has done it again in her new book, *Shake Up Shared Reading!* In it, she takes a familiar and often underutilized strategy and shows us how to implement it in new and important ways. It is a much-needed update of how the practice of shared reading can be used to invite active participation, support multilingual learners, and playfully teach foundational skills. From the first page to the last, this book is packed with practical and simple ways to shake up shared reading using a variety of thoughtfully curated books that will create and nurture communities of readers.

—**April Larremore**, Instructional Strategy Coordinator
Dallas Independent School District

This book is a gift to early literacy educators yearning to infuse more joyful and engaging learning experiences into our classrooms. By introducing us to 50 of the latest and greatest picture books, Maria Walther provides the tools and structure needed to bridge read-aloud and shared-reading interactions.

—**Jill Culmo**, Instructional Strategy Coordinator
Early Learning Department, Dallas ISD

Maria Walther has done it again! *Shake Up Shared Reading* is exactly the book I needed at exactly the right time. Teaching in a pandemic has been tough, but one saving grace has been our read-aloud time. Maria makes shared reading easy, engaging, and more importantly, exciting!

—**Vera Ahiyya**, Kindergarten Teacher
Author, *Rebellious Read Alouds*

*Shake Up Shared Reading* is an absolute must-read for anyone who finds themselves having the honor of reading to and with children. In this postpandemic time of varying entry-point levels, *Shake Up Shared Reading* allows practitioners to meet both individual and group needs for the oral language, critical discourse, and understanding of literary elements needed to propel student learning forward. Maria Walther provides engaging and focused reading interactions that lead to increased comprehension and fluency, while also strengthening learning applications for writing. Being intentional with our text interactions allows for a shared experience where students can confidently bridge scaffolded reading skills to independence, all while fostering a love of reading! *Shake Up Shared Reading* levels the playing field while concurrently elevating it for all, ensuring an equitable learning environment.

—**Hilda Martinez**, NBCT
Early Literacy Resource Teacher and RTI Coordinator
2020 San Diego County Teacher of the Year

*Shake Up Shared Reading* is a practical resource for teachers who are looking to connect their interactive read-aloud experiences to their shared-reading experiences. Maria Walther shares units with loads of read-aloud titles and short bursts of shared-reading experiences with the same titles to engage young readers in phonological awareness, fluency building, comprehension strategies, vocabulary building, attention to punctuation, and even the noticing of authors' craft moves. I can't wait to have this book in my hands, as I know I will turn to it whenever I work with teachers of early literacy.

—**Whitney La Rocca**, Literacy Consultant
Coauthor, *Patterns of Power*

Maria Walther's *Shake Up Shared Reading* is a breath of fresh air in a world where literacy instruction felt cloudy in the years of pandemic teaching. I can't remember the last time a professional reading ignited my excitement to plan a classroom lesson. It is evident that Walther wrote this book with the educator in mind by creating a resource that is both informational and enlightening. Educators will understand the importance of shared reading; they will get ideas for how to shake up shared reading all year long, and best of all, they will discover book recommendations.

—**Juan E. Gonzalez Jr.**
Elementary School Teacher, Speaker, and Social Media Content Creator

Shared reading is one of the most powerful, high-leverage instructional strategies for early readers. In her fabulous new book *Shake Up Shared Reading*, Maria Walther provides a deep dive into ways to make shared reading happen with purpose and meaning in your classroom. With a comprehensive menu of shared reading interactions, Maria walks teachers through the steps for providing deep, rich lessons. My favorite part? Designed to be "short bursts," sessions allow shared reading to fit into already busy schedules. So whether you are using shared reading often already or looking for ideas to start, *Shake Up Shared Reading* is a must-have guide for all early literacy educators.

—**Matt Halpern**, Education Consultant, Speaker and Author

# SHAKE UP SHARED READING

*To picture-book creators whose words and illustrations radiate off the page
and into the hearts and minds of children.*

Featuring
**100**
Shared Reading
Lessons

# SHAKE UP SHARED READING

♥ ♥ ♥

## Expanding on Read Alouds to Encourage Student Independence

♥ ♥ ♥

## Maria Walther

CORWIN Literacy

FOR INFORMATION:

Corwin

A SAGE Company

2455 Teller Road

Thousand Oaks, California 91320

(800) 233-9936

www.corwin.com

SAGE Publications Ltd.

1 Oliver's Yard

55 City Road

London EC1Y 1SP

United Kingdom

SAGE Publications India Pvt. Ltd.

B 1/I 1 Mohan Cooperative Industrial Area

Mathura Road, New Delhi 110 044

India

SAGE Publications Asia-Pacific Pte. Ltd.

18 Cross Street #10-10/11/12

China Square Central

Singapore 048423

President:  Mike Soules

Associate Vice President and
 Editorial Director:  Monica Eckman

Executive Editor:  Tori Mello Bachman

Content Development Editor:  Sharon Wu

Editorial Assistant:  Nancy Chung

Project Editor:  Amy Schroller

Copy Editor:  Sarah J. Duffy

Typesetter:  C&M Digitals (P) Ltd.

Proofreader:  Lawrence W. Baker

Indexer:  Integra

Cover Designer:  Gail Buschman

Marketing Manager:  Margaret O'Connor

Printed in the United States of America

*Library of Congress Cataloging-in-Publication Data*

Names: Walther, Maria P., author.

Title: Shake up shared reading, grades PreK-3 : expanding on read alouds to encourage student independence / Maria Walther.

Description: Thousand Oaks, California : Corwin, 2022. | Series: Corwin literacy | Includes bibliographical references and index.

Identifiers: LCCN 2021048222 | ISBN 9781071844830 (paperback) | ISBN 9781071872222 (epub) | ISBN 9781071872215 (epub) | ISBN 9781071872192 (pdf)

Subjects: LCSH: Reading (Elementary) | Oral reading. | Picture books for children—Educational aspects.

Classification: LCC LB1573.5 .W353 2022 | DDC 372.4—dc23/eng/20211103
LC record available at https://lccn.loc.gov/2021048222

This book is printed on acid-free paper.

22 23 24 25 26 10 9 8 7 6 5 4 3 2 1

# Contents

Acknowledgments                                                                xi
About the Author                                                               xiii

## Introduction                                                                1

Share the Book, Share the Learning                                             1
Keep It Simple! Short Bursts of Shared Reading                                 2
Ten Reasons to Shake Up Shared Reading                                         4

   Creates Camaraderie                                                         4
   Elevates Texts and Celebrates Rereading                                     6
   Invites Active Participation                                                7
   Engages All Learners                                                        7
   Expands Oral Language Development                                           8
   Strengthens Story Sense                                                     9
   Fosters Fluency                                                             9
   Demonstrates the Reading Process                                            10
   Supports Multilingual Learners                                             11
   Offers a Supportive Instructional Context                                   11

Build Bridges—Connect Read-Aloud Experiences
   and Shared Reading Interactions                                             11

   Read Aloud and Shared Reading: All About Conversation                       12
   A Quick Peek at a Read-Aloud Experience                                     13
   What's New?                                                                 13
      Key Vocabulary: Kid-Friendly Definitions                                 13
      Extend the Experience                                                    13

Three Steps to Successful Shared Reading Interactions                          16

   Step 1: Highlight a Literacy Skill or Strategy                              16
      • Listen for Sounds (Phonological Awareness)                             17
      • Match Letters to Sounds (Phonics)                                      19
      • Spotlight High-Frequency Words                                         20
      • Ponder Punctuation                                                     20
      • Reread for Fluency                                                     20
      • Wonder About Words                                                     21
      • Reread to Boost Comprehension                                          21
      • Notice Writer's Craft Moves                                            21

Step 2: Select Irresistible Texts     22

Step 3: Plan the Short Burst     25

     Before Reading     25

     During Reading     25

     After Reading     25

**Four Ways You Might Use This Book**     **27**

Strengthen the Read Aloud–Shared Reading Connection     27

Enhance Your Literacy Curriculum     27

Joyfully Teach Foundational Skills and Strategies     27

Share Quick Snippets of Clear Instruction Virtually     28

## ① Chapter 1: Reading, Learning, and Talking Together     31

**A Year of Promise and Possibility**     **31**

**Menu of Shared Reading Interactions**     **32**

**Develop Self-Awareness**

     Be Who You Are: *A Normal Pig* (Steele, 2019)     34

     Be Your Best Self: *I Promise* (James, 2020)     38

**Identify Feelings and Emotions**

     Infer Characters' Feelings: *Watch Me* (Richards, 2021)     42

     Empathize With Characters' Feelings:
       *Not Quite Snow White* (Franklin, 2019)     46

**Think Flexibly**

     Notice Characters' Decisions: *Harlem Grown: How One Big
       Idea Transformed a Neighborhood* (Hillery, 2020)     50

     Notice Characters' Reactions: *When Grandpa
       Gives You a Toolbox* (Deenihan, 2020)     54

**Strategically Problem Solve**

     Make a New Plan: *Dirt Cheap* (Hoffman, 2020)     58

     Consider the Consequences: *The Last Tree* (Haworth-Booth, 2020)     62

**Persist**

     Keep Trying: *Oona* (DiPucchio, 2021)     66

     Be Patient: *Jabari Tries* (Cornwall, 2020)     70

**Empathize**

     Show You Care: *What's the Matter, Marlo?* (Arnold, 2020)     74

     Work to Understand Others: *I Talk Like a River* (Scott, 2020)     78

**Build Relationships**

     Notice How Relationships Begin: *Swashby and the Sea* (Ferry, 2020)     84

     Notice How Relationships Change: *The Arabic Quilt* (Khalil, 2020)     88

## Chapter 2: Converse About Comprehension–Fiction　93

**Reading Between the Lines and Beyond the Page**　93

**Menu of Shared Reading Interactions**　94

### Describe and Understand Characters

Consider Characters' Actions: *Catch That Chicken!* (Atinuke, 2020)　96

Connect Characters' Actions to Character Traits: *Rocket Says Clean Up!* (Bryon, 2020)　102

### Study Story Structure

Identify Story Elements: *The Purple Puffy Coat* (Boelts, 2020b)　106

Use Story Elements to Predict and Retell: *The Pirates Are Coming!* (Condon, 2020)　110

### Engage in Illustration Study

Discover Details in Realistic Texts: *Simon at the Art Museum* (Soontornvat, 2020)　114

Discover Details in Imaginative Texts: *Lift* (Lê, 2020)　118

### Predict Using Evidence

Use Picture Clues to Predict: *Thank You, Omu!* (Mora, 2018a)　122

Predict Characters' Actions: *Harold Loves His Woolly Hat* (Kousky, 2018)　126

### Visualize Using Senses and Feelings

Spot Sensory Language: *My Papi Has a Motorcycle* (Quintero, 2019)　130

Use Your Imagination: *Milo Imagines the World* (de la Peña, 2021)　134

### Ponder Point of View

Notice Who's Talking: *I'm Sticking With You* (Prasadam-Halls, 2020)　138

Notice Characters' Opinions: *We Love Fishing!* (Bernstein, 2021)　142

### Read Between the Lines

Infer Big Ideas: *Outside In* (Underwood, 2020)　146

Learn Lessons From Characters: *Big Papa and the Time Machine* (Bernstrom, 2020)　150

## Chapter 3: Converse About Comprehension–Nonfiction　155

**Bringing the Outside Inside**　155

**Menu of Shared Reading Interactions**　156

### Spot Nonfiction Text Structures

Notice the Question-Answer Structure: *Whose House Is That?* (Tekiela, 2021)　158

Notice Unique Structures: *My Thoughts Are Clouds: Poems for Mindfulness* (Heard, 2021)　162

Integrate Information From Text and Images

Learn From Illustrations: *Flying Deep: Climb Inside Deep-Sea Submersible ALVIN* (Cusolito, 2018) — 166

Explore With Illustrations: *Red Rover: Curiosity on Mars* (Ho, 2019) — 170

Identify Main Topics and Key Details

Discover Details—Expository Nonfiction: *The Beak Book* (Page, 2021) — 174

Discover Details—Narrative Nonfiction: *Star of the Party: The Solar System Celebrates!* (Carr, 2021) — 178

Ask and Answer Questions

Wonder Before, During, and After Reading: *If Bees Disappeared* (Williams, 2021) — 182

Wonder as You Learn: *DROP: An Adventure Through the Water Cycle* (Moon, 2021) — 186

Consider the Author's Purpose

Take Action: *Sometimes People March* (Allen, 2020) — 190

Understand Important Events: *Outside, Inside* (Pham, 2021) — 194

# Chapter 4: Inspire Writers! 201

**Sharing Our Stories** — **201**

**Menu of Shared Reading Interactions** — **202**

Uncover Ideas

Write About Memories: *In a Jar* (Marcero, 2020) — 204

Write About Observations: *Ten Beautiful Things* (Griffin, 2021) — 208

Tell a Story

Tell a Real-Life Story: *Sunrise Summer* (Swanson, 2020) — 212

Tell a Make-Believe Story: *Octopus Stew* (Velasquez, 2019) — 216

Play With Patterns

Riddles: *A New Green Day* (Portis, 2020) — 220

Days of the Week Pattern: *I Want to Ride the Tap Tap* (Joseph, 2020) — 224

Try Out a Text Structure

Explain How To: *How to Find a Bird* (Ward, 2020) — 228

Share Facts in Creative Ways: *13 Ways to Eat a Fly* (Heavenrich, 2021) — 232

Collect Words

Point Out Playful Language: *Hello, Rain* (Maclear, 2021) — 236

Spot Sensory Language: *Over and Under the Rainforest* (Messner, 2020b) — 240

Pen a Poem

Learn From Poets: *Write! Write! Write!* (VanDerwater, 2020) — 246

Try Out Techniques: *The Last Straw: Kids vs. Plastics* (Hood, 2021) — 250

**References** — **255**

**Index** — **259**

# Acknowledgments

When I was quarantined in my home with only one other person, my husband, I had a lot of time for self-study and reflection. So, I want to begin my acknowledgments with the one I believe is the most important. I acknowledge that I've lived a life of white privilege, and although I strived throughout my teaching career to be responsive to the students in my care, I know I fell short in many areas. I own those shortcomings and am committed to doing the work necessary to unlearn and relearn. I welcome colleagues to call me into conversations that invite me to examine my missteps so that I can continue to grow toward being a responsive educator for the children and teachers whom I learn alongside.

While I was writing this book, the read-aloud area morphed into a Zoom screen, and collegial collaboration took place across the miles rather than around a table. Even so, and perhaps because of those changes, I was supported in my work by dedicated professionals and organizations who literally and figuratively shared their books and shared in my learning:

- Katherine Phillips-Toms: I'm so grateful to you for inviting me into your at-home classroom to observe virtual kindergarten learning and into your "Room and Zoom" classroom to wrap up the year. Seeing you in action during pandemic teaching was awe-inspiring. Your positivity and dedication to students is unmatched. Thanks, my friend, for continuing to be my thinking partner.

- The friends, colleagues, and students I've had the pleasure of learning alongside in my thirty-three-year career in Indian Prairie School District 204: The accumulated wisdom I gained from you permeates these pages.

- Karen Biggs-Tucker: Whenever I needed a book idea or a bit of encouragement, you were always a phone call or text message away—even while learning with fifth graders during a pandemic. I can always count on you to be the one who helps me find just the right book. I owe you!

- My #Here4Teachers colleagues, Pamela Koutrakos, Melanie Meehan, and Julie Wright: What can I say? We came together to figure our way through pandemic teaching and a community was born. Every interaction we shared made me smarter.

- The Writing Zone members, Nawal Qarooni Casiano, Pamela Koutrakos, Melanie Meehan, Christina Nosek, and Julie Wright: Although still in its infancy, this writing group has already pushed me to reflect on my process and embrace the messiness of writing (hard for this perfectionist!).

- My dear editor, Tori Bachman: I appreciate all the times you listened to me lament about pandemic writer's block and, in your own quiet way, encouraged me to keep at it. I don't know if this book would exist if it wasn't for those gentle nudges.

- Lisa Luedeke, Sharon Wu, Nancy Chung, and the rest of the Corwin team: I greatly appreciate the way you supported your authors during the pandemic and am grateful for your continued enthusiasm for my work.

- The following publishers who provided me with many of the titles that I included in this book: Candlewick, Disney/Hyperion, Macmillan Publishing Group, Penguin Random House, and Scholastic.

- The librarians at the West Branch of the Aurora Public Library: Without knowing it, you helped me out so much. Week after week, I ordered the picture books you had just processed so that I could stay on top of the latest and greatest. You cheerfully delivered them to our car even on the coldest of days. Kudos to you and to librarians everywhere!

As I put the finishing touches on this manuscript, I would be remiss if I didn't take a moment to thank my husband, Lenny, and our daughter, Katie, for the life we share. Whether we're hiking through the snow, cuddled up reading, or enjoying a meal out, every small moment we spend together brings me joy.

## Publisher's Acknowledgments

Corwin gratefully acknowledges the following reviewers:

Paula Bourque
Literacy Coach/Author
Gardiner, ME

Hilda Martinez
Response to Intervention Coordinator
San Diego, CA

Viviana Tamas
AIS Reading Teacher/Literacy Coach
White Plains, NY

# About the Author

Teacher, author, literacy consultant, and children's literature enthusiast, **Maria Walther** taught first grade for 34 years. Maria partners with teachers in their classrooms and inspires colleagues through engaging professional learning experiences. What educators appreciate most about Maria is her enthusiasm for teaching and her realistic approach toward classroom instruction. Maria earned a doctorate at Northern Illinois University and was named The Outstanding Literacy Alumni by the Department of Literacy Education for professionalism, service, and career success. Maria has been a longtime advocate of reading aloud. She was honored as *Illinois Reading Educator of the Year* and earned the *ICARE for Reading Award* for fostering the love of reading in children. The award that Maria cherishes the most is *The Most Influential Educator* given to her by one of her former first-grade students who is now a colleague. Maria is a prolific professional writer. She strives to create practical resources for busy teachers. Her best-selling book, *The Ramped-Up Read Aloud*, promotes joyful read aloud experiences. Learn more about her books at mariawalther.com and follow her on Twitter @mariapwalther.

*Excitement, engagement, joy, and learning all wrapped into one.*

*That's the beauty of a shared reading interaction.*

# INTRODUCTION

## Share the Book, Share the Learning

The lights are dimmed, there's a hush in the room as you turn the page of the book you're projecting on the interactive whiteboard. The minute a new page appears, kids immediately begin pointing to the words at the end of each line to confirm their prediction that the text will continue to rhyme. Excitement, engagement, joy, and learning all wrapped into one. That's the beauty of a shared reading interaction.

Rooted in the gradual release model (Pearson & Gallagher, 1983), shared reading offers children the opportunity to hear expressive oral reading that furthers their development as fluent readers (Allington, 2009). Then, with each successive rereading, learners deepen their understanding of how to process and comprehend text. Shared reading surrounds students at the beginning stages of literacy development with the language of stories and wealth of information found in nonfiction texts. If we think of gradual release as *I do, we do, you do,* shared reading is one component of the *we do* phase that bridges the teacher modeling that happens during the read-aloud experience and the application that occurs when we guide readers in small groups. Together, these essential literacy practices lead students toward independence.

As their collection of shared texts grows, so do students' abilities to apply the learning from these interactions to small-group learning experiences and to their personal reading and writing. Shared reading is a community event that welcomes children of all abilities and experiences to learn from and with each other (Fisher & Medvic, 2000). When readers join their voices together with their teacher and classmates, their competence and confidence grows. Therefore, shared reading not only strengthens students' literacy skills but also helps foster the relationships that are essential in a healthy classroom environment. Because shared reading provides the "cognitive lure of productive effort" (Burkins & Yaris, 2016, p. 53), it engages learners in the act of processing text and promotes a growth mindset. In fact, Regie Routman (2018) encourages us to do more shared reading because "the support of a shared-reading experience allows the use of more challenging content for all students, a crucial equity-access issue" (p. 144). With benefits like these, you can see why shared reading is an essential component of powerful reading instruction.

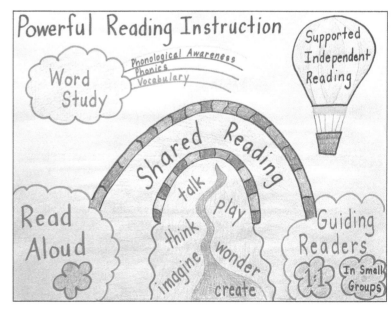

*Shared reading is an essential component of powerful reading instruction.*

# Keep It Simple! Short Bursts of Shared Reading

If you're thinking, "That all sounds great, Maria, but I don't have time to squeeze shared reading into my busy teaching day," I hear you! Classroom life has always been busy, but during the pandemic my colleagues and I lamented about having *even* less time. My solution to maximizing instructional time is—keep it simple!

With simplicity in mind, I'll share my take on shared reading, which stands on the shoulders of the shared reading advocates who came before me and meets the needs of today's learners and classrooms: Shared reading is a time when you collaborate with your students to reread and study key pages of a familiar text. During a shared reading interaction, the text is projected or is large enough for all learners to see. Together, you and students investigate the text to bring a transferable literacy skill or strategy to light—a behavior learners can approximate and apply as they read or write. A shared reading interaction can occur face-to-face or virtually with the whole class, a small group, or sitting beside an individual learner.

In this resource, you will find 100 short, laser-focused bursts of shared reading. Among the many benefits, these targeted shared reading interactions invite students to dig deeper, with a precise aim in mind. They are a perfect fit for virtual settings as they are clear and to the point (Fisher et al., 2021). Each short burst follows a predictable structure that you can easily use or adapt.

## The Benefits of Short Bursts of Shared Reading

- Responds to students' curiosities
- Invites wonder
- Nudges students to dig deeper
- Moves learners from understanding to application
- Builds on and broadens the read-aloud experience
- Bridges whole-group and small-group instruction
- Focuses on a wide range of literacy skills and strategies, including author's craft

As you're rereading, you will invite learners to pause and ponder at three key points in the book. Why three key points? First, zeroing in on three key pages or sections in the book keeps the interaction brief and engaging. Second, the three key pausing points are set up in a way that will guide you and your learners from teacher-led demonstration to student-led discovery using a *my turn*, *our turn*, *your turn* structure.

Each shared reading interaction is connected to and planned as a follow-up to a read-aloud experience. In other words, the read-aloud experience provides the foundation for the shared reading interaction that follows. Based on your schedule, the shared reading interaction can occur later that day, the next day, or whenever you notice your students are in need of that particular strategy. For each of the 50 read-aloud experiences featured in this book, I've designed two different short bursts of shared reading. The two shared reading options offer flexibility to respond to your students. Use your professional judgment to decide whether to do both bursts, choose the one that matches that needs and interests of your students, or create one of your own.

Keep reading to discover ten reasons to shake up shared reading along with actionable strategies to make shared reading work, whatever your learning context may be.

# Ten Reasons to Shake Up Shared Reading

Creates camaraderie

Elevates texts and celebrates rereading

Invites active participation

Engages all learners

Expands oral language development

Strengthens story sense

Fosters fluency

Demonstrates the reading process

Supports multilingual learners

Offers a supportive instructional context

# Ten Reasons to Shake Up Shared Reading

## Creates Camaraderie

Like adults, children bond over shared interactions. You might have fitness buddies or fellow sports enthusiasts. Each time you sweat or cheer together, the connection is strengthened. The same holds true for learners as they gather around a text in pursuit of better understanding the intricacies of reading or craft choices that writers make. Together, students can dip their toes into the reading pool and test out newly acquired strategies, with you and their peers buoying them up. You might choose to begin the year with a community-building book like *Where Are You From?* (Méndez, 2019). When you return to the first few pages to ponder the author's use of punctuation, both the theme of the story and the act of shared reading communicate to students, "We are in this together."

During shared reading interactions, children are "collaboratively negotiating meaning" (Parkes, 2000, p. 15). While teaching your students to work together in this way, you are also fostering the social-emotional learning (SEL) competencies identified by the Collaborative for Academic, Social, and Emotional Learning (CASEL). When you reframe your thinking about shared reading interactions in this way, they become a huge time saver because you're creating literacy lessons and a social-emotional learning experiences all rolled into one. The chart that follows is just a snapshot of the language you might use during shared reading to foster SEL competencies. Some of the questions and prompts are book-related, while others support learners in developing self-awareness and positive relationships. The shared reading interactions in Chapters 1 through 4 include language and ideas to continue the SEL conversation throughout the year.

*During shared reading children collaboratively negotiate meaning.*

## Foster SEL Competencies Through Shared Reading Interactions

| To Foster . . . | Say . . . | Try This Book . . . |
|---|---|---|
| **Self-awareness:** The ability to understand how one's feelings, thoughts, and actions guide behavior. To have an honest view of one's abilities. To be confident, optimistic, and possess a growth mindset. | • Can you infer how that character is feeling?<br>• If you were that character, how might you be feeling?<br>• You figured that out by yourself! That's what readers do!<br>• Thumbs up if using that strategy was a bit challenging.<br>• We can do this together! | *Gustavo the Shy Ghost* (Drago, 2020)<br><br>In her debut picture book, Mexican-born author and illustrator Flavia Z. Drago introduces readers to Gustavo, a violin-playing ghost who is terrified to make friends. In the end, he wins them over by inviting them to a Day of the Dead violin concert (held in a cemetery, of course!). |
| **Social awareness:** To be aware of the importance of perspective-taking and empathy. To celebrate diversity and respect others. | • Can you put yourself in that character's shoes?<br>• What would you have done in that situation?<br>• Notice how we all thought about that in different ways.<br>• Is your opinion the same as or different from your friend's opinion?<br>• Did something your friend said make you change your thinking? | *Watercress* (Wang, 2021)<br><br>This moving story shows how a young girl's embarrassment evolves into understanding when her mother shares a story of loss from her childhood in China. Andrea Wang's author's note explains, "This story is both an apology and a love letter to my parents." |
| **Responsible decision making:** To practice decision-making processes that weigh consequences and consider the well-being of oneself and others. | • What's the problem?<br>• What's one way we can work together to solve this problem?<br>• Are there other ways?<br>• What can we learn from trying out different solutions?<br>• How might our solution impact others?<br>• If we try something and it doesn't work, our brain will grow. | *Amara and the Bats* (Reynolds, 2021)<br><br>Bat-loving Amara moves to a new neighborhood and discovers that bats no longer inhabit the park. After sharing this issue with her classmates, the whole community pitches in to advocate for a nature reserve and create a bat-friendly sanctuary. Backmatter enhances the story with additional bat facts and ideas for helping bats. |
| **Self-management:** To self-regulate one's feelings, thoughts, and actions in a variety of situations. | • How was the character feeling?<br>• Have you ever felt that way?<br>• What do you do when you feel like that?<br>• How were the character's feelings and actions connected?<br>• Are there other ways the character could have reacted to that emotion? | *A Little Space for Me* (Olson, 2020)<br><br>A girl who lives with a busy multigenerational family realizes she needs some space. At school, she climbs to the top of the monkey bars to gather a bit of the universe above. After collecting so much "space" there's no room for anyone else, she discovers the importance of balance. |
| **Relationship skills:** To initiate and maintain healthy relationships with diverse individuals. | • Actively listen to your friend's idea.<br>• Ask your friend to share their thinking. How is it the same as or different from yours?<br>• What can you say if you don't agree?<br>• When you and your friend want to say something at the same time, what can you do? | *Listen* (Snyder, 2021)<br><br>A girl takes readers on a listening walk through her day. Along the way, she demonstrates how we attend to individual sounds, to words in a story, to friends' thoughts and feelings, and to the voice inside us. Backmatter explains some additional information about listening. |

## Elevates Texts and Celebrates Rereading

It doesn't come as a surprise that the treasured texts you read aloud and return to for shared reading quickly become the best sellers in your classroom library. A popular poem in my classroom starts this way: "Books to the ceiling, Books to the sky" (Lobel, 1985). After a few repetitions, learners have it memorized, actions and all. Like a catchy jingle, the shared texts children chant, sing, and read become ingrained in their memories, providing the harmony that accompanies and helps unlock the print they encounter in books. Think of it this way: if you increase the volume of text you're rereading in a shared format, you are giving students a leg up as independent readers. As an added bonus, you are showing learners the secrets they can uncover when they reread.

When we approach rereading with excitement and curiosity, our learners will quickly see the many reasons they might choose to do it. To begin the yearlong conversation about rereading, I teach students the piggyback song I wrote with my daughter. (See *"Rereading for Different Reasons" Reproducible Song Page* on the companion website, resources.corwin.com/shakeupsharedreading.) Then, as we engage in shared reading interactions, we record the different reasons on an ongoing chart, such as what's shown in the figure on page 7.

# Rereading for
## Different Reasons

**Tune: "Do Re Mi"** (*from The Sound of Music*)
**Written by Maria Walther and Katie Walther**

**Reread to help you understand.**

**Reread a story you adore.**

**Reread to notice something new**

**or discover even more.**

**Answer questions that you have.**

**Find the meaning of a word.**

**Read with style and pizzazz.**

**When you open up a book**

**One**

**more**

**time . . .**

*"Rereading for Different Reasons" Reproducible Song Page*

Because each short burst of shared reading has a clear purpose, students' time spent rereading is maximized. In each short burst, I've indicated three key pages or sections to pause and ponder with your learners. It's up to you to determine whether you want to reread the text in its entirety, stopping on key parts, or, if time is tight, spend all of your instructional minutes focused solely on rereading the three key sections.

## Invites Active Participation

Shared reading lessons, by nature, are designed to bring learners together around a shared purpose and piece of text. In Don Holdaway's (1982) words, "This learning environment is trusting, secure, and expectant" (p. 815). I love Holdaway's description of a shared reading experience—trusting, secure, expectant. In learning spaces where making mistakes is encouraged and approximations are celebrated, children jump in because they trust themselves, each other, and, of course, you. As they reread, they confidently test their theories about print. When you intentionally plan to reveal surprises found between the covers of a book, readers are expectant, on the edge of their seats, sure that something interesting is about to be uncovered. By actively participating in a shared reading experience, the learning is coming at them from all sides—your modeling, the insights of their peers, and your intentional focus on strategies that they can apply to future interactions with text.

> **Reasons We Reread**
> ✓ Figure out unknown words
> ✓ Check if the word is right
> ✓ Notice if we skipped a word
> ✓ Self-correct a miscue
> ✓ Understand a word's meaning
> ✓ Read with expression
> ✓ Ponder what's happening
> ✓ Notice writers' choices
> ☺ Because it's FUN!!

*Reasons to Reread Chart*

## Engages All Learners

It's nearly impossible to stay quiet when everyone's chanting, "Tickle, tickle in a pickle," one of the many catchy phrases in Yasmeen Ismail's (2020) rhyming romp *Joy*. When you pick texts that are custom-made for shared reading, your learners can't help but join in. Whether it's rhyming text, repetitive words or phrases, a familiar story structure, or an engaging nonfiction topic, children draw on their experiences with oral language to engage in the reading task at hand. The brevity of a short burst of shared reading makes it an ideal lesson to slip in when you find small time gaps in your schedule. The high engagement factor means it will work well at any time of the day.

## Trusted Techniques for Inviting Engagement

- Keep the interaction brief, focused, and joyful

- Invite inquiry

- Encourage collaborative problem solving

- Celebrate approximations

- Give focused feedback

## Expands Oral Language Development

For most children, the literacy learning process actually begins with speaking—talking about themselves and about what's happening around them. Conversing about experiences widens a child's background knowledge and, in turn, boosts their language development. As their bank of known words increases, they become more adept at expressing their observations and insights. Visualize an upward spiral—the more a child's actions are surrounded by language-expanding conversation, the richer their vocabulary becomes, and so on. Language-expanding conversations occur both at home with caregivers and at school. As you'll see in the examples shown in the table on page 9, language-expanding conversations invite children to do the following:

- notice

- make connections from new to known

- add details

- make comparisons

- wonder

In a literacy-rich classroom, the basis for many of these conversations is shared learning experiences and the texts you read together. It is through spoken language that children learn to organize their thinking, listen to how their peers respond to their ideas, and notice how others add to or expand on their initial thoughts (Hammond, 2015). As students bounce ideas off each other, prompts like the ones that follow help children actively use oral language as they hone their reading skills:

- Tell us about something you discovered on this page.

- Show us how you figured that out.

- Explain to your neighbor what you just learned.

- Ask a friend about what they notice on this page.

- Repeat that smart thinking so that we can all hear it.

When you think of your role as their teacher during these interactions, subscribe to the wisdom of *Hamilton*'s Aaron Burr: "Talk less. Smile more."

## Language-Expanding Conversations

| | |
|---|---|
| Language-Expanding Conversation Outside on an Autumn Day | Look at all of the leaves on the ground! (Notice) |
| | Where did they come from? (Connect) |
| | What colors do you see? Pick them up. How do they feel? What do they smell like? (Add sensory details) |
| | Do all of the trees have colorful leaves? (Compare) |
| | Why do you think some of them are still green? (Wonder) |
| Language-Expanding Conversation While Reading *Goodbye Summer, Hello Autumn* (Pak, 2016)<br><br>A girl walks through her neighborhood greeting all the signs that autumn is approaching. Each creature or object from the natural world responds to her "Hello" with one of their own, creating a see-saw structure. Because of this, readers have to pay attention to the varying points of view. | What do you notice? (Notice) |
| | Does this remind you of any other books we've read? (Connect) |
| | What are some of the things she said hello to? (Add details) |
| | Are all of the two-page spreads the same? (Compare) |
| | Why do you suppose the author chose to use this pattern? (Wonder) |

## Strengthens Story Sense

Kate Read's (2019) counting-book thriller opens with "One famished fox" and concludes with "One frightened fox." In between, readers delight at the suspenseful story with a surprise ending. When revisiting this book during shared reading, you might draw readers' attention to the number words or Read's clever choice of adjectives. Be confident that because these high-frequency words and parts of speech are wrapped in the package of an engaging tale, students are developing their story schema, or story sense. I liken story schema to a stick person drawn by a youngster. A child who is developing story schema is learning the basic elements of a story. Similarly, a young artist knows the essential parts of a human—body, arms, legs, and head. Story after story, readers add to this schema by adding details they've learned from questioning, conversation, and reflection—eventually progressing into a rich understanding of the inner workings of stories. In the same way, the budding artist learns to add details when drawing pictures of themselves, their friends, and family members.

## Fosters Fluency

Fluent readers read connected text accurately and effortlessly. They read at a conversational rate with phrasing and expression, while at the same time grasping the meaning of the text. One way that children develop fluency is by listening to a fluent model (you!) read aloud, hence the critical importance of the read-aloud experience. Shared reading has long been seen as the ideal context for immersing students in another key fluency development practice—repeated reading. There are many effective ways to reread during the short bursts of shared reading. As you're savoring texts together, try some of these proven fluency-building methods:

- Choral reading: Voices join together to read a text.

- Echo reading: Teacher reads a line, and children echo the line back.

- Tag-team reading: Teacher reads a line or page, learners read a line or page, and so on.

- Fill in the blank: Teacher reads and leaves out a word, and listeners use letter clues, context clues, or rhyming patterns to fill-in-the-blank.

In addition to shared fluency-focused interactions with text, children need quiet time to read, read, and read some more, with the voices of their teachers and peers in their heads coaching them along.

*To build fluency, children need time to read.*

## Demonstrates the Reading Process

View shared reading as an opportunity for learners to peek behind the curtain and see the invisible actions of a reading brain. As you think aloud about the reading process, you shine the spotlight on what otherwise might seem like a mystery. In the *my turn* portion of the short burst of shared reading, take the stage and explicitly model the target skill or strategy. Then, during *our turn* time, scaffold and support students as they take on those skills or strategies in a low-risk, yet cognitively demanding, environment. Modeling, scaffolding, and clarifying what we want our readers to do is culturally relevant and supports student learning (Souto-Manning et al., 2018). Whether you're demonstrating how to orthographically map a word by matching letters to sounds or how readers infer a character's feelings, clear language devoid of verbal clutter is the key. I've written each shared reading interaction using the same straightforward language I use with young learners to model for you how to clearly communicate the reading process.

## Supports Multilingual Learners

As the term implies, shared reading is about the give-and-take relationship between readers and a text and among the learners who are enjoying it together. For students who have the asset of being multilingual, a give-and-take relationship means honoring their existing linguistic knowledge and inviting them to interact with the text and with each other in the languages with which they are the most comfortable (España & Herrera, 2020). Building on students' funds of knowledge, shared reading invites inquiry-based learning that expands students' experience with the English language. In the company of their peers, multilingual learners grow their English vocabulary knowledge, deepen their comprehension, and get a glimpse into the nuances of English.

## Offers a Supportive Instructional Context

The power of the shared reading context lies in its simplicity—a reader, a goal, a text, and a conversation. Like building blocks, one shared reading experience stacked on another supports students' understanding of increasingly complex texts. For readers at the beginning stages, this language-rich setting provides the perfect backdrop for learning how print works and much more. After you set the stage and model the actions of a proficient reader, students can lean on each other as they unravel the mysteries that lie between the covers of a book. While students are negotiating meaning, they are also learning how to listen to one another, build on the thinking of their peers, and push back when they disagree—essential conversational competencies. The skills and strategies students discover during shared reading are put into action when you are guiding readers in small groups and when they're reading on their own. To sum it up, the in-depth study of a small portion of text embedded in a meaningful whole results in the pleasurable end goal of understanding.

## Build Bridges—Connect Read-Aloud Experiences and Shared Reading Interactions

When used effectively, shared reading is the bridge between read aloud and guided reading (Burkins & Yaris, 2016) and a brick on the pathway toward independence. In fact, Gay Su Pinnell and Irene Fountas (1998) dub shared reading as a *transition tool* that helps learners increase their understanding of the inner workings of the reading process. Yet in my thirty-five years in education, I was unable to find a professional resource that explicitly tied read aloud and shared reading together. So, I wrote one! The book experiences that follow in Chapters 1 through 4 will guide you in building sturdy bridges between read aloud and shared reading. They will assist you in leveraging shared reading as a transition tool to guide readers in small groups and support them as they read independently. By providing coherent, connected learning experiences for children, you are offering them clear pathways to proceed forward in their literacy learning with confidence and competence.

## Read Aloud and Shared Reading: All About Conversation

What you're aiming for during read-aloud experiences and shared reading interactions is conversation that promotes what Peter Johnston and his colleagues (2020) dub "dialogic engagement—the idea that when multiple perspectives are actively and equitably taken up, people are more engaged, build new knowledge, and think more positively about their peers" (p. 5). To move toward dialogic engagement, intentionally model the language of conversation by asking the following questions:

- What do you notice?

- What are you thinking?

- Can you link your thinking to your friends' thinking?

- Do you want to push back at their thinking?

- Does someone have the same thinking?

- Does anyone have different thinking?

After posing one of the questions above, do what I find the toughest part of all—keep quiet and *listen*! Provide time for *all* students to think and reflect before inviting responses. Once learners are conversing, soak in what they're saying and record their insights in whatever manner works best for you. Step into the conversation only when needed, and then quickly back away. I realize this is much easier to do in a face-to-face setting than in a virtual setting, so the figures below and on page 13 offer a few tips to keep responses and conversation lively through a screen.

---

### Student Response Options in Virtual Settings

- Use colored response cards. (Students make a red, yellow, green, and blue card, or find items in those colors. Assign the colors a meaning that matches your purpose and conversation, like agree = red, disagree = blue. Children respond by displaying a card.)

- Type into the chat.

- Post their thinking on a Google Jamboard.

- Write their thoughts on a small dry-erase board and hold it up to the camera.

- Record an audio or video reaction.

## A Quick Peek at a Read-Aloud Experience

In the early days of the COVID-19 pandemic, when schools were shuttered and learning shifted from in person to online, we were all scrambling to figure out the best ways to stay connected to our students. Above the din, teachers cried out to trade book publishers, "Help! We have to keep reading aloud, what can you do?" Publishers relaxed copyright guidelines and creators posted videos reading aloud. Thanks to the ingenuity and will of teachers, the relationship-building practice of read aloud thrived. To me, this is a true testimony to the power of the read-aloud experience. In *The Ramped-Up Read Aloud* (2019), I shared 101 read-aloud experiences. Listening to the feedback from teachers and students, I've added a few new features to the read-aloud experiences in this book.

# Chatting About Books

- Type a 1-word or 1-sentence answer to our question.
- Add a 1-word or 1-sentence book-related comment.
- Ask a question.
- Link your thinking to a friend's thinking.
  - I agree with _____.
  - I want to add _____ to _____'s thinking.

*Virtual Settings: Chatting About Books*

## What's New?

### Key Vocabulary: Kid-Friendly Definitions

When teaching children individual words, it is essential to provide kid-friendly definitions (Cobb & Blachowicz, 2014). Easier said than done. I often find myself stumped to formulate an on-the-spot definition. I've included child-friendly definitions comprising words that young children generally know. To enhance the definition, you might add an example that is relevant to your learners or display an image.

### Extend the Experience

The extension will differ based on where the text and conversation naturally lead. For consistency and to assist you with your planning, they will follow this pattern: The first extension will align with the learning target and purpose statement. The second extension may take the conversation in a different direction and, periodically, include one of the following:

- Compare and Contrast! Multigenre text set that addresses the main theme or topic. Students can independently read these texts to consider how they are similar to or different from the featured title.

- Meet the Creator! Author and/or illustrator study insights.

- Be an Observer! How to use the featured book as the impetus for an inquiry-based learning center or station.

If you're acquainted with the read-aloud experiences found in *The Ramped-Up Read Aloud* (Walther, 2019), then the infographic on pages 14–15 will look familiar. If not, it will briefly explain my thinking behind the structure of a read-aloud experience.

# Read-Aloud Experiences at a Glance

## Read-Aloud Experience Title:

To assist you in intentionally selecting picture books for your read-aloud experiences, I've categorized each read-aloud title by strategy and learning target. A complete list of titles and learning targets appears in the Learning Target Chart found on the companion website (resources.corwin.com/shakeupsharedreading). It's nearly impossible to put a well-crafted picture book neatly into one category. My hope is to give you a starting point knowing that you'll let your students and their responses to the books be your guide.

## Book Title: The 50 titles featured in this resource were
selected to represent a range of recently published books and spotlight those written and illustrated by people who are from underrepresented and/or marginalized backgrounds.

## About the Book: Here I include a teacher-focused summary
of any insights I've learned about the author, illustrator, or behind-the-scenes tidbits about the creation or design of the book.

## Learning Targets: This section will help you zero in on
what you are aiming for students to be able to know and do as a result of the experience.

---

Read-Aloud Experience: Be Who You Are

**Book Title:** *A Normal Pig* (Steele, 2019)

**About the Book:** Pip the pig is satisfied being her normal self until a new pig joins the class. After the new pig teases Pip about her lunch and her artwork, she comes home upset and lashes out at her family. Pip's wise mom senses the problem and suggests a family trip to a museum in the city. There, Pip realizes that being "normal" doesn't mean being the same as everyone else.

To find a book like this one, look for the following:

- Characters developing self-awareness
- Stories with themes that will resonate with your learners

 Comprehension Conversation

**Before Reading**

**Notice the Cover Illustration**

What do you suppose the pigs on the cover are doing? [Taking a class picture.] What else do you notice? Which pig would you say is the "normal" pig? [Listen to students' thoughts.] There are some hints on the book casing, the endpapers, and the title page that might make you rethink your first answer. [Glance at those book parts, and then discuss any new insights students have gleaned from the illustrations.]

**Set a Purpose:** The title of this book is *A Normal Pig*. While enjoying this story together, we're going to ponder the meaning of the word *normal*.

**During Reading**

- *Then one day, a new pig came to school* page: What changed on this page? How do you think the new pig's comments made Pip feel?
- *When her parents asked her what was wrong* page: Is it Pip's parents' fault she's upset? Notice what she is drawing. [A house.] Why do you suppose she's drawing a house? [Maybe because the new pig made fun of her unique house drawing in art class.]
- *At the playground, all the pigs looked so different* page: Why do you think Pip's mom wanted to take her to the city? When you compare the kids on the city playground to the ones on Pip's school playground, what do you notice? [Flip back to the first page to compare. Listen and respond to students' insights about rich diversity found in the city park compared to that found on Pip's school playground.]
- *When they got home, Pip was feeling better* page: Which events do you think caused Pip to change her mind about wanting a "normal" lunch? Think and talk about this question with a friend.

**Learning Targets:**

- I notice the words and actions of characters in a book.
- I think about how my words and actions make me who I am.

34 ● Shake Up Shared Reading

---

# Comprehension Conversation

## Before Reading

### Notice the Cover Illustration:

Take a moment to glance at the book cover that appears with each read-aloud experience. In this part, I guide you in previewing the book. This preview might include noticing the artistic and design techniques used on the book jacket and, if applicable, on the book casing (the hard cover underneath the paper book jacket), pondering the connection between front and back cover, discussing the title, and exploring other ideas to build excitement and invite wonder.

**Set a Purpose:** View the purpose statement like an invitation to your listeners to inquire and investigate something in the book. The purpose statement will align with the learning target(s).

### Bracketed Text

The text that appears in brackets includes teaching tips and other insights that are directed at you, the teacher, rather than the students.

## During Reading

Because most picture books don't have page numbers, I use the first few words on the top of the left-hand page to point you in the right direction. As to not disrupt the flow of your read aloud, I've included only a handful of questions at critical key points. In my opinion, asking too many questions distracts your listeners. It is better to let the author and illustrator magic do the job!

## Develop Self-Awareness

**1**

### After Reading

- Can you infer that the author, K-Fai [Kay-Fy] Steele, was trying to teach you about the word *normal*? If someone asks you what the word *normal* means, what would you say?
- Let's go back to the museum page to translate what the pigs are saying in their own languages. [The author provides translations on the copyright page.]

### Extend the Experience

- On this blank sheet of paper, draw or write any big ideas or lessons you learned from listening to this story.
- Remember the page when Pip was thinking about all of the things she could do when she grew up. Divide a piece of paper into half, and write or draw about two things you want to do when you grow up. For an extra challenge, flip to the back and share two other possibilities.

### Similar Titles

*Avocado Asks: What Am I?* (Abe, 2020)
**About the Book:** A little girl points at Avocado and asks, "Is an avocado a fruit or a vegetable?" This sends Avocado on a journey of self-discovery. Just when Avocado is feeling lost and alone, Tomato helps Avocado celebrate being a unique individual. This book pairs nicely with *Ogilvy* (Underwood, 2019a).

*Fred Gets Dressed* (Brown, 2021)
**About the Book:** Fred bounds through his house "naked and wild and free" until he comes to his parents' closet. When the clothes on his dad's side don't quite work, he has better luck with one of his mom's outfits. After he adds some lipstick (on his cheek), his parents find him and, without judgment or hesitation, join in the dress-up fun.

**Key Vocabulary and Kid-Friendly Definitions:**

- *respond:* to answer or react in some way
- *usual:* the most common way

online resources

View the author talking about *A Normal Pig* resources.corwin.com/shakeupsharedreading

---

**Key Vocabulary and Kid-Friendly Definitions:** When highlighting vocabulary during a read aloud, it is helpful to provide kid-friendly definitions. In this feature, you will find key words along with a definition to share with your learners.

**Extend the Experience:** The extension will differ based on where the text and conversation naturally lead. For consistency and to assist you with your planning, they will follow this pattern: the first extension will align with the learning target and purpose statement, and the second extension will vary (for a brief explanation, see page 13.)

**Similar Titles:**

I scoured my independent bookstore and public library shelves to find related titles with comparable themes that lead students to similar read-aloud conversations. You might choose to read these titles to reinforce learning targets, compare and contrast with the featured title, or continue the conversation with a small group of students. Note that when a text set is featured, the similar titles section does not appear.

### After Reading

The concluding questions and conversation starters bring the experience full circle by drawing students' attention back to the purpose of the read aloud (other than simply for fun!). Their intention is to prompt students to apply what they've learned from this book to their lives, their learning, or their own writing.

# Three Steps to Successful Shared Reading Interactions

Teachers are planners. If you're like me, you write and rewrite lists just so you can check things off. Sometimes that planning mentality works to my benefit; other times it gets in the way of the flexibility needed to center students' needs and voices. Flexibility is also the key when organizing your classroom space for shared reading. Depending on your current guidelines, you can either draw students close to the text or project the text so that they can view it from a safe distance. Remember, based on your purpose and students' needs, shared reading interactions can take place in the whole group, with a small group of learners, or even with one student.

Shared reading can also occur in any setting; it just takes a little ingenuity to make it work virtually. For virtual shared reading interactions, I recommend using a document camera to project the book. With a real book under the camera, you can draw students' attention to key parts simply by using your finger. In addition, you can quickly jot students' thoughts or ideas about the book on sticky notes and keep them in the book for future reference.

Whether you are gathering learners together virtually or face-to-face, you will need the same supplies at your fingertips. Keep the fluidity of teaching in mind as you proceed through the next part of this introduction. View the plan you create as a rough sketch, with your students' thoughts and reactions filling in the details and color.

## At My Fingertips During a Shared Reading Interaction

- Sticky notes
- Sentence strips
- Small magnetic whiteboard
- Dry-erase markers
- Magnetic letters
- Removable highlighter tape

## Step 1: Highlight a Literacy Skill or Strategy

For each short burst of shared reading, I offer two possible literacy skills or strategies to highlight from this list of options, which are detailed in the following pages:

- Listen for sounds (phonological awareness)
- Match letters to sounds (phonics)
- Spotlight high-frequency words

- Ponder punctuation

- Reread for fluency

- Wonder about words

- Reread to boost comprehension

- Notice writer's craft moves

My selection is based on what I've learned from decades of sitting beside emergent readers and my career-long study of children's literature. You add a vital piece of information that I'm lacking—knowledge of your learners. You will be able to use the information you've gained from formative assessment sources to determine what your readers need next to nudge them toward independence. Lean into that knowledge as you select from the two possible choices I offer or create one of your own.

## Formative Assessment Sources

- Running records

- Spelling inventories

- Analyzing students' written work

- Conferring

- Kid watching

- Observations during read-aloud experiences

### Listen for Sounds (Phonological Awareness)

Over thirty years ago, Marilyn Adams's (1990) research called attention to the essential role phonological awareness plays in the development of a literacy learner. When you invite learners to listen for sounds during a shared reading interaction, you draw their active attention to the fact that language comprises small speech sounds called *phonemes*. To strengthen students' phonological awareness, guide them to notice sounds that are the same and those that are different, and also to consider the number and order of those sounds in words. Provide opportunities for readers to segment (or take the sounds of a word apart) and blend the separate sounds together. The most important thing to remember when you are spotlighting sounds is to revisit the text *orally* without showing the words and invite students to *listen* rather than read. To find key pages to reread with a focus on phonological awareness, choose those that include rhyme, alliteration, word play, onomatopoeia, and memorable repeated phrases. On page 18, I have provided an example of each.

## Finding Key Pages to Listen for Sounds

| Look For . . . | Say . . . | Try This Book . . . |
|---|---|---|
| **Rhyme**<br><br>Possible focus: Strengthen children's ability to hear rhyme, the most basic form of phonological awareness. | [Reread sentences where the rhyming pattern will help listeners predict the word.] *I'm going to read some sentences from the book and leave some words out. Listen to see if you can figure out and say the missing words.* | *Secret, Secret Agent Guy* (Bigwood, 2021)<br><br>The Franklin brothers are on a mission: Operation Lollipop. Working as a team, with their kid-created spy gear, they almost succeed. That is, until they are double-crossed by their secret-agent sister. Read to the tune of "Twinkle, Twinkle, Little Star." |
| **Alliteration**<br><br>Possible focus: Students listen for sounds that are the same and then match that sound to a letter. You could also play with the words by deleting or substituting other beginning phonemes. | *I'm going to say some words. Tell me what you notice. Yes! They start with the same sound. What sound do you hear at the beginning of each word? What letter stands for this sound? When authors repeat the beginning sound, it's called alliteration. It makes words fun to say. Let's try another one!* | *Catch That Chicken!* (Atinuke, 2020)<br><br>After speeding through a West African village to catch chickens with Lami, reread to listen carefully for the author's use of repetitive beginning sounds. [See Book Experiences in Chapter 2 on pages 96–101.] |
| **Word Play**<br><br>Possible focus: Listeners enjoy and repeat the tongue-twisting words found in books, poems, songs, and other texts that play with words. | *Listen to the words in this book. What do you notice? Can you repeat them with me? Say them fast. Say them slow. Say them high. Say them low.* | *Atticus Caticus* (Maizes, 2021)<br><br>You may need a bit of practice before reading this tongue-twisting book aloud. I did! A boy wakes up "Atticus Cat-ticus" with a "rat-a-tat-tat-icus" of his cardboard box drum. Then, with rollicking rhymes, he follows him throughout the day. |
| **Onomatopoeia**<br><br>Possible focus: Begin by building listening skills as students match the sound words to the object or action they represent. Then depending on the phonic elements contained in the word, focus beginning or ending sounds, blends, digraphs, and more. Focus on activities where children are segmenting and blending sounds. | *Listen to these sound words, "Plunk, plunk, plunk." What might be happening in the story if you hear those words? The word plunk begins with the /pl/ blend. Let's play a /pl/ blend game.* [Give students four cubes, chips, or blocks. Say the first word in a pair below. Students repeat the word and represent it with blocks. Then, say the second word. Students add a block to the beginning to represent the first sound in blend. Repeat the pair *lay-play-lay-play* as they remove and add blocks. Continue in the same fashion with another word or two.]<br><br>lay – play<br><br>lot – plot<br><br>lug – plug<br><br>lace – place<br><br>lane – plane<br><br>lump – plump | *Double Bass Blues* (Loney, 2019)<br><br>Little Nic makes an onomatopoeia-filled journey with his beloved double bass on his back. He leaves orchestra practice at his suburban school, travels through the city, and arrives at his granddaddy's house just in time to jam. |
| **Memorable Repeated Phrases**<br><br>Possible focus: Use the repetitive lines to concentrate on listening to and separating words in sentences. | [Give each child five to seven cubes, blocks, or counting chips.]<br><br>*I'm going to repeat a sentence from our favorite part of this book so we can think about how many words are in the sentence.* [Repeat a memorable line.] *Say the sentence slowly and put one marker down for each word.* [Continue in this same fashion for a few more sentences.] | *The Pirates Are Coming!* (Condon, 2020)<br><br>"The pirates are coming! Pirates are coming! Quick! Everybody hide!" Tom shouts each time he thinks he spots a pirate ship. Along with the familiar repeated phrase, your readers will love the surprise ending in this swashbuckling "The Boy Who Cried Wolf" reboot. [See Book Experiences in Chapter 2 on pages 110–113.] |

## Match Letters to Sounds (Phonics)

Consonants. Short vowels. Long vowels. Blends. Digraphs. By themselves the individual sounds lack meaning, but when writers use them to form words, they take on a life of their own. Helping learners match letters to sounds so that they can unlock the meaning of the text is essential. There are abundant opportunities to draw students' attention to letter–sound correspondences during shared reading. Some might sound like these:

- *The character's name begins with the /r/ sound. Which of our friends' names begin with the same sound? Which letter makes the /r/ sound?*

- *Wait! I'm not sure how to read this word. Let me slide through the sounds to figure it out. Listen and watch as I point and slide.*

- *Look! All of the words on this line begin with the same letter. What letter is it? What sound does it make? Let's say the words together as I point to the beginning sound.*

In my dissertation, I called these contextualized conversations about the features of written language *phonics talk* (Walther, 1998). Purposeful phonics talk during shared reading interactions helps children understand how print works (Hiebert & Raphael, 1998). This implicit phonics instruction complements and extends the explicit phonics instruction that takes place at other times during the day. Addressing the ins and outs of explicit phonics instruction for our youngest learners is beyond the scope of this book, but I can point you toward a few professional reads that you might find helpful:

- *How to Prevent Reading Difficulties: Proactive Practices for Teaching Young Children to Read PK–3* (Weakland, 2021)

- *Letter Lessons and First Words: Phonics Foundations That Work PK–2* (Mesmer, 2019)

- *Shifting the Balance: 6 Ways to Bring the Science of Reading Into the Balanced Literacy Classroom* (Burkins & Yates, 2021)

*Look for opportunities to draw students' attention to letter-sound connections.*

### Spotlight High-Frequency Words

I'm always amazed by the fact that if children can recognize and write these ten high-frequency words—*the, of, and, a, to, in, is, you, that,* and *it*—they know almost one quarter of all of the words they will read and write (Cunningham, 2013, p. 88). If that is not a reason to ensure our readers learn high-frequency words, I don't know what is! Further, automatic recognition of high-frequency words is one of the hallmarks of fluency. Many high-frequency words have no meaning in isolation. In addition, some are not pronounced or spelled in logical ways. This poses a challenge for all learners, particularly our multilingual learners. Shared reading provides an opportunity for you to give children repeated exposure to contextualized high-frequency words in a playful manner.

| We can read and write these words... | am | an | and | at | be |
|---|---|---|---|---|---|
| big | can | do | go | he | in |
| is | it | me | my | no | on |
| see | so | the | to | up | we |

*Shared reading offers learners repeated exposure to contextualized high-frequency words.*

### Ponder Punctuation

Notice the title of this section—Ponder Punctuation. Why do authors use punctuation? What is its role in reading and writing? How does that particular mark impact the way we read the text? Why did the author choose to punctuate the text that way? Questions like these are the ones I want children to be able to answer after engaging in conventions-focused learning events like shared reading. If you keep your conversations keyed in on the purposes of punctuation, it helps learners view conventions from the perspective of a reader and writer, rather than seeing punctuation as "something I have to add because my teacher said so."

### Reread for Fluency

In their resource *The Megabook of Fluency*, Tim Rasinski and Melissa Cheesman Smith (2018, p. 8) offer the helpful acronym EARS to use when focusing on fluency during shared reading interactions. Fluency is the ability to read with the following:

**E**xpression

**A**utomatic word recognition

**R**hythm and phrasing

**S**moothness

With this acronym in mind, we model fluent reading during our read-aloud experiences and then offer learners an authentic context for repetitive reading during shared reading. The end goal when supporting students as they reread with fluency is that they move from accurate decoding to automatic decoding.

## Wonder About Words

Word wonder is just that: approaching the study of words with curiosity. In the shared reading context, you dip back into the book to inquire and guide students as they do the following:

- study the sound–letter correspondences

- figure out the meaning of words

- explore different parts of speech

- consider how words make them feel

- notice figurative language

- borrow words for writing

The goal in harvesting and analyzing words from a familiar text is to not only help students better understand that particular text but also transfer the different aspects of word knowledge they've gained to future encounters with similar words as they read and write (Rawlins & Invernizzi, 2019).

## Reread to Boost Comprehension

Picture the students in your learning space who can easily answer questions beginning with *who, what, where,* and *when* but balk when you dig deeper and ask, "Why?" Guiding readers to think beyond literal-level comprehension and progress toward inferential understanding takes time and scaffolded instruction. During comprehension-focused shared reading interactions, children take a second look at key pages that offer clues to a character's actions or reactions. They apply comprehension strategies in real time and surrounded by a "sea of talk" (Britton, 1983, p. 11), centering two critical elements to comprehension instruction—application and socialization.

## Notice Writer's Craft Moves

Admiring the way LeUyen Pham (2021) makes every single word count in *Outside, Inside* or marveling at Dan Santat's imaginative illustrations in *Lift* (Lê, 2020). Wondering, "How did the creator do that? How can I do that in my own writing?" This is the thought process of a writer who looks to mentor authors and illustrators for inspiration. Shared reading provides a beautiful opportunity to blend the best of both worlds—the intensive study of a text that happens during a shared reading interaction and the learning and transfer that occurs when children study books from a writer's point of view. To help you see these blendings, I've included short bursts of shared reading that illuminate authors' craft moves.

*Young writers look to mentor authors and illustrators for inspiration.*

## Step 2: Select Irresistible Texts

I began my teaching career in the era of the big book and pocket charts. Over the years, I created and collected a wealth of giant-sized texts to share with students. Now that big books and pocket charts are not as readily available, we have to rethink the way we enlarge a text to share with students. Here are a few suggestions that have worked for me, and I'm sure you can add to this list ideas that work well in your teaching context:

- Select picture books with large font size.
- Project the text using a document camera.
- Display e-books on an interactive whiteboard.
- Access and view a text from an online database.
- Photocopy poems and other short texts. (Remember to follow copyright guidelines.)
- Cowrite texts to reread (classroom charts, books, songs, and/or poems).

When considering texts to include in this resource, I used these criteria:

- **Rhythm and rhyme**: When gathering books with rhythm, seek out poetic picture books and those that make your toes tap as you read aloud, like *A Hippy-Hoppy Toad* (Archer, 2018). Rhythmic books draw listeners in and, during shared reading, are ideal for choral reading. As you've probably noticed, there are many picture books with rhyming patterns like those found in Markette Sheppard's (2020) *My Rainy Day Rocket Ship*, which is about a boy who needs to find something to do because "Mom says it's too rainy to play outside today, so I'll have to find my fun another way." You might select this book because, in addition to its rhyming text, it stresses the importance of imagination leading to conversations and extensions that include creative play.

- **Memorable language**: Skilled writers use words and sentences in creative ways. These words create vivid images that help readers put themselves in the setting or feel the mood of the story. When searching for books with memorable language, be on the lookout for those words or phrases that will stick with readers long after the book experience. For instance, after reading Christina Soontornvat's (2021) *Ramble Scramble Children*, kids are sure to be looking for things to "proper up!" Books in this category often include word play and figurative language. Take, for example, *When Lola Visits* by Michelle Sterling (2021), a simile-filled description of a girl's summer visits with Lola, her grandmother from the Philippines. For the girl, summer smells like "mango jam simmering on the stove" and "a freshly opened can of tennis balls" (n.p.). The memorable language found in picture books like these is just begging to be savored and celebrated during shared reading interactions.

- **Repeated words or phrases**: Predictable text has long been the preferred fare for shared reading. Books, songs, and poems with repetition or a predictability in the language structure are supportive of emergent readers because they can leverage their experiences with spoken language and apply them to the reading task. On top of that, repetition encourages children to join in. Readers can sing along with the repeated refrain of Lucky Diaz's (2021) *Paletero Man:* "RING! RING! Can you hear his call? Paletas for one! Paletas for all!" On another day, they might join the dog in repeatedly asking, "You want to help a pumpkin grow?" as it nurtures pumpkins from seed to pie in *How to Help a Pumpkin Grow* (Wolff, 2021). Repetitive texts are also helpful to young writers because they can use the repeated part as a jumping-off point for their own text innovation.

- **Rich vocabulary**: Books with rich vocabulary help promote word wonder and provide opportunities to practice word-solving using strategies to better understand the meaning of words. To promote word wonder when teaching about the consonant *s*, share Charles Trevino's (2021) *Seaside Stroll* and saunter alongside a girl and her mother on a wintry beach walk. Children will marvel at the fact that the entire book is written using only words that begin with s. Reach for expository nonfiction texts when demonstrating strategies for understanding word meanings. Readers can practice using text features, visual images, and the glossary to boost their word knowledge. To build background knowledge for an upcoming content area unit, you might choose books with topic-specific vocabulary. For instance, when studying forces and motion in science, transportation buffs will learn words like *conducting, piloting*, and *captaining* as their imagination takes them on trains, planes, boats, and many other vehicles in *On the Go Awesome* (Detlefsen, 2020). If your social studies topic is identifying feelings, then the book *Big Feelings* (Penfold, 2021) would be ideal; it is told using words that describe emotions. Revisiting books with rich vocabulary during shared reading provides students with authentic experiences with language.

*Books with rich vocabulary help promote word wonder.*

- **Ideas to ponder**: When focusing on comprehension, look for books that invite deep thinking. Stories filled with action, excitement, suspense, and conflict. These will be books that your students can connect to and perhaps debate with the author's message. Zetta Elliott's (2020) timely and moving poem *A Place Inside of Me* leads to conversations about a boy's emotional change throughout the year that his community is wounded by a police shooting. Another route you might take when selecting texts to boost comprehension is curating text sets for students to compare and contrast. If you're exploring the theme of kindness, for example, children could compare *A Small Kindness* (McAnulty, 2021a) with *The Power of One: Every Act of Kindness Counts* (Ludwig, 2020). To help you get started, you'll find text sets sprinkled throughout the lessons in this resource.

- **Interesting topics**: Sneaking a little content area teaching into your shared reading interactions is a win-win for you and your students. For you, it conserves instructional minutes. For learners, informational texts spark interest in topics and build background knowledge. When rereading key pages of these texts, you can zero in on supporting learners in using text features, identifying text structures, understanding topic-related words, and more. A winner in my classroom was Melissa Stewart's (2018) *Pipsqueaks, Slowpokes, and Stinkers: Celebrating Animal Underdogs*, particularly the stinkers! Chapter 3 is dedicated to nonfiction texts to guide you in building students' content knowledge and language comprehension. In the other chapters, you'll find two simple ways to weave information texts into literacy instruction. The first way is to curate multigenre text sets that extend learning beyond the featured book. Add to that the opportunity for learners to further explore a topic in an Observer Center stocked with books and related resources. When you come across the text sets or ideas for the Observer Center in the chapters that follow, view them as exemplars to guide you as you create your own extensions to highlight topics that are of interest to your students.

Layered on top of these criteria was the intentional selection of books that are written and illustrated by creators from underrepresented or marginalized populations.

To support you in selecting books for shared reading, the following table pairs text types with possible teaching points.

| Matching Texts to Literacy Skill or Strategy Focus | |
|---|---|
| **Text Selection Criteria** | **Possible Literacy Skill or Strategy Focus** |
| Rhythm and rhyme | Listen for sounds<br>Ponder punctuation<br>Notice writer's craft moves |
| Memorable language | Wonder about words<br>Reread for fluency<br>Notice writer's craft moves |
| Repeated words or phrases | Reread for fluency<br>Ponder punctuation<br>Notice writer's craft moves |
| Rich vocabulary | Wonder about words |
| Ideas to ponder | Wonder about words<br>Reread to boost comprehension |
| Interesting topics | Wonder about words<br>Reread to boost comprehension |
| Mentor texts for writers | Notice writer's craft moves |

## Step 3: Plan the Short Burst

When you're planning a short burst of shared reading, sketch out what will happen before, during, and after you reread the text together. To prepare for the *before reading* portion, decide how you will welcome students into the learning space and clearly communicate the purpose for rereading the text. Next, to plan what will happen *during reading*, select three key places to pause, reread, and investigate the text. The key pages should help learners uncover new understandings that directly relate to the instructional focus. The *during reading* part of the lesson concludes with an explicit nudge toward independence to direct students in applying what they've learned to their independent reading and/or writing. Finally, if it makes sense for your learners and goals, *after reading* you can invite students to innovate on the text. In other words, invite students to write or draw something that mirrors or builds on the words, concepts, or structure of the book. I'll add a few details to this planning structure in the pages that follow.

### Before Reading

- **Welcome students**. Since every minute is precious, as students are gathering for shared reading, begin with a brain-grabbing or, as Zaretta Hammond (2015) calls it, "igniting" activity. This might be a new or familiar song, chant, or rhyme. Perhaps an image or video clip that relates to the book, focus skill, or strategy. Consider starting as soon as the first few students arrive rather than waiting for everyone to be settled. This warm-up invites everyone to the shared reading experience in a welcoming manner. If you are sharing songs and poems, you might consider reproducing your students' favorite welcoming texts to add to a "Song, Poems, and Rhymes" binder or notebook. Then, reread this collection of treasured tunes and rhymes when you have an extra minute or, occasionally, when guiding readers in small groups. Readers can also access this collection of familiar texts during independent reading.

- **Set the stage**. Once learners are settled in, invite them into the experience by quickly drawing their attention to your instructional focus or learning target. Setting the stage helps children see the purpose and importance of rereading the text. I've included a *setting the stage* statement you can use in each of the short bursts of shared reading. Your aim is to meet the needs of your readers. I encourage you to adjust the targets based on your students' interests, questions, or misunderstandings.

### During Reading

- **Investigate key pages**. To keep shared reading interactions short and engaging, I've selected key stopping points for close study. The three points provide an opportunity for you to demonstrate the skill or strategy (My Turn), invite students to try it out with you (Our Turn), and apply it on their own or with a friend (Your Turn). After each stopping point, rely on your observations of students to guide the next steps. The formative data you collect from kid watching may lead you to linger a bit longer in developing a shared understanding or indicate the need to revisit your demonstration.

- **Nudge toward independence**. The overarching goal of a shared reading interaction is for students to gain a deeper understanding of literacy skills and strategies with an eye toward applying them on their own. A nudge toward independence is a question or prompt that circles back to the instructional focus and offers learners ideas about how to put something they learned into practice. Prompts that nudge learners toward independence can begin in many ways, including these:

  o *Think about how you might . . .*

  o *You can practice this by . . .*

  o *Use this anchor chart/tool to help you . . .*

  o *It's helpful to . . .*

  o *To use what you learned today . . .*

You'll find additional teacher talk to encourage students to continue their learning in each short burst of shared reading.

### After Reading

- **Innovate on Text.** Young learners who have frequent opportunities to engage in purposeful writing view it as a way to express their ideas. As children listen to, reread, and investigate a text together, they learn a great deal about being a reader and, as an added benefit, they gain insights into the craft of writing. It makes sense to show students how to apply these insights to a text innovation. Text innovations take the shared reading interaction to the next level by inviting learners to create a piece of writing (or drawing) based on an idea, concept, pattern, phrase, or illustration found in the book. You can innovate together in a shared or interactive writing format, or students can write with a partner or on their own. Some additional ways to use or adapt the ideas contained in the innovate on text section include the following:

  o Introduce and demonstrate the innovation, and then place the materials needed in a writing center or station.

o Use an online platform for students to photograph and/or video record their completed innovations.

o Invite each child to write one page, and then put all the pages together in a class book.

o Set up a literacy notebook (Walther & Biggs-Tucker, 2020) for students to record innovations and other responses from read-aloud and shared reading experiences.

The shared reading interactions found in Chapters 1 through 4 suggest an innovation that can help learners apply what they've learned from the interaction while strengthening the reading–writing connection. Often, your learners will lead you in a different direction and suggest an innovation of their own. When that happens, follow their lead and see where it takes you.

## Four Ways You Might Use This Book

View this book as a multipurpose literacy resource. Each read-aloud experience is designed in a consistent two-page spread so that you can quickly locate the sections that will be most helpful to your students. The short bursts of shared reading are designed in a similar manner. Together they create a connected learning sequence that can support your literacy learners in the following ways.

### Strengthen the Read Aloud–Shared Reading Connection

When shared reading interactions stem from and enhance a robust read-aloud experience, learners begin by enjoying the book in its entirety. Then, later in the day or week, as you seamlessly transition from a read aloud to a short burst of shared reading, students can examine parts of a book in the context of the whole-book experience. Funneling learning from whole to part makes it easier for students to grasp literacy-related concepts. I intentionally planned the ideas for the two teaching contexts so that they dovetail from one to another and still leave plenty of room for students to continue to explore on their own.

### Enhance Your Literacy Curriculum

Whether you organize your literacy instruction around units, have a core reading program, or design your own curriculum, this book will extend and enhance students' literacy learning. Every book experience is aimed at helping your students make sense of standards-based learning targets. You can easily do this by matching your students' learning targets to those found in the Learning Target Chart located on the companion website (resources.corwin.com/shakeupsharedreading). The Learning Target Chart is a comprehensive list of the featured titles, additional titles, learning targets, key vocabulary, and related links. In addition, the chart details learning goals for each of the two bursts of shared reading.

### Joyfully Teach Foundational Skills and Strategies

Why download a printable when a picture book can provide the real thing—contextualized literacy learning. Read aloud and shared reading are authentic contexts for learners to study and apply skills and strategies in a purposeful and joyful manner.

Short bursts of shared reading tap into students' curiosities. Approach each shared reading interaction as a puzzle to complete, a problem to solve. An inquisitive approach not only honors and celebrates what learners already know about the particular skill or strategy but also models reading behaviors you hope they will adopt as they interact with books on their own. Welcoming students into the unraveling process helps them take ownership that will transfer to their personal literacy experiences.

## Share Quick Snippets of Clear Instruction Virtually

During the pandemic, I joined a group of colleagues to read and discuss *The Distance Learning Playbook* (Fisher et al., 2021). One of the tenets I found most helpful when working with learners at a distance was teacher clarity—ensuring every aspect of my virtual instruction was clear. Teacher clarity is critical whether in person or in a virtual learning environment! For this reason, I've designed the experiences in this resource to support you in creating coherent reading experiences in two ways. First, to guide you in stating your learning intentions, each read-aloud experience has a kid-friendly purpose statement that is directly tied to the learning targets. Similarly, the short bursts of shared reading begin with an explicit *Set the Stage* statement that highlights the learning goal. Second, to weave formative assessments into the experience, I've included *Extend the Experience* options. Many of the options can be completed face-to-face on a blank sheet of paper or sticky note; therefore, the response ideas are easily translated to electronic response options like a Google Slide, Google Jamboard, video or audio recordings, or a variety of other digital tools.

*Teacher clarity is critical whether in person or in a virtual learning environment.*

It's time to dim the lights and let the power of read aloud and shared reading do the work—read, talk, ponder, react. I hope you and your learners find as much pleasure reading the books in this resource as I did when selecting them. I wish you hours of joy and wonder as you share the books and share the learning.

My Favorite Texts and Resources for Shared Reading

"I promise to cross bridges, and break down walls, to rise with the sun and learn from the falls."

—I Promise by LeBron James and Nina Mata

# Reading, Learning, and Talking Together

## A Year of Promise and Possibility

I'll let you in on a little secret: I'm wild about school supplies. I can barely walk past the aisle without grabbing the latest shade of markers or another journal . . . just in case. When the back-to-school sales begin, earlier and earlier it seems, I'm waiting outside the door. I wonder, "Is it the school supplies I crave or the anticipation of a brand-new year?" In *The Book Tree,* Paul Czajak (2018) writes, "Beginnings were always the best part. They smelled as if anything were possible" (n.p.). I do love the beginning of the school year with its promise and possibility.

In this chapter, I've curated a collection of books ideal for the first weeks of school because they shine the spotlight on some essential social-emotional competencies. As you read and discuss these books with children, you'll engage in dialogue that lays the groundwork for a healthy, caring community. Glance at the menu of shared reading interactions on page 32. Notice that in the short bursts of shared reading that follow the read-aloud experiences, you'll have the option to zero in on a range of skills and standards. Select the short bursts that meet your students where they are and move them forward.

The book experiences in this chapter will guide your students to do the following:

- Develop self-awareness
- Identify feelings and emotions
- Think flexibly
- Strategically problem solve
- Persist
- Empathize
- Build relationships

Along with my gratitude for inviting me to join you in your teaching space, I'm sending you strength, positivity, and joy as you open the world of possibility that lies between the covers of a book. And, if I knew your name and address, I would send you a bouquet of newly sharpened pencils, too!

# Menu of Shared Reading Interactions

| Book Title | Shared Reading Focus 1 | Shared Reading Focus 2 |
|---|---|---|
| *A Normal Pig* (Steele, 2019) | Listen for Sounds: Clap Syllables | Notice Writer's Craft Moves: Transition Words and Phrases |
| *I Promise* (James, 2020) | Listen for Sounds: Rhyme or Not? | Reread to Boost Comprehension: Read Between the Lines |
| *Watch Me* (Richards, 2021) | Match Letters to Sounds: Word Families *-ook* and *-all* | Reread for Fluency: Join in on a Repeated Phrase |
| *Not Quite Snow White* (Franklin, 2019) | Wonder About Words: Act Out Expressive Words | Reread to Boost Comprehension: Notice How Characters' Feelings Change |
| *Harlem Grown* (Hillery, 2020) | Ponder Punctuation: Commas in a Series | Notice the Writer's Craft Moves: Repeated Phrase |
| *When Grandpa Gives You a Toolbox* (Deenihan, 2020) | Wonder About Words: Compound Words | Reread to Boost Comprehension: Detail Detectives |
| *Dirt Cheap* (Hoffman, 2020) | Reread to Boost Comprehension: Enjoy the Funny Parts | Notice Writer's Craft Moves: Unseen Narrator |
| *The Last Tree* (Haworth-Booth, 2020) | Ponder Punctuation: Ellipses | Reread to Boost Comprehension: Consider Cause and Effect |
| *Oona* (DiPucchio, 2021) | Ponder Punctuation: Parentheses | Notice Writer's Craft Moves: How Dialogue and Inner Thinking Help Readers Understand Characters |
| *Jabari Tries* (Cornwall, 2020) | Reread to Boost Comprehension: The Magic of Three | Reread for Fluency: Join in on Expressive Words |
| *What's the Matter, Marlo?* (Arnold, 2020) | Reread for Fluency: Speech Bubbles | Reread to Boost Comprehension: What's the Reason for the Feeling? |
| *I Talk Like a River* (Scott, 2020) | Wonder About Words: Similes | Notice Writer's Craft Moves: First-Person Point of View |
| *Swashby and the Sea* (Ferry, 2020) | Match Letters to Sounds: Look for Chunks | Wonder About Words: Adjective Trios |
| *The Arabic Quilt: An Immigrant Story* (Khalil, 2020) | Wonder About Words: Different Ways Authors Write "Says" | Notice Writer's Craft Moves: Transition Words and Phrases |

My Favorite Texts and Resources for the First Weeks of School

## Read-Aloud Experience: Be Who You Are

**Book Title:** *A Normal Pig* (Steele, 2019)

**About the Book:** Pip the pig is satisfied being her normal self until a new pig joins the class. After the new pig teases Pip about her lunch and her artwork, she comes home upset and lashes out at her family. Pip's wise mom senses the problem and suggests a family trip to a museum in the city. There, Pip realizes that being "normal" doesn't mean being the same as everyone else.

To find a book like this one, look for the following:

- Characters developing self-awareness
- Stories with themes that will resonate with your learners

## Comprehension Conversation

**Before Reading**

**Notice the Cover Illustration**

What do you suppose the pigs on the cover are doing? [Taking a class picture.] What else do you notice? Which pig would you say is the "normal" pig? [Listen to students' thoughts.] There are some hints on the book casing, the endpapers, and the title page that might make you rethink your first answer. [Glance at those book parts, and then discuss any new insights students have gleaned from the illustrations.]

**Set a Purpose:** The title of this book is *A Normal Pig*. While enjoying this story together, we're going to ponder the meaning of the word *normal*.

### During Reading

- *Then one day, a new pig came to school* page: What changed on this page? How do you think the new pig's comments made Pip feel?

- *When her parents asked her what was wrong* page: Is it Pip's parents' fault she's upset? Notice what she is drawing. [A house.] Why do you suppose she's drawing a house? [Maybe because the new pig made fun of her unique house drawing in art class.]

- *At the playground, all the pigs looked so different* page: Why do you think Pip's mom wanted to take her to the city? When you compare the kids on the city playground to the ones on Pip's school playground, what do you notice? [Flip back to the first page to compare. Listen and respond to students' insights about rich diversity found in the city park compared to that found on Pip's school playground.]

- *When they got home, Pip was feeling better* page: Which events do you think caused Pip to change her mind about wanting a "normal" lunch? Think and talk about this question with a friend.

---

**Learning Targets:**

- I notice the words and actions of characters in a book.

- I think about how my words and actions make me who I am.

## After Reading

- Can you infer that the author, K-Fai [Kay-Fy] Steele, was trying to teach you about the word *normal*? If someone asks you what the word *normal* means, what would you say?

- Let's go back to the museum page to translate what the pigs are saying in their own languages. [The author provides translations on the copyright page.]

### Extend the Experience

- On this blank sheet of paper, draw or write any big ideas or lessons you learned from listening to this story.

- Remember the page when Pip was thinking about all of the things she could do when she grew up. Divide a piece of paper into half, and write or draw about two things you want to do when you grow up. For an extra challenge, flip to the back and share two other possibilities.

## Similar Titles

 ***Avocado Asks: What Am I?* (Abe, 2020)**

**About the Book:** A little girl points at Avocado and asks, "Is an avocado a fruit or a vegetable?" This sends Avocado on a journey of self-discovery. Just when Avocado is feeling lost and alone, Tomato helps Avocado celebrate being a unique individual. This book pairs nicely with *Ogilvy* (Underwood, 2019a).

 ***Fred Gets Dressed* (Brown, 2021)**

**About the Book:** Fred bounds through his house "naked and wild and free" until he comes to his parents' closet. When the clothes on his dad's side don't quite work, he has better luck with one of his mom's outfits. After he adds some lipstick (on his cheek), his parents find him and, without judgment or hesitation, join in the dress-up fun.

**Key Vocabulary and Kid-Friendly Definitions:**

- *respond*: to answer or react in some way

- *usual*: the most common way

View the author talking about *A Normal Pig* at resources.corwin.com/shakeupsharedreading

## Short Bursts of Shared Reading: *A Normal Pig*

### Focus 1–Listen for Sounds: Clap Syllables

#### Before Reading

**Set the Stage:** As we reread *A Normal Pig,* we are going to pause on key pages to clap the syllables of certain objects that appear in the pictures. [If this phonological awareness activity is new to students, you may want to introduce syllable clapping by teaching them how to listen for and clap the syllables in their first name.]

#### During Reading

#### Investigate Key Pages

#### My Turn

*Pip was a normal pig who did normal stuff* page: I'm going to reread this page. Now, I'll point to a picture and clap the syllables. First, I'll clap the syllable in *Pip*. Pip is a one-clap or one-syllable word. Next, I'll clap the syllables in *playground. Playground* is a two-clap or two-syllable word.

#### Our Turn

*Pip hadn't changed, but she started to feel different* page: On this page, I will point to the instruments and say their names, and then you'll clap:

- drum
- tuba
- clarinet

What do you notice about the number of syllables in each of those words?

#### Your Turn

*When her parents asked her what was wrong* page: As we reread the next four pages, I'm going to choose one item on each page for you to clap.

- refrigerator
- subway
- museum
- swing

[Reread the rest of the book without pausing to clap syllables.]

#### After Reading

#### Nudge Toward Independence

Clapping syllables helps tune your ears into the sounds of words. You can practice this at school or at home by saying the names of your favorite objects and then clapping to find out how many syllables their names contain.

## Focus 2–Notice Writer's Craft Moves: Transition Words and Phrases

### Before Reading

**Set the Stage:** In *A Normal Pig,* K-Fai Steele uses a technique to move a story through time. Instead of writing words like *and* or *and then* over and over, writers add transition words or phrases. Transition words or phrases are like a bridge that gets you from one part of the story to the next.

### During Reading

### Investigate Key Pages

### My Turn

*Then one day, a new pig came to school* page: I notice that the author started this page with a transition phrase. The phrase "Then one day" helps me know that it is a new day.

### Our Turn

*On Saturday, Pip's mother had an idea* page: Reread the first sentence on this page. How did this transition help move the story through time?

### Your Turn

*At the playground, all the pigs looked so different* page: What is different about this transition? Does it tell you *when* or *where?* [Continue to guide students to notice the transitions and the fact that they are often followed by a comma.]

### After Reading

### Nudge Toward Independence

A *transition* is a word or a group of words that carries the reader from one part of the story to the next. I'm going to write some of the transitions we found on this chart in case you want to use them when you are writing. [On an anchor chart, record phrases like *Then one day; On Saturday; At the playground; When they got home;* and *On Monday.*]

> **Innovate on Text:** In the story, we learn that Pip enjoys making art and cooking with her family. What do you like to do? On a blank sheet of paper, draw a self-portrait. Around the picture of your face, draw and label a few things you enjoy doing.

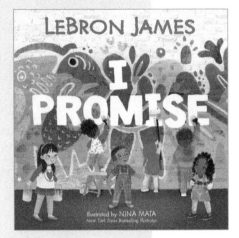

## Read-Aloud Experience: Be Your Best Self

**Book Title:** *I Promise* (James, 2020)

**About the Book:** Meet a group of children in school and beyond who are living up to the promises they've made to themselves. This book is based on the practice of creating a set of self-promises that occurs in LeBron James's Promise School located in his hometown of Akron, Ohio.

To find a book like this one, look for the following:

- Themes that lead to conversations about self-awareness and positivity
- Messages that promote a growth mindset

## Comprehension Conversation

### Before Reading

### Notice the Cover Illustration

One thing I love about this book is Nina Mata's bright, colorful illustrations. She created them using digital tools—isn't that amazing? What are the kids on the cover busy doing? It looks to me like they are working together as a team. Would you agree?

**Set a Purpose:** Have you heard of the basketball player named LeBron James? Here's his picture on the back of the book. [Display back cover.] Along with being a basketball player, he also donates his time and money to help others. For children in his hometown, he worked with folks to open a Promise School. As we read, we'll learn about the kinds of promises we can make to ourselves. A promise is when you tell yourself or someone else that something will happen or will get done.

### During Reading

- *I promise to go to school* . . . page: What do you think LeBron James means by "respect the game plan"? [Discuss different "game plan" or "group plan" scenarios like working with friends to complete a task or helping family members clean up after a meal.]
- *I promise to run full court* . . . page: On this page, when LeBron James talks about your *magic,* he means everything that makes you unique. What are different ways you can let your magic shine? Picture some of them in your mind.
- *I promise to wear a big smile* . . . page: There are two words on this page that might be puzzling to you. Let's take a look. The first word is *humble.* On this page, *humble* means that if you win a game, you don't brag or show off. The second word is *defeat.* Defeat is the opposite of win; it means to lose.
- *I promise to ask questions* . . . page: Let's talk about *second chances.* A second chance is when you tried something once, it didn't work, so you try it again. Sometimes you even need more than two chances! Have you ever given something a second chance? How did it go? Ask a neighbor how it went for them.
- *I promise to respect my elders and peers the same* page: You can use the picture clues to help you figure out the puzzling words on this page. *Elders* are people who are

## Learning Targets:

- I notice the words and actions of characters in a book.
- I think about how my words and actions make me who I am.
- I talk, write, or draw about how I can use what I learned from this book in my own life.

View the book trailer at resources.corwin.com/shakeupsharedreading

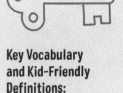

older than you and *peers* are people who are about your same age. In our class-room, smile at an elder. Give an elbow bump to a peer.

## After Reading

- What are some of the words or actions from this book that stuck with you? [If needed, flip back through the pages to spark students' conversation.]

- Which of the promises in the book are similar to promises you've made to yourself?

## Extend the Experience

- In this book, you heard a lot of different personal promises—promises you can make to yourself. Now it's your turn. Write down two prom-ises: a promise you plan to keep at school and one you want to work on at home. See *Personal Promise Reproducible Response Page* located on the companion website (resources.corwin.com/shakeupsharedreading).

- Work together in a shared or interactive writing format to cocreate a class promise.

## Similar Titles

 ***Remarkably You*** **(Miller, 2019)**

**About the Book:** This uplifting book showcases positive messages. The big takeaways readers will learn from this book are that they have the power to change the world and they should look for ways to celebrate their uniqueness and share their gifts with others.

 ***When We Are Kind*** **(Smith, 2020)**

**About the Book:** This book, written by a team of Indigenous creators, highlights the reciprocal relationship between performing acts of kindness and the positive feelings one gains from being kind. Available in a dual-language edition in Diné and English, a French edition, and an English edition.

### Key Vocabulary and Kid-Friendly Definitions:

- *courageous*: to be brave

- *humble*: not bragging or showing off about the things you have or can do

- *respect*: to be polite and nice to others

View the author reading *When We Are Kind* aloud at resources.corwin.com/shakeupsharedreading

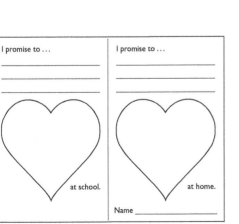

*Personal Promise Reproducible Response Page*

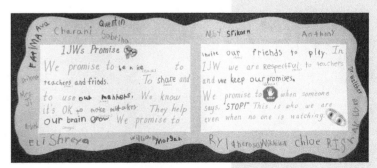

*Cocreated Class Promise*

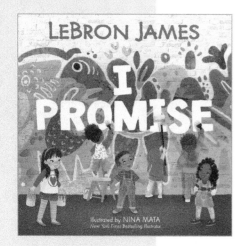

## Short Bursts of Shared Reading: *I Promise*

### Focus 1–Listen for Sounds: Rhyme or Not?

### Before Reading

**Set the Stage:** The book *I Promise* has a rhythm and a flow. It sounds that way because LeBron James sprinkles in some rhyming words. Get ready to reread, listen, and decide whether the two words at the end of the lines rhyme.

### During Reading

### Investigate Key Pages

### My Turn

*I promise to work hard . . .* page: [Reread the page.] The two words we're going to listen to are *right* and *life*. To help me tune in to the word endings, I will bounce the rhymes. That means I pretend to put the first word in my left hand and say, "right, -ight, -ight," while bouncing my hand up and down. Then, put the second word in my right hand and say, "life, -ife, -ife," while doing the same thing. When I listen carefully to the sounds at the end of the two words, I hear that *right* and *life* do not rhyme.

### Our Turn

*I promise to go to school . . .* page: [Reread the page together.] The two words we're going to listen to are *can* and *plan*. Let's bounce the rhymes. Put the first word in your left hand and say, "can, -an, -an." Then, put the second word in your right hand and say, "plan, -an, -an." Do the two words rhyme?

### Your Turn

[Continue in the same fashion as you reread a few more pages. To help students make the sound–letter connection, you can revisit the word pairs and use a variation of Cunningham's (2017) *Rounding Up the Rhymes* strategy:

- Write the word pairs on two separate index cards or Google Jamboard sticky notes.
- Listen for rhymes.
- If they rhyme, keep them displayed.
- If they don't rhyme, tear up the cards (kids love this!) or delete the Jamboard sticky notes.

Here are the word pairs from the book to explore:

| | | |
|---|---|---|
| time–shine | right–fight | same–came |
| things–bring | got–spot | walls–falls |
| speak–defeat | | |

### After Reading

### Nudge Toward Independence

Listening to and noticing rhyming words will help you both as a reader and as a speller.

## Focus 2–Reread to Boost Comprehension: Read Between the Lines

### Before Reading

**Set the Stage:** Our focus for rereading is to stop on key pages to read between the lines. That means we have to think beyond the picture and word clues and use our schema to try to piece together what LeBron James is trying to help us understand.

### During Reading

#### Investigate Key Pages

#### My Turn

*I promise to work hard and do what's right* . . . page: When I first read the words *be a leader* on this page and look at the picture clues, I might think LeBron James is telling me to be a line leader. But when I read the rest of the sentence, I revise my thinking. The word clues help me see that he means much more than that. I infer he is saying that I should lead in different ways, like being the first to invite a new friend to play.

#### Our Turn

*I promise to run full court* . . . page: In basketball, when someone runs full court, they run from one basket to the other, but the picture shows kids playing soccer, so I'm thinking he means more than running back and forth on a basketball court. Can you infer what *run full court* means? [Try your best, finish what you start, don't give up.]

#### Your Turn

*I promise to cross bridges* page: Okay. The last line on this page reads, "learn from the fall." Even though the picture shows a child falling, your challenge is to think beyond that meaning. Put your head together with a partner and see if you can infer what he might be telling us to do. [Learn from mistakes.]

### After Reading

#### Nudge Toward Independence

Sometimes we have to think beyond the words and picture on the page to understand the author's message. This takes time and practice. When you are doing this on your own, it is helpful to talk about the ideas in your books with another reader.

> **Innovate on Text:** Writers use different patterns or structure to create texts. LeBron James used a list pattern to write *I Promise*. If you want to write a list book, think of your own topic or use one of these ideas:
>
> - Leaders are . . .
> - I'd like to try . . .
> - I'm special because . . .

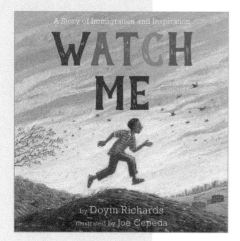

## Read-Aloud Experience: Infer Characters' Feelings

**Book Title:** *Watch Me* (Richards, 2021)

**About the Book:** Based on the true story of Doyin Richards's father, readers meet Joe, who emigrated from Sierra Leone to America in pursuit of his dreams. Whenever Joe encounters doubters or challenges, he persists while saying, "Watch me." In the end, he becomes a doctor.

To find a book like this one, look for the following:

- Characters experiencing a wide range of emotions
- Characters who overcome challenges

## Comprehension Conversation

### Before Reading

#### Notice the Cover Illustration

**Learning Targets:**

- I use pictures, words, and my schema to infer how a character is feeling.
- I talk, write, and draw about how the characters felt.

What do you notice about the landscape on the cover? [To the left of the boy, there are mountains and he's running toward a city.] Think about the title *Watch Me*: what are some possible activities we could watch this boy do? Joe Cepeda painted the illustrations in this book with oil paint. If you look closely, you can see the texture of his brushstrokes.

**Set a Purpose:** The subtitle of this book is *A Story of Immigration and Inspiration*. *Immigration* is when people move into a new country. *Inspiration* is what happens when you see another person do something and it gives you the feeling that you could do it too. Now that you know the meaning of the subtitle, do you want to revise or add to your thinking about what you might watch the boy do?

### During Reading

- *Joe had goals and dreams, like you* page: Can you infer Joe's friends' thoughts about his dream of going to America? What clues led you to this inference?
- *His friends and family were right* page: How do you suppose Joe might be feeling on this page? What would you have said if you heard someone teasing Joe?
- *It hurt Joe to be hated for things he couldn't control* page: Which adjectives would you use to describe Joe? Joe is . . . [brave, persistent, determined].
- *How do I know?* page: Talk about what you learned on this page. Did the fact that this book is about the author's dad surprise you?

### After Reading

- Explain how Joe's emotions changed throughout the book. What was Joe's attitude at the beginning of the story? How did his feelings change when he arrived in America? Can you imagine how he felt when he became a doctor?
- Choose one word that best describes how you felt after reading this book. Share that word with a neighbor. Ask your neighbor about their word. Are your words the same or different?

### Extend the Experience

- Use the *Inferring a Character's Feelings Reproducible Response Page* found on the companion website (resources.corwin.com/shakeup sharedreading) to write and draw about how Joe's feelings changed throughout the story.

- The people Joe met when he came to America were not very welcoming. Throughout your life, you are going to be in many situations where you will have the chance to warmly welcome someone. What are some different ways to make others feel welcome? Let's work together to create a list of welcoming actions that we can practice.

**Key Vocabulary and Kid-Friendly Definitions:**

- *achieve*: to get something you've been working for

- *doubted*: thought something might not be true

- *prove*: to show that something is true or correct

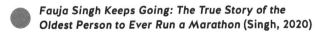

## Similar Titles

● ***Fauja Singh Keeps Going: The True Story of the Oldest Person to Ever Run a Marathon* (Singh, 2020)**

**About the Book:** Like Joe in *Watch Me*, Fauja defies the expectations of naysayers throughout his long, happy life. Beginning in his childhood when his relatives think he is too weak to walk and continuing until age 100 when he completes the Toronto Waterfront Marathon, Fauja persists. The repeated refrain "Fauja did not listen and Fauja did not stop" reveals the theme of this book. This biography begins with an inspiring letter from Fauja Singh and ends with additional background information, including his running accomplishments.

● ***Nya's Long Walk to Water: A Step at a Time* (Park, 2019)**

**About the Book:** In the picture book companion to Linda Sue Park's (2010) novel *A Long Walk to Water*, set in South Sudan, we meet Nya (pronounced as one syllable: nyah) and her sister Akeer. They are on their way home from fetching water when Akeer falls ill. With no help in sight, Nya has to carry both Akeer and the water on the long walk back to their village.

*Ways to Welcome Chart*

Name _____

**Inferring a Character's Feelings**

| In the beginning ... | In the middle ... | At the end ... |
|---|---|---|
| The character felt | The character felt | The character felt |
| because | because | because |

*Inferring a Character's Feelings Reproducible Response Page*

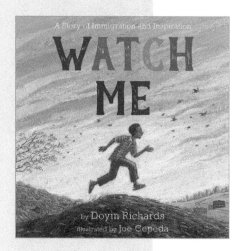

## Short Bursts of Shared Reading: *Watch Me*

### Focus 1—Match Letters to Sounds: Word Families *-ook* and *-all*

### Before Reading

**Set the Stage:** Word detectives, get ready to tune your ears to the end of words by listening for and looking at rhyming patterns or word families. If you can read and spell one word in the word family, it will help you read and spell all of the other words with the same pattern.

### During Reading

### Investigate Key Pages

### My Turn

*Do you watch them learn and study, surrounded by books?* page: I notice that the words at the end of these two questions rhyme. The words are *looks* and *books*. Why do you suppose Doyin Richards chose to have this section of the book rhyme? The words *look* and *book* are in the same word family. I'm going to write them on a word family chart so that you can see the spelling pattern at the end of the word.

### Our Turn

*Do you watch them throw an awesome curveball?* page: Can you find two words from the same word family? [*curveball* and *hall*.] Look at the end of each word as I write it on the word family chart. What do you notice? Listen to how the ends of the words sound when you say them aloud.

### Your Turn

[Divide the class into two groups, one for the *-ook* word family and one for the *-all* word family. Invite students in each group to work with a partner or on their own to brainstorm and write down as many words as they can think of that have the same spelling pattern. Students may jot words on a whiteboard, Google Jamboard, or piece of paper. Share and add the words to your class word family chart. Chant the words together to listen for the ending sound.]

| Word Family Chart | |
| --- | --- |
| **-ook Family** | **-all Family** |
| look | ball |
| book | hall |

### After Reading

### Nudge Toward Independence

Using the rhyming patterns in words or word families to help you decode and spell words is a smart strategy. If you would like a small copy of the word family chart we made to keep in your notebook, let me know.

## Focus 2—Reread for Fluency: Join in on a Repeated Phrase

### Before Reading

**Set the Stage:** When we read this book the first time, we noticed that the author repeated the phrase "Watch me." I'm going to reread, and you're going to join in on the words "Watch me."

### During Reading

### Investigate Key Page

### My Turn

*He was different* page: When I read the words "Watch me," I'm going to imagine I'm Joe talking to his friends and family.

### Our Turn

*But Joe's dreams didn't hang out with "safe" and "easy"* page: Pretend you're Joe. How would you say, "Watch me" to the people who are doubting him?

### Your Turn

*Many of his teachers and classmates thought he wouldn't graduate* page: Think about what is happening on this page before reading, "Watch me."

### After Reading

### Nudge Toward Independence

Why do you suppose the author repeated the words "Watch me"? How does the repeated phrase help you understand Joe's story? What other phrases could Joe have repeated that would have a similar meaning?

> **Innovate on Text:** Has anyone ever told you that you can't do something that you know you have the ability to do? Think about activities that are safe and healthy for you to do. Use this sentence stem to write about your experience: When someone tells me I can't _____, I will say, "Watch me!"

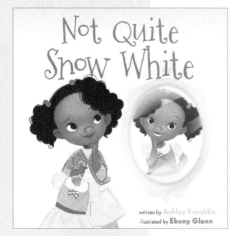

written by **Ashley Franklin**
illustrated by **Ebony Glenn**

## Read-Aloud Experience: Empathize With Characters' Feelings

**Book Title:** *Not Quite Snow White* (Franklin, 2019)

**About the Book:** Tameika's life is filled with music and movement. She loves being on stage but has never played the part of a princess. At school, when she sees a poster advertising auditions for the princess in *Snow White,* she's the first one in line. During auditions, she overhears kids whispering reasons why she shouldn't get the part. When her father finds out what happened, he reassures Tameika that she is "just enough of all the right stuff" to be a princess. With her confidence buoyed, Tameika nails the audition and gets the part.

To find a book like this one, look for the following:

- Illustrations that clearly reflect characters' feelings
- Characters who display a range of emotions
- Characters who overcome challenges

### Learning Targets:

- I use pictures, words, and my schema to infer how a character is feeling.
- I think about how I would feel in the same situation.
- I talk, write, and draw about how the characters felt.

online resources

View the author talking about the book at resources.corwin.com/shakeupsharedreading

## Comprehension Conversation

### Before Reading

#### Notice the Cover Illustration

Compare the picture of the girl with her reflection in the mirror. What do you notice? Why do you suppose that the illustrator, Ebony Glenn, made the two images look different? Talk about it with a friend. If you were going to write words in a thinking bubble above each image of the girl, what would each bubble say?

**Set a Purpose:** Ponder the title *Not Quite Snow White.* What do you think the author means? [That the girl is not Snow White yet.] Readers, as we read to find out whether the girl gets to be Snow White, notice how she is feeling and consider how you might react if you were in the same situations.

### During Reading

- *Tameika had a hip-rolling happy dance* page: Look at Tameika's face and body in these pictures. Can you find clues to help you infer her mood? [Discuss her body language and facial features.]

- *After the audition, Tameika heard some of the other kids whispering* page: Imagine what is going through Tameika's mind right now. What would you be thinking and feeling?

- *Tameika slouched and sucked in her belly* page: Wow! Tameika sure looks different here than she did at the beginning of the story. What caused her mood to change? Ask a neighbor how they would be feeling if they were in a similar situation.

- *"Besides," said her dad, "Snow White is just pretend"* page: Let me reread her dad's encouraging words: "You're just enough of all the right stuff." Tell a friend what you think he means.

## After Reading

- What words would you use to describe Tameika's emotions at the end of the story?

- Think about the sentence on the last page. Where have you read that sentence before? [They were the encouraging words her dad told her at bedtime.]

## Extend the Experience

- What do you think Tameika learned about herself in this book? Write and/or draw to explain your thinking.

- I noticed when we were discussing this book, we were using words like *happy, sad,* and *mad* to describe Tameika's feelings. I think we can challenge ourselves to more accurately describe characters' emotions if we have a range of words to use. [Gather books that highlight the feelings *happy, sad,* and/or *mad*. Over the next few days, read a book featuring one particular feeling. Then, using a thesaurus, help students brainstorm a list of synonyms for each word. In small groups, invite learners to put the synonyms in order of intensity. Record words on a chart or electronic document to display near read-aloud area.]

## Similar Titles

 ***Amazing Grace* (Hoffman, 1991)**

**About the Book:** When I finished the last page of *Not Quite Snow White*, I immediately thought of *Amazing Grace*. Like Tameika, Grace wants to act in a play as Peter Pan, but two children tell her she can't because she is Black and she's a girl. Buoyed by the positivity of her mother and grandmother, she auditions and gets the lead role.

 ***The Bug Girl (A True Story)* (Spencer & McNamara, 2020)**

**About the Book:** Sophia loves bugs. When Sophia brings a grasshopper to school, her friends tease her and kill the bug. Seeing Sophia's passion dampened, her mother reaches out to a group of entomologists. This request for a "bug pal" results in an outpouring of bug-related advice and opportunities. Backmatter includes "More Bug Facts."

*Synonyms for Happy and Mad*

## Short Bursts of Shared Reading: *Not Quite Snow White*

### Focus 1—Wonder About Words: Act Out Expressive Words

#### Before Reading

**Set the Stage:** Tameika is an energetic girl. We know that because of the words Ashley Franklin used to describe her actions. Let's read, think about, and act out some of the words in *Not Quite Snow White*.

#### During Reading

#### Investigate Key Pages

##### My Turn

*Tameika had a hip-rolling happy dance* page: I'm noticing the words *swayful* and *stomping*. They communicate two very different actions. A swayful dance would be more flowing and quiet, like ballet. On the other hand, I might stomp to a rap or hip-hop song. Let me show you how I would act out both dances. Now, try it with me.

##### Our Turn

*Tameika slouched and sucked in her belly* page: Reread the first sentence on this page. What does it mean to slouch? Show me your slouchy look. Why do you suppose Tameika was slouching?

##### Your Turn

*It was Tameika's turn at last* page: When Tameika was on stage, her legs were *jittery*. Stand up and act out what jittery legs might look like. Have you ever had jittery legs?

#### After Reading

#### Nudge Toward Independence

When you read characters' actions, imagine yourself doing the same action. Notice if doing that helps you connect with and understand the character.

**Innovate on Text:** If you could act in a play or a movie, what role would you want? Why? Write, draw, or video record your answer.

## Focus 2–Reread to Boost Comprehension: Notice How Characters' Feelings Change

### Before Reading

**Set the Stage:** Our purpose for rereading is to notice the changes in Tameika's emotions throughout the story. We're also going to think about where the story took a turn.

### During Reading

### Investigate Key Pages

### My Turn

*Tameika was so excited that she went to both days of auditions* page: I'm going to choose precise adjectives to describe Tameika's feelings at the beginning of the story. Up to this point in the story, I would say that Tameika is joyful, confident, and excited. I will write those adjectives on the *How Characters' Feelings Change* chart.

### Our Turn

*For the first time, she didn't feel like dancing or singing* page: If you had to describe Tameika's feelings now, what adjectives would you choose? Let's jot them on the chart.

### Your Turn

*Maybe she was just enough of all the right stuff* page: Talk with a friend. Brainstorm some adjectives you would use to describe Tameika's mood at the end of the story. Tell your friend about the event that happened in the middle of the story that caused her feelings to change. That event is called the *turning point*. I'll mark it on the chart.

### After Reading

### Nudge Toward Independence

Today we studied how Tameika's feelings changed over the course of the story and noticed the turning point of a story. Noticing the turning point helps you better understand how a character grows and changes as they learn new things. To use what we practiced today, you might mark the turning point in your book with a sticky note. Then, talk about it with a friend to notice the character's feelings before and after the turning point. Ponder the lessons the character learned along the way.

*How Characters' Feelings Change Chart*

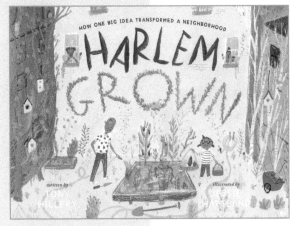

## Read-Aloud Experience:
## Notice Characters' Decisions

**Book Title:** *Harlem Grown: How One Big Idea Transformed a Neighborhood* (Hillery, 2020)

**About the Book:** Based on the inspiring true story of how Tony Hillery worked alongside children to plant the Harlem Grown gardens in New York City.

To find a book like this one, look for the following:

- Characters or people who figure out how to solve problems
- Characters or people who work with others to improve their community

### Learning Targets:

- I notice how characters make decisions when they have a problem.
- I think about how I make decisions when I have a problem.

## Comprehension Conversation

### Before Reading

### Notice the Cover Illustration

Jessie Hartland included a lot of details in her cover illustration. Tell a friend three details you see. Ask them if they can find three different details. The title of this story is *Harlem Grown*. Notice there are words above the title. This is the subtitle of the book: *How One Big Idea Transformed a Neighborhood*. The subtitle adds more information about the topic of the book. The word *transformed* means to change something. Put together what you've learned from the title, subtitle, and illustration to predict what the big idea might be.

**Set a Purpose:** I guess we better start reading to see if your predictions match the author's ideas! I'm also curious to find out why something in the neighborhood needed a change and what decisions people made that transformed the neighborhood.

### During Reading

- *Once, in a big city, in a bustling neighborhood, there was Nevaeh's school* page: What have you learned so far about the setting for this book? Do you notice any problems?

- *One day a man came to PS 175* page: What's his idea? Is your prediction the same as it was before we started reading, or have you revised it based on what we've read?

- *Her friends came too* page: Wow! They planted 400 seedlings. Do you think all of them will grow?

- *Then the kids watered and weeded, and their plants began to grow* page: Hmmm! What's the problem? [Nevaeh's plants aren't growing.] What does Mr. Tony decide to do? [Plant something different.] Do you think it will work?

- *Wood* page: What is Mr. Tony's new plan? Have you ever seen a raised bed garden? How might this type of garden help? [Fewer weeds, keeps critters out, better soil.]

## After Reading

- What was the big idea that transformed the neighborhood?
- Talk about the decisions Mr. Tony made to create the garden.

### Extend the Experience

- Now that the garden is growing, what else could Mr. Tony and the kids do with the food from the garden? Write, draw, or video record your ideas.
- In this book, Mr. Tony and the kids planted a garden and watched it grow. We are going to do a little experiment to learn more about how seeds grow. Let me show you how to make a "germinator." [For a how-to video by PBS Learning Media, see https://bit.ly/3x9WRSL. The figure below lists directions for quick reference.]

## Similar Titles

 **Big Feelings (Penfold, 2021)**

**About the Book:** The kids in *Big Feelings* decide to spruce up an empty lot in their neighborhood. As they are working, they experience conflict and have to compromise to come up with a solution. Ultimately, they accomplish their goal of creating a playground only to have a storm make a mess of their hard work. Once again, they have to find a way to look on the bright side. Most of the story is told through the illustrations, making this an ideal book for inferring both the plot and characters' feelings.

 **A Garden to Save the Birds (McClure, 2021)**

**About the Book:** After a bird crashes into the window of Callum's house, Callum, his mom, and his sister Emmy set out to make their yard more bird-friendly. The more they do and learn, the more they want to spread their knowledge. Soon, their whole block has become more welcoming to birds. Eventually, Callum's neighborhood is designated as a certified wildlife habitat. The backmatter includes suggestions for creating safe areas for birds.

### Key Vocabulary and Kid-Friendly Definitions:

- *bustling*: everything moving quickly, a busy place
- *cluttered*: filled with lots of different things
- *tended*: to have taken care of something

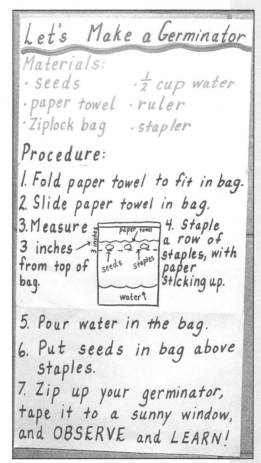

*Let's Make a Germinator*

**Materials:**
- seeds
- paper towel
- Ziplock bag
- $\frac{1}{2}$ cup water
- ruler
- stapler

**Procedure:**
1. Fold paper towel to fit in bag.
2. Slide paper towel in bag.
3. Measure 3 inches from top of bag.
4. Staple a row of staples, with paper sticking up.
5. Pour water in the bag.
6. Put seeds in bag above staples.
7. Zip up your germinator, tape it to a sunny window, and OBSERVE and LEARN!

*How to Make a Germinator*

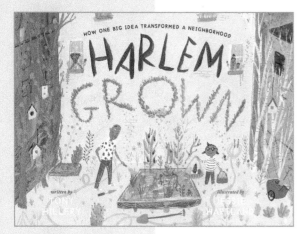

## Short Bursts of Shared Reading:
### *Harlem Grown*

### Before Reading

**Set the Stage:** Today we're going to look for and learn about commas. A comma looks like a period with a tail on it. Let's study the commas in this book to see what we can discover.

### During Reading

### Investigate Key Pages

### My Turn

*Nevaeh called it the haunted garden* page: Here is a list of the items that are cluttering the haunted garden. I notice that each item is followed by a comma. That signals me to rest or pause after reading each item. Listen to how that sounds. [Reread the page aloud.] Writers use commas to separate a list of three or more things.

### Our Turn

*Four hundred seedlings went into the ground, one for each kid* page: This is a list of the spices they planted. What do you notice after each spice in the list? [A comma.] Read the list using what you know about commas.

### Your Turn

*and at last . . .* page: Wow! Do you see this gigantic list? I'll read it first, and then you can echo read it after me. Notice the comma after each food.

### After Reading

### Nudge Toward Independence

What did you learn about commas? When writers use commas between items in a list, the convention is called *commas in a series*. I bet you'll start noticing commas between items in a list in the books you're reading. Remember that a comma is a signal to pause while you're reading.

## Focus 2–Notice Writer's Craft Moves: Repeated Phrase

**Before Reading**

**Set the Stage:** Authors repeat words or phrases to emphasize a point or help us remember important parts of the story. Let's see if that's true in *Harlem Grown*.

**During Reading**

**Investigate Key Pages**

**My Turn**

*Once, in a big city called New York* page: When we read this book the first time, I noticed that Tony Hillery repeated some of the words on this page a few more times in the book. On this page, the words tell me about the setting and the problem of the story. Those are important elements to remember.

**Our Turn**

*Once, in a big city* page: Reread this page with me. Which words are the same as the first page, and which are different? Why do you suppose Tony Hillery repeats a similar phrase here?

**Your Turn**

*Once, in a big city called New York* page: What do you notice about the repeated words on this page? [Discuss how Tony Hillery "bookended" the story by using a similar beginning and end. Also, draw students' attention to how this page summarizes the story.]

**After Reading**

**Nudge Toward Independence**

Tony Hillery isn't the only author who uses repeated phrases. As you're reading, notice how other authors use repetition to make certain words or ideas stand out. Think about how you might use repeated phrases in the stories you are writing.

**Innovate on Text:** In the backmatter, there is a page that says you can start a garden anywhere. If you were going to start a garden, where would it be? What would you plant? Draw and label a picture of your garden.

## Read-Aloud Experience:
## Notice Characters' Reactions

**Book Title:** *When Grandpa Gives You a Toolbox*
(Deenihan, 2020)

**About the Book:** It's the boy's birthday, and instead of getting what he wished for—a house for his dolls—his grandpa gives him a toolbox. The boy is polite but not excited about his new gift. When he sees a bird without a nest, it sparks an idea. With his grandpa's help, he builds a birdhouse. The boy comes to appreciate and enjoy the toolbox one project at a time.

To find a book like this one, look for the following:

- Characters who make the best of a difficult situation
- Intergenerational relationships

## Comprehension Conversation

### Before Reading

### Notice the Cover Illustration

The title of this book is *When Grandpa Gives You a Toolbox.* What can you infer from looking at the cover? [It's the boy's birthday. He's unhappy about getting a toolbox.] Look carefully at the title. It's almost as if it has been written on graph paper; it looks like a blueprint or design for building something. People use this kind of paper when they are planning a project. Hmmm. Any thoughts?

**Set a Purpose:** I'm curious to know what the boy is going to make using the tools in his toolbox. Do you have any predictions? Share them with a classmate. Readers notice what characters say, how they act, and how they react to different situations. Let's open the book and get this story started!

### During Reading

- Front endpapers: What is happening on the endpapers? [Grandpa is pulling into the boy's driveway with a gift in the bed of his truck.] After reading, we'll compare the front endpapers to those in the back to decide if they're the same or different.

- *Next, compliment Grandpa as he shares photos . . .* page: How did the boy react to his gift? [He listened patiently, complimented Grandpa, and gave him a hug.] Let's talk about his reaction. We know he was disappointed, but he was still patient and kind. What does this tell you about the boy?

- *It'll be easy to forget about Grandpa's toolbox* page: Can you infer what is going on here? Look carefully at the illustrations. Whisper your prediction to a neighbor.

- *With guidance and lots of practice, you'll discover . . .* page: Remember the blueprint we saw on the cover. What are they designing on this page? [Birdhouse plans.]

- *You and Grandpa will work together measuring and sawing* page: Hmmm! Can you predict what they are building this time?

## Learning Targets:

- I notice how characters react to problems or situations.
- I think about how I react to problems or situations.

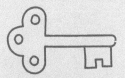

## After Reading

- Recall the boy's feelings at the beginning of the story, and compare them to the way he felt at the end. What changed? Do you think that would have happened if the boy had a different reaction to the toolbox?

- How are the front and back endpapers alike? How are they different?

## Extend the Experience

- When the boy got the toolbox, he wasn't excited but reacted by being patient, complimenting his grandpa, and giving him a hug. There will be many times in your life when you will be faced with situations that do not go the way you expect, so it's helpful to think through ways to deal with disappointment. Imagine I told you we were going on a field trip, but when you got to school you found out that the trip was cancelled. Work with a partner to come up with different ways you could react to this unexpected event. Then, we'll share.

- In this story, the boy and his grandpa built a birdhouse, a house for his dolls, and a tree house. If you had a toolbox, what would you build? Write your idea and make a plan on the *Toolbox Reproducible Response Page* located on the companion website (resources.corwin.com/shakeupsharedreading). Look on the last page of *When Grandpa Gives You a Toolbox* for some ideas.

## Key Vocabulary and Kid-Friendly Definitions:

- *complain*: to say that you are not happy with something

- *handy*: something that helps you

- *patient*: staying calm when you have to wait a long time or something isn't going your way

View the illustrator of *Drawn Together* discussing his process at resources.corwin.com/shakeupsharedreading

## Similar Titles

 **Drawn Together (Lê, 2018)**

**About the Book:** When a young boy goes to visit his grandfather, they have difficulty communicating because they speak different languages. Just when they give up trying, they discover a new way to connect—through their shared love of drawing.

 **When Grandma Gives You a Lemon Tree (Deenihan, 2019)**

**About the Book:** When Grandma gives a little girl a lemon tree for her birthday, she makes lemonade out of lemons while teaching readers a few helpful life lessons. In the end, instead of using the money she's earned from selling lemonade to buy the electronics on her wish list, the girl buys more plants and installs a community garden.

*Ways to React to Disappointment Chart*

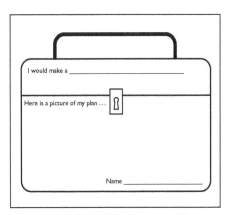

*Toolbox Reproducible Response Page*

## Short Bursts of Shared Reading:
### *When Grandpa Gives You a Toolbox*

Focus 1—Wonder About Words:
Compound Words

### Before Reading

**Set the Stage:** Compound words are two separate words put together. When they are joined together, they make a new word. Sometimes the compound word has a new meaning. Other times, you can figure out the meaning of the word by using the two small words. Let's listen for and clap the two parts of the compound words in this book.

### During Reading

### Investigate Key Pages

### My Turn

*But, surprise!* page: The word *toolbox* is made from the words *tool* and *box*. I'm going to put my left hand up and say *tool,* my right hand up and say *box,* and clap them together to form *toolbox.* I can figure out the meaning of that word by putting the two words together. A *toolbox* is a box for tools.

### Our Turn

*What should you do when Grandpa gives you a toolbox for your birthday?* page: The word *birthday* is also a compound word. It is made from the words *birth* and *day*. I'm going to put my left hand up and say *birth,* my right hand up and say *day,* and clap them together to form *birthday.* Your turn. Clap the words *toolbox* and *birthday.* Can you use the two small words to figure out the meaning of *birthday?*

### Your Turn

*It'll be easy to forget about Grandpa's toolbox* page: Here are two more compound words. Show me how you would clap *forget* and *someone.* [If you want to give students more practice clapping compound words, here are a few more compound words that end with *box: lunchbox, mailbox, sandbox.*]

### After Reading

### Nudge Toward Independence

Let's review by clapping all of the compound words we found in this book and then thinking about the meaning of the words. Do these words have new meanings, or can we figure out the meaning by using the two small words?

| toolbox | birthday | backyard |
|---------|----------|----------|
| forget | someone | treehouse |

## Focus 2–Reread to Boost Comprehension: Detail Detectives

### Before Reading

**Set the Stage:** The illustrations in this book are filled with details that I didn't notice the first time around. I need to reread and look carefully at each picture to pay better attention to them. Get ready to be a detail detective.

### During Reading

#### Investigate Key Pages

#### My Turn

*DO NOT: launch it into outer space* page: The first time I read this page, I didn't realize that the boy's outfits match the situation in each of the four scenes. Even his dog is wearing different kinds of hats in each scene and an eye patch when they are burying treasure! I also see that, in the outer space scene, the neighbor's doghouse is broken. That detail is important later in the story, but the illustrator gave us a preview here.

#### Our Turn

*With guidance and lots of practice, you'll discover . . .* page: Let's flip back to the beginning of the book. Notice the boy always has his superhero doll nearby. Where is it on this page? Hmmm! Let's watch for the doll as we continue rereading.

#### Your Turn

*You and Grandpa will work together measuring and sawing* page: Look at the details in the four illustrations on this page. Tell a friend what you notice. [If you look in the background through the window, you can see evidence that it has taken them a year to build this project together. The illustrations show that the seasons are changing.] How are the details in these illustrations helpful in figuring out what is going on in the story?

### After Reading

#### Nudge Toward Independence

Whether in the pictures or words, details make a story more meaningful. Think about how much we might have missed if we didn't reread this book! Rereading the pictures to notice the details is something you can do to make sense of what happened in the book. When you're writing, adding details to your words or pictures will keep your readers interested.

**Innovate on Text:** You can borrow the author's idea to write your own version of this story. Think about a time when someone gave you something. What happened after they gave it to you.

Use this sentence stem to get started: When _____ gave me a _____, . . .

## Read-Aloud Experience: Make a New Plan

**Book Title:** *Dirt Cheap* (Hoffman, 2020)

**About the Book:** Birdie really wants the XR1000 Super Extreme Soccer Ball, but she doesn't have any money. Helped by an interactive narrator, she decides to sell the dirt from her yard. Once she lowers the price to twenty-five cents, she makes enough money to buy the soccer ball. In an unexpected twist, she realizes she has dug up her whole lawn and therefore has no place to play soccer. Fortunately, resourceful Birdie has a solution—she opens a lawn care service.

To find a book like this one, look for the following:

- Characters who are innovative problem solvers
- Characters who design, build, and/or innovate

## Comprehension Conversation

### Before Reading

**Notice the Cover Illustration**

Can you figure out what this girl is doing? [She's digging up the grass and selling dirt.] Let me show you the whole wraparound cover. See how it is just one big scene that wraps around the whole book. What is happening on the back cover? [A dog is digging up another yard.] How might these two pictures be related? Turn and tell a friend what you're thinking.

**Set a Purpose:** Why do you suppose the girl is selling dirt? [Listen to students' ideas.] What do you think she'll do with the money she earns? [Listen to students' thoughts.] Okay, curious readers. There's only one way to find out. Let's read *Dirt Cheap* to learn the reason this girl is selling dirt and whether it works out the way she plans.

### During Reading

- Front endpapers: Take a careful look at the houses and yards pictured on the front endpapers. What do you notice? We're going to come back to these endpapers after reading the story.

- Title page: Notice that there are two different people talking on this page. It seems like one is the narrator—the narrator's words look like they are typed. Birdie's words look different. Sometimes the different fonts or ways the words are printed help us determine who is talking in the story. Let's see if that is true in this story.

- *Well, soccer balls cost money* page: Explain Birdie's problem. What do you think of the narrator's solution? If you were in Birdie's situation, what would you choose to sell?

- *DIRT FOR SALE!* page: Turn and tell a neighbor your opinion. Do you think twenty-five dollars is too much for a bag of dirt?

- *I used to love playing soccer in my yard* page: Oh my! Can you infer what Birdie's problem is now? How might she go about solving it?

**Learning Targets:**

- I notice how characters think and act to solve problems.
- I look for new and different ways to solve my own problems.

## After Reading

- What did you think of Birdie's new solution? Talk about it with someone nearby.

- Back endpapers: Let's compare and contrast the front and back endpapers. How are they the alike? What's different? What do you think Mark Hoffman is trying to show us?

## Extend the Experience

- In this story, Birdie was faced with many problems. Each time a problem arose, she had to figure out a new solution. What does that tell you about Birdie's personality? If you remember and write down her problems and solutions, it can help you retell the story.

- *And those are just a few of the ways to do it* page: In this story, Birdie's neighbors paid her twenty-five cents using different coin combinations. Can you show different coin combinations to make ___ cents? [Divide students into partners or small groups, and provide each group with real coins or access to digital manipulative coins. Invite each group to show the different combinations to make a specific amount of money. Choose amounts that make sense for the students in each group.]

## Similar Titles

 ***Jabari Tries* (Cornwall, 2020)**

**About the Book:** After overcoming his fears in *Jabari Jumps* (Cornwall, 2017), Jabari sets out to design a flying machine. His sister Nika wants to help. When Jabari resists, his dad steps in and encourages him to view his sister as his inventing partner. After a few attempts, a bit of frustration, and some wise advice from their dad, Jabari and Nika finally find success. [See book experiences in Chapter 1 on pages 70–73.]

 ***The Little Red Fort* (Maier, 2018)**

**About the Book:** This girl-powered version of *The Little Red Hen* begins as Ruby, who is filled with ideas, finds some pieces of wood and asks her brothers to help her build a fort. When they refuse to help, Ruby plans and constructs a fort with assistance from her dad, mom, and grandma. After her brothers finally add some amenities to her fort, she lets them join in the fun. The backmatter includes fort building ideas.

### Key Vocabulary and Kid-Friendly Definitions:

- *hefty*: a big amount of money, a high price

- *plenty*: a lot of something

- *spare*: extra or leftover

| *Dirt Cheap* by Mark Hoffman ||
| :--- | :--- |
| **Problem** | **Solution** |
| Birdie wants a soccer ball but doesn't have money. | She has a yard sale. |
| No one comes to the yard sale. | She sells dirt. |
| The price of dirt is too high. | She lowers the price. |
| Birdie can't play soccer because she dug up her yard. | She starts a lawn service to buy more dirt. |

Dirt Cheap *Problem-Solution Chart*

## Short Bursts of Shared Reading: *Dirt Cheap*

### Focus 1–Reread to Boost Comprehension: Enjoy the Funny Parts

**Before Reading**

**Set the Stage:** This story made me laugh and smile the first time we read it. The author did a few things to make it funny. Get ready to investigate!

**During Reading**

**Investigate Key Pages**

**My Turn**

*Hold up. How cheap?* page: When I reread Birdie's sign, it makes me laugh. It's witty because it is a play on words. When something is *dirt cheap* that means it hardly costs any money, but it's funny here because she's actually selling dirt. Get it?

**Our Turn**

*I used to love playing soccer in my yard* page: Let's read these pages together the way the characters would say them. What made these pages humorous? [The fact that she no longer has a yard!]

**Your Turn**

*Well . . . hmmm!* page: This one is a little trickier, but I think you can figure it out. Reread, think about what the store clerk says, and talk with a friend. [Now she can't afford to buy dirt—the store never sells it that cheap!]

**After Reading**

**Nudge Toward Independence**

To add humor to stories, authors sometimes use a play on words like *dirt cheap* or create funny situations. Humor makes us smile and laugh while we're reading. Notice if you're drawn to stories with humor or prefer more serious ones. Perhaps you enjoy both but at different times.

### Focus 2—Notice Writer's Craft Moves:
### Unseen Narrator

#### Before Reading

**Set the Stage:** In this story there was a character that we never saw. We just heard their words. Let's reread to notice how this affected the story.

#### During Reading

#### Investigate Key Pages

#### My Turn

*Hold up. How cheap?* page: Birdie and the boy are talking, then the narrator interrupts to tell Birdie something important. I think if the narrator weren't a part of this story, Birdie might not have realized that there were different ways to make twenty-five cents. In this story, the narrator is kind of like her friend or helper.

#### Our Turn

*How much did you make, Birdie?* page: This time, I'll read the narrator's words and you read Birdie's words. While we're doing that, picture the narrator. Who do you picture?

#### Your Turn

*So this is it, huh?* page: Read this page to yourself. Then read it aloud the way you think the characters are talking. [Discuss the different ways this page could be interpreted. Is Birdie excited about the soccer ball or having second thoughts? It depends on how you read it!]

#### After Reading

#### Nudge Toward Independence

When you're reading, it is helpful to think about who is saying the words and how they would say them. Writers give us signals with punctuation and sometimes with different fonts or ways the words are printed. As a writer, you can think about how you might use these techniques to help your readers know who is talking and how you want their words to sound.

**Innovate on Text:** Write about something you've always wanted and what you might do to get it.

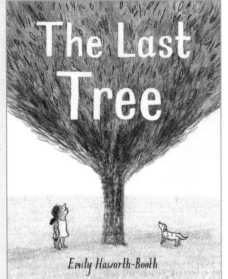

Emily Haworth-Booth

**Learning Targets:**

- I notice how characters think and act to solve problems.

- I think about the consequences of characters' decisions.

- I look for new and different ways to solve problems.

## Read-Aloud Experience: Consider the Consequences

**Book Title:** *The Last Tree* (Haworth-Booth, 2020)

**About the Book:** A group of friends who are searching for the perfect place to settle down find a forest. In the summer, they are happy living among the trees. As the seasons change, they begin cutting down the trees to solve the problems they encounter. Little by little, all but one tree is replaced by houses and a towering wall. When the villagers send their children out to cut down the last tree, they learn an important lesson. Notice that the words on the copyright page are shaped like a tree!

To find a book like this one, look for the following:

- Plots where decisions lead to consequences
- Books with an environmental message

## Comprehension Conversation

### Before Reading

### Notice the Cover Illustration

Why do you suppose the girl and the dog are looking at the tree that way? [Notice that some of the leaves on the tree are shiny.] Think about the title *The Last Tree*. Do you think the tree on the cover is the last tree? Give me a thumbs up or thumbs down to show your answer.

**Set a Purpose:** What do you suppose would happen if there were only one tree left in the world? Talk about it with your friend. Let's notice the decisions the characters in this book make and what happens as a result of those decisions.

### During Reading

- *When summer returned, the sun blazed down and there weren't enough trees left to shade them* page: What is wrong now? [There isn't enough shade, and the fall winds are blowing everything around.] How might the villagers go about solving these problems? What advice would you give them?

- *They needed a new plan* page: One of the villagers said a barrier is the answer. A *barrier* keeps things in or out, like a fence or a wall. What kind of barrier do you predict they are going to build? What do you suppose will happen once the barrier is built? Will it solve their problems once and for all? Give me a thumbs up or thumbs down.

- *Meanwhile, each night the parents asked their children why they hadn't brought back wood* page: Where do you think the children are getting the wood? [Perhaps from the wall.] What makes you think that?

- *In the bright daylight they remembered that they were old friends, not enemies* page: What do you predict the villagers will do next?

- *What fun they had taking down the wall, and how proud they were when it was done!* page: Do you remember when they built the wall? What lesson do you think the villagers learned?

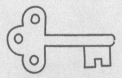
## After Reading

- When the characters in this book tried to solve their problems, their decisions had consequences; that means something happened because they made a certain decision. Do you think this is true in life? [Discuss the fact that consequences can be positive, like seeing someone smile when you do something kind, or negative, like making someone sad by using unkind words or actions.]

- What are other ways the villagers could have solved their problems?

## Extend the Experience

- What could the villagers do if it gets too windy again? Write or draw your solution.

- On this sticky note, write a big idea, lesson, or moral that you learned from reading this story.

## Similar Titles

 ***Kate, Who Tamed the Wind*** **(Scanlon, 2018)**

**About the Book:** A man lives alone in "the creaky house on the tip-top of a steep hill" where the wind blows and blows. When he shouts, "What to do?" Kate hears his cry for help and figures out a way to block the wind—plant trees. So, she and the man plant trees around his house. Over the years, the trees grow and so does the friendship between Kate and her neighbor.

 ***The Tree*** **(Layton, 2016)**

**About the Book:** A couple have a wonderful plan to build a house, but a tree stands in their way. As they begin to cut down the tree, they realize that it is home to many animals. Thinking flexibly, they revise their original house plan and create homes for the creatures who share their tree.

### Key Vocabulary and Kid-Friendly Definitions:

- *clever*: smart, a problem-solver

- *pleasant*: nice and enjoyable

- *remind*: help someone remember to do something

View the author reading *Kate, Who Tamed the Wind* at resources.corwin.com/shakeupsharedreading

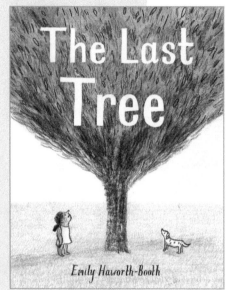

## Short Bursts of Shared Reading: *The Last Tree*

### Focus 1—Ponder Punctuation: Ellipses

#### Before Reading

**Set the Stage:** Ellipses are a punctuation mark that has three dots. Writers use an ellipsis when a word or phrase is missing. They also use an ellipsis to keep readers in suspense—to signal that more text or ideas are coming.

#### During Reading

#### Investigate Key Pages

#### My Turn

*Once upon a time, a group of friends were looking for a place to live* page: At the end of this two-page spread, I notice an ellipsis. The three dots signal that there is more text coming on the next page. An ellipsis makes me want to turn the page to see what is going to happen next.

#### Our Turn

*I saw the neighbors looking at me strangely yesterday* page: What do you notice at the end of the words on this page? [An ellipsis.] Do you remember what those marks mean? What do you see at the beginning of the next page?

#### Your Turn

*that they ran outside and saw that despite all their new wood . . .* page: Look at the ellipsis at the end of this page. Why do you suppose the author put it here?

#### After Reading

#### Nudge Toward Independence

Notice ellipses as you are reading. Think about why the author used them and how they affect the meaning of the story. You also might look for places in your writing where you can use an ellipsis to add suspense.

## Focus 2—Reread to Boost Comprehension: Consider Cause and Effect

### Before Reading

**Set the Stage:** We can reread this book to study cause-and-effect relationships. When the friends tried to solve a problem, their solution caused something else to happen. Their solution is the *cause,* and the result of that decision is the *effect.*

### During Reading

### Investigate Key Pages

### My Turn

*When winter came, the breeze turned colder, and they took a few branches for firewood* page: I can clearly see the cause-effect relationships on this page. As I reread, I'm going to record them on the cause-effect chart.

### Our Turn

*But with nothing to look at but the wall, something happened to the people, too* page: What was the effect of building the wall? Let's add it to the chart. What do you suppose the author means by "they had walls around their hearts"?

### Your Turn

*In the bright daylight they remembered that they were old friends, not enemies* page: What is the effect that seeing the last tree had on the villagers? Talk with a friend. Then, we'll add your ideas to the chart. [If time or interest permits, invite learners to add the cause-effect relationships that occur as the story continues.]

### After Reading

### Nudge Toward Independence

Writers use cause and effect to help us see connections between events. As readers, noticing those connections helps us better understand the problems, solutions, and consequences in a story.

### *The Last Tree* by Emily Haworth-Booth

| When . . . | Then . . . |
|---|---|
| They took branches for firewood. | The rain put out their fires. |
| They chopped down trees to build shelters. | The forest grew colder. |
| They built the wall. | They had walls around their hearts. |
| They saw the last tree. | They remembered how things used to be. |
| **Cause** | **Effect** |

The Last Tree *Cause and Effect Chart*

**Innovate on Text:** Emily Haworth-Booth chose to call this story *The Last Tree.* If you were going to give this book a different title, what would it be? Create your own title for this story, and use ideas from the book to explain the reasons you chose that title.

## Read-Aloud Experience: Keep Trying

**Book Title:** *Oona* (DiPucchio, 2021)

**About the Book:** Oona the mermaid is a treasure hunter. She and Otto, her pet sea otter, are always searching for trinkets. The treasure Oona really wants is the unreachable sparkly crown that lies at the bottom of the rift. With persistence and a little ingenuity, Oona retrieves the crown and learns that sometimes the quest is as rewarding as the find.

To find a book like this one, look for the following:

- Characters who display persistence and ingenuity
- Characters who overcome challenges

## Comprehension Conversation

### Before Reading

#### Notice the Cover Illustration

What words or feelings come to mind when you look at the wraparound cover of *Oona*? Think about the colors that Raissa [RI-Zuh] Figueroa chose for her digital illustrations. Where do you think this story takes place? What are the clues? I predict the main character is named Oona. Do you agree? Why or why not?

**Set a Purpose:** From looking at the cover illustration, we have an idea about the character and setting of this story. We also know that in many stories the main character wants something. Let's dive into the sea and discover what Oona wants and how she is going to go about getting it.

### During Reading

- *But there was one special treasure Oona could never quite reach* page: What does Oona want? If you were Oona, what would you do to get it? The crown was stuck deep inside the *rift*. A rift is a deep hole in the ocean.

- *Her next plan was a good one* page: Study the illustrations. Can you figure out what she is planning to do? What did the squid do?

- *A seashell washed ashore* page: Even though she gave up and took a break, Oona is ready to try again. Do you think she'll finally get the sparkly crown?

- *She dove to the bottom of the murky rift* page: Can you infer how Oona is feeling? Do you predict the rift will gobble her up?

### After Reading

- Did Oona get what she wanted?
- What lessons can we learn from Oona? What might she do differently next time?

## Learning Targets:

- I notice how characters think and act to get what they want.

- I use what I learn from characters when I need to keep trying.

online resources

View the author read aloud at resources.corwin.com/shakeupsharedreading

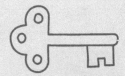

## Extend the Experience

- In the book, the author describes Oona as *brave, curious, and determined.* Can you find clues in her words or actions? Let's use the Character–Trait–Clues chart to record what we learned about Oona's personality. You can use the same chart to record the traits of characters in the books you're reading. See *Character–Trait–Clues Reproducible Response Page* on the companion website (resources.corwin.com/shakeupsharedreading).

- Compare and Contrast! Multigenre Text Set—Under the Sea

  Reading *Oona* got me thinking about the other books you might enjoy that take place in or teach you about the ocean. So, I started a collection of under-the-sea texts and put them in this basket. Read and think about how these texts are the same as or different from *Oona*. I'll leave some sticky notes here so you can write down what you notice. If you find other texts about life under the sea, please add them to the collection.

**Key Vocabulary and Kid-Friendly Definitions:**

- *determined*: wanting to do or get something
- *murky*: dark and cloudy, hard to see through
- *peer*: to look closely so you can see something better

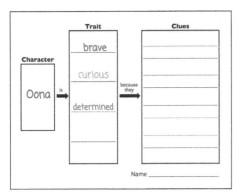

Character-Trait-Clues Chart for Oona

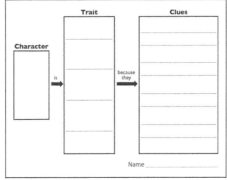

Character–Trait-Clues Reproducible Response Page

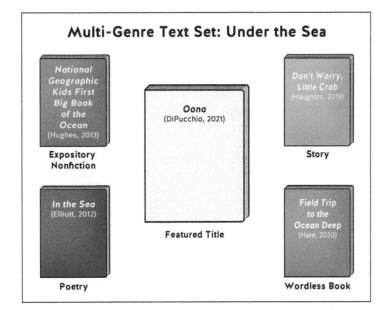

## Short Bursts of Shared Reading: *Oona*

### Focus 1—Ponder Punctuation: Parentheses

#### Before Reading

**Set the Stage:** Writers use conventions to communicate meaning and to make writing clear and understandable. Parentheses are a pair of punctuation marks that look like curved lines and are placed before and after information that is not part of the sentence. The word or words in parentheses add extra information or make the idea in the sentence clearer.

#### During Reading

#### Investigate Key Pages

##### My Turn

*When Oona was just a baby (no bigger than a scallop)* page: Here are a pair of parentheses. Kelly DiPucchio placed parentheses before and after the words that explain how small Oona was when she was a baby. Sometimes I imagine that the words in the parentheses are like a little secret the author is whispering to me. So, I'm going to put my hands on either side of my mouth and read the words in parentheses.

##### Our Turn

*And if that loooong ship plank hadn't bumped her head (hard!)* page: Zoom in on this page and find the parentheses. Let's reread this sentence together. What extra information do we learn from the words in parentheses?

##### Your Turn

*Through the commotion Oona could hear something in the distance* page: As we read this page, think of a place where you could add extra information between a pair of parentheses. Tell me what you would add, and I'll put it in the book on a sticky note.

#### After Reading

#### Nudge Toward Independence

As a reader, notice how conventions, like parentheses, add to the meaning of the text. When you're writing, you may want to add extra information by using parentheses.

## Focus 2–Notice Writer's Craft Moves: How Dialogue and Inner Thinking Help Readers Understand Characters

### Before Reading

**Set the Stage:** To help you better understand the character, authors add dialogue or words the characters say and inner thinking or ideas the character thinks.

### During Reading

#### Investigate Key Pages

#### My Turn

*Poor Oona* page: Let me read you the words Oona says on this page. When Oona shouts the angry words into the pit, it helps me imagine exactly how she is feeling.

#### Our Turn

*She got right to work* page: When Oona peers into the rift, we hear her thinking. What might you say to yourself if you were looking into the rift?

#### Your Turn

*"We did it!" Oona cheered* page: How is Oona feeling now? Say her dialogue the way she would say it. Do you see how dialogue helps you relate to the character?

### After Reading

#### Nudge Toward Independence

Authors want you to feel like you know their characters, like they are your friends. To do this, they let you hear what the characters are saying or thinking. Try adding dialogue and inner thoughts to your own writing. See if it helps your readers get to know your characters.

> **Innovate on Text:** Okay, treasure hunters. If you could dive into the sea to find a treasure, what would it be? Draw a picture and write a sentence or two to tell us about your treasure.

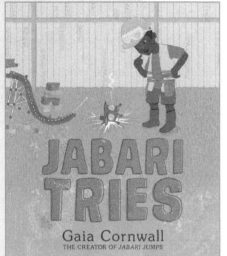

Gaia Cornwall
THE CREATOR OF *JABARI JUMPS*

## Learning Targets:

- I notice how characters think and act to solve problems.
- I use what I learn from characters when I need to keep trying.

## Read-Aloud Experience: Be Patient

**Book Title:** *Jabari Tries* (Cornwall, 2020)

**About the Book:** After overcoming his fears in *Jabari Jumps* (Cornwall, 2017), Jabari sets out to design a flying machine. His sister Nika wants to help. When Jabari resists, his dad steps in and encourages him to view his sister as his inventing partner. After a few attempts, a bit of frustration, and some wise advice from their dad, Jabari and Nika find success. If students like this book, you can find a read-aloud experience for *Jabari Jumps* on page 106 of *The Ramped-Up Read Aloud* (Walther, 2019).

To find a book like this one, look for the following:

- Characters who display persistence and ingenuity
- Characters who overcome challenges

## Comprehension Conversation

### Before Reading

#### Notice the Cover Illustration

Have you ever tried doing something and it didn't turn out the way you expected? Can you tell what Jabari is trying to do? [If you can display the hardcover book casing under the paper book jacket, notice the other flying machines Jabari has designed.]

**Set a Purpose:** Since the title of this story is *Jabari Tries,* we are going to focus on the word *tries*. Study Jabari's actions to see what you can learn from him that might help you when you are trying to do something.

### During Reading

- Title page: Do you see the series of illustrations across the title page? Take turns with a friend to tell the story of these pictures. Start with, "One day . . ."
- *Jabari built an excellent ramp* page: What happened? What could Jabari do to solve the problem?
- *After a lot of building and stacking and hammering and sticking, Jabari was ready* page: Oh no! Not again! Should Jabari give up? What would you do?
- *Jabari gathered up all his patience* page: What did Jabari do to persist or keep going? Have you ever used any of these strategies? What other strategies help you keep trying?

### After Reading

- Do you think Jabari is going to let Nika help him build a rocket to Jupiter?
- What did you learn from Jabari that might help you next time you're trying to do or make something?

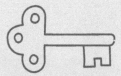

## Extend the Experience

- Think about Jabari's actions in this book. What are some of the things he did when he was faced with a problem? Let's record some tips we learned from Jabari on a chart so we can use them next time we're faced with a problem.

- Are you ready to be an engineer? Here are the supplies you can use. [Gather natural materials from outside or simple materials from your classroom, like math cubes, popsicle sticks, rubber bands, yarn, tape, and so on.] Draw a picture to help you figure out what supplies you'll need. Gather your supplies and get started. Don't forget, engineers often have to build, rebuild, and change their designs before they get them to work. Be persistent and patient! [Provide time for students to plan, create, and share their design.]

## Similar Titles

 ***Nia and the New Free Library*** (Lendler, 2021)

**About the Book:** When the Littletown library gets carried away in a tornado, the townspeople are ready to replace it with something else until a book-loving girl named Nia comes up with a plan. Nia begins rewriting her favorite library books and cleverly lures the townspeople to join her. When books are spilling into the street, a new library has to be built.

 ***A Plan for Pops*** (Smith, 2019)

**About the Book:** Every Saturday, Lou visits Grandad and Pops. Grandad favors plain food and science, while Pops enjoys spicy food and rock and roll. After Pops takes a fall and has to use a wheelchair for mobility, he doesn't want to leave his bedroom. Using the three Ps she's learned from Grandad–perseverance, persistence, and patience–Lou makes a plan to cheer up Pops.

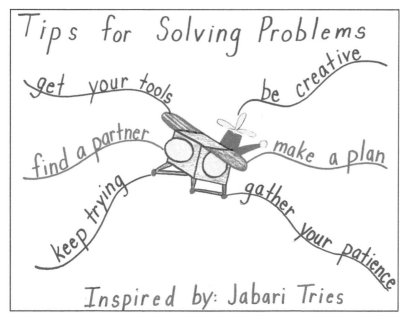

*Tips for Solving Problems Chart*

### Key Vocabulary and Kid-Friendly Definitions:

- *concentrating*: focusing on or thinking about only one thing

- *frustrated*: feeling upset or angry when you can't do something or solve a problem

- *patience*: staying calm when something is taking a long time or there is a problem

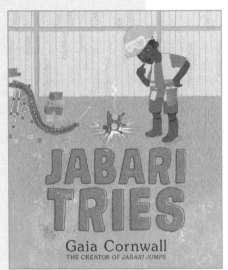

## Short Bursts of Shared Reading: *Jabari Tries*

### Focus 1—Reread to Boost Comprehension: The Magic of Three

#### Before Reading

**Set the Stage:** You might have noticed that in some of the picture books that we read, when the character has a problem, they will try three different ways to solve it. Then, on the fourth attempt, they solve the problem. Writers call this the rule of three or the magic of three. Let's see if Gaia Cornwall uses this technique in *Jabari Tries*.

#### During Reading

#### Investigate Key Pages

#### My Turn

*Jabari built an excellent ramp* page: I see that this is Jabari's first attempt to get his flying machine to go. But it didn't work. Let's see what he tries on his second attempt.

#### Our Turn

*After a lot of building and stacking and hammering and sticking, Jabari was ready* page: For Jabari's second try, he decided to make a bigger ramp. Tell a friend whether this strategy worked or not.

#### Your Turn

- *"Maybe we need more power, Nika," said Jabari* page: What happened on Jabari's third attempt? If Gaia Cornwall used the magic of three, we know that Jabari will solve the problem on his next try. Do you remember what happens next?

- *The partners thought and thought together* page: This is the fourth time Jabari has tried to fly his machine. Talk with a friend about whether you think Gaia Cornwall used the magic of three.

#### After Reading

#### Nudge Toward Independence

Recognizing that some stories use the magic of three will be helpful as you read more and more books. Can you think of other books we've read that have used the magic of three?

## Focus 2–Reread for Fluency:
## Join in on Expressive Words

### Before Reading

**Set the Stage:** Have you noticed that when I read aloud, my voice changes? Sometimes I read quietly and other times I read VERY LOUDLY! When I read with expression, it helps me better comprehend or understand what is happening in the story. Rereading while paying attention to the signals the author gives you will help you be even more fluent readers.

### During Reading

### Investigate Key Pages

### My Turn

*Jabari built an excellent ramp* page: Listen to how I read the words that describe how Jabari's flying machine traveled. I notice the punctuation and the way the text is arranged on the page to help me read with expression.

### Our Turn

*After a lot of building and stacking and hammering and sticking, Jabari was ready* page: Join me in reading the words that describe the flight path. Notice the commas and the exclamation mark.

### Your Turn

*Whoosh, UP, "Wheeeee!" said Nika* page: It's your turn! Read this page the way it's written.

### After Reading

### Nudge Toward Independence

Fluent readers, like you, notice the clues the authors give them. They use those clues to help them read with expression. Some of those clues might be punctuation marks or big and bold words.

**Innovate on Text:** Write the next book in the Jabari series about a "rocket to Jupiter."

**WHAT'S THE MATTER, MARLO?**

**Andrew Arnold**

**Learning Targets:**

- I notice characters who show empathy.
- I talk, write, or draw about ways to show empathy.

## Read-Aloud Experience: Show You Care

**Book Title:** *What's the Matter, Marlo?* (Arnold, 2020)

**About the Book:** Marlo and Coco are inseparable best friends. On this particular day, when Coco asks Marlo to play, he tells her to "go away." She tries to cheer him up with dog jokes, but this only upsets him more. Eventually, she discovers the problem—Marlo's dog has passed away. Coco comforts Marlo the way best friends do, with a hug.

To find a book like this one, look for the following:

- Characters who offer kindness or comfort
- Characters who display empathy

## Comprehension Conversation

### Before Reading

#### Notice the Cover Illustration

The title of this story is the question *What's the Matter, Marlo?* Which character could be Marlo? Why do you think that? Does the cover illustration give you any hints about what might be wrong with Marlo?

**Set a Purpose:** It looks like we are going to have to read the book to learn the answer to the question in the title. As we read *What's the Matter, Marlo?* notice what Marlo's friend says and does. I think we can learn some helpful lessons from her.

### During Reading

- Front flap: I notice that the first sentence on the front flap tells us some important information: Marlo's friend's name is Coco.

- *But not today* page: Look at the way Marlo is sitting. Notice his facial expression, or the look on his face. Which word would you use to describe how he's feeling? Whisper a word to a friend. Listen to hear your friend's word.

- *Marlo got angrier* page: Let's go back a page and compare. How have Marlo's feelings changed? [First, he looked sad, and now he seems angry.] Put yourself in Coco's shoes—what would you do or say?

- *At first I didn't know what to do* page: When Coco says she can *find* Marlo, I'm thinking that she means she can find out where he went. She also might be able to find a way to help him because that's what friends do. What are your thoughts?

- *When I did, I realized that Marlo wasn't just mad, he was sad, too* page: Oh no! Can you use the picture to help you explain what's the matter with Marlo? [His dog passed away.] By saying, "I'm sorry, Marlo," Coco is letting her friend know she understands how he is feeling; she is showing *empathy*.

### After Reading

- Once Coco realized what was wrong with Marlo, she cried with him. Even though it wasn't her dog, she empathized with her friend. Have you ever been in a situation where a friend was sad? What did you do?

- How would the story have been different if Coco hadn't taken the time to "find" Marlo?

### Extend the Experience

- Hugging is one way to show a friend you care, but some people might not want a hug. Let's write a list of some other ways you might show understanding and kindness toward another person. [Collaborate with student to cocreate a list of ideas. Once the list is created, use the sentence stems below to role play different scenarios.]

- How did the ending of the story make you feel? What do you predict will happen next? Talk about that with a friend.

What's the Matter, Friend?

| **Ways to Comfort a Friend Chart** | | |
| --- | --- | --- |
| _____ happened | My friend felt _____ | I can help them by _____ |

### Similar Titles

 ***A New Kind of Wild*** (Hoang, 2020)

**About the Book:** Ren loves his vibrant rainforest home. When he and his mother leave the rainforest and move to the city, Ren feels lost and alone. Fortunately, Ren's neighbor Ava loves the city. Although she's never lived anywhere but the city, Ava empathizes with Ren and helps him discover its hidden beauty.

 ***Let's Play! A Book About Making Friends*** (McCardie, 2021)

**About the Book:** Sukie is starting at a new school. Using her quest to find and maintain friendships as a model, the book teaches lessons like friendliness is catching and true friends are brave, loyal, and supportive. Readers will empathize with Sukie as they learn valuable social-emotional learning lessons.

*Ways to Comfort a Friend Chart*

**Key Vocabulary and Kid-Friendly Definitions:**

- *eventually*: at a time in the future

- *realized*: suddenly understood something

- *replied*: spoke or wrote an answer

View the author reading *A New Kind of Wild* at resources.corwin.com/shakeupsharedreading

**Andrew Arnold**

## Short Bursts of Shared Reading: *What's the Matter, Marlo?*

### Focus 1—Reread for Fluency: Speech Bubbles

#### Before Reading

**Set the Stage:** Andrew Arnold uses speech bubbles in interesting ways in this book. Let's investigate to see what you notice to help you as a reader.

#### During Reading

#### Investigate Key Pages

#### My Turn

*Our favorite game is hike-and-seek* page: Coco is looking for Marlo and calling his name. The two speech bubbles on this page are different. The first one is small, so I can infer that I read it as I'm calling Marlo's name in a regular voice. The second speech bubble is larger and has his name spelled with a lot of Os. I will read it as if I'm calling someone who is far away.

#### Our Turn

*But not today* page: I'm going to reread these two pages. When I get to the speech bubbles, you can join in. What kind of voice will you use? [A sad voice.] Yes! We can infer that Marlo is sad from looking at his face. Look at the speech bubbles. What do you notice? [The outline is shaky, like a sad voice might be.] Ready? Let's give it a try.

#### Your Turn

*So I looked* page: Now it's your turn. You're going to be Coco as she looks for Marlo. Look at the speech bubble, and read it in the way you think Coco would. [Continue until Coco finds Marlo.]

#### After Reading

#### Nudge Toward Independence

In *What's the Matter, Marlo?* Andrew Arnold changed the shape and the size of the speech bubbles and also the appearance of the words inside of them to help you read as if you were feeling the same emotions as the characters. When you come across speech bubbles in the books you're reading, pay attention to how they look. Noticing the way speech bubbles are designed will help you make sense of how to read them.

## Focus 2—Reread to Boost Comprehension: What's the Reason for the Feeling?

### Before Reading

**Set the Stage:** When we read this story the first time, we used clues to infer Marlo's emotions. Today we're going to reread to investigate the reasons for his feelings. We will connect the reasons to the feeling by using the words *cause* and *effect*. The reason is the *cause,* and the feeling is the *effect.*

### During Reading

### Investigate Key Pages

### My Turn

*Marlo is my best friend* page: I'm going to reread the first three pages of the story to show you how I piece together clues to explain the reasons for a character's feelings. [Point out facial expressions and other reasons that Marlo is joyful.] When I'm done, I can say or write:

In the beginning, Marlo was playing with his friend Coco. This made him feel joyful. Playing is the cause. Feeling joyful is the effect.

### Our Turn

*But not today* page: Wow! Marlo is feeling different on these pages. Do we know what caused this feeling yet? [No.] We could say or write:

In the middle, something happened that made Marlo feel upset and angry. We have to keep rereading to find the cause.

### Your Turn

*When I did, I realized that Marlo wasn't just mad, he was sad, too* page: Now it's your turn. How would you complete this sentence:

In the end, _____ made Marlo feel _____. Tell a neighbor which is the cause and which is the effect.

### After Reading

### Nudge Toward Independence

Noticing the cause-and-effect relationships between reasons and feelings can help you empathize with a character's feelings. Understanding the connection between reasons and feelings is also helpful when you are working and playing with your friends. If something happens that makes your friends feel upset, you can be like Coco and show them you care.

**Innovate on Text:** In this book, Marlo and Coco enjoyed telling each other jokes. Jokes can cheer your friends up. Write the beginning of a joke on the front side of the paper and the answer to the joke on the back. Once you're finished, we'll put them together into a class book of jokes. If you don't know any jokes, you can start one with "Why did the chicken cross the road?" and then make up a funny reason.

**Book Title:** *I Talk Like a River* (Scott, 2020)

**About the Book:** As a boy, Jordan Scott's father took him to the river on what he called "bad speech days"—the days when his classmates laughed at his dysfluent speech. This unforgettable book tells the story of a caring dad's healing and encouraging words.

To find a book like this one, look for the following:

- Characters who overcome challenges
- Characters who celebrate their unique qualities

## Comprehension Conversation

### Before Reading

#### Notice the Cover Illustration

Take a moment to appreciate Sydney Smith's painting on the wraparound cover. What words come to mind as you look at it? In this book, he used watercolor paints, ink, and gouache. Goauche is kind of like watercolor paint, but it's opaque, or not as see-through as watercolors. I think his illustrations are stunning. We'll see if you agree.

**Set a Purpose:** [If possible, play river sounds as students are gathering.] When you listen to a river, what do you hear? [Invite students to share the sounds they hear.] *I Talk Like a River* is based on the author's experiences as a child. Let's read to better understand what Jordan Scott means when he writes that he talks like a river.

### During Reading

- *At school, I hide in the back of class* page: Put yourself in the boy's shoes. Imagine that you're hiding in the back of the class. What thoughts might be going through your head? How might you feel? Share with a friend.

- *I feel a storm in my belly; my eyes fill with rain* page: Can you think of a time when you had a similar feeling as the one the boy is having? What could you say or do if you saw him feeling this way?

- *This is what I like to remember* page: What has changed? [His dad gave him a mantra, or something to say to himself when he is having a bad speech day.]

### After Reading

- How did the boy's emotions change from the beginning to end of the story? How does thinking about his feelings help you understand or empathize with him?

- What do you understand about the boy now that you didn't before we read the story?

**Learning Targets:**

- I work to understand book characters by empathizing with their feelings or situations.

- I work to understand others by empathizing with their feelings or situations.

online resources

View the author talking about the book at resources.corwin.com/shakeupsharedreading

### Extend the Experience

- How did this story make you feel? Draw an emoji on a sticky note. Then, find a friend with the same emoji, and talk with them about why you both had the same feeling about the story. When I say "switch," find a friend with a different emoji and discuss why you each reacted differently about the story.

- The boy's favorite place was the river. The closest river to us is _____. Would anyone like to team up to research and learn three interesting facts about the river? As a group, decide how you want to present the facts and report back to us about what you discover. Let me know what I can do to help you.

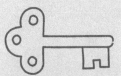

**Key Vocabulary and Kid-Friendly Definitions:**

- *proud*: feeling happy about something you have or do

- *shore*: the land next to an ocean, sea, lake, or river

- *tangled*: mixed up or knotted

### Similar Titles

 **A Friend for Henry (Bailey, 2019)**

About the Book: Henry enters Classroom Six hoping to make friends but quickly discovers it is not that easy to find others with similar interests. Finally, he meets Katie. When reading the author's note, you discover that Jenn Bailey wrote this book after watching one of her sons, who is on the autism spectrum, navigate the process of finding a friend.

 **I Will Dance (Flood, 2020)**

About the Book: Eva was born prematurely, has cerebral palsy, and uses a motorized wheelchair for mobility. Her greatest desire is to dance. Eva's dream comes true when one of her moms finds Young Dance, a studio where all are welcome.

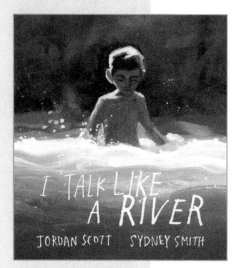

## Short Bursts of Shared Reading:
## *I Talk Like a River*

### Focus 1—Wonder About Words: Similes

### Before Reading

**Set the Stage:** When the dad tells his son that he talks like a river, he uses a *simile.* He compares his son's speech patterns to a river. His dad's comparison gives the boy more confidence. Writers use similes to compare two things in an interesting way so that you can picture what they are saying. Similes often have the words *like* or *as.*

### During Reading

### Investigate Key Pages

#### My Turn

*My dad says I talk like a river* page: [Reread from here to the end of the book.] We all have our own unique speech patterns. If I were to make a simile about mine, I would say, "I talk like the wind" because I speak quietly and sometimes people can't hear me. What would you say?

#### Our Turn

*I wake up in the morning with these word-sounds stuck in my mouth* page: I'm going to read this page to you. Listen for the simile. [I stay quiet as a stone.] Let's reread the simile together. Can you think of another animal or object you would use to describe quiet?

#### Your Turn

*I go to school and tell the class about my favorite place in the world* page: The last two sentences in this book are very similar. Which one is a simile? How can you tell?

### After Reading

### Nudge Toward Independence

During shared reading, we learned about similes, or phrases that compare two things using the word *like* or *as.* Now that you know more about similes, notice them in the books you're reading. You might even experiment with them when you're writing!

## Focus 2—Notice Writer's Craft Moves: First-Person Point of View

### Before Reading

**Set the Stage:** Authors choose to tell their stories from different points of view. That means that they decide who will be telling the story. We'll be rereading with point of view in mind.

### During Reading

#### Investigate Key Pages

#### My Turn

*I wake up each morning with the sounds of words all around me* page: When I'm trying to figure out point of view, I notice who is talking. Here, I see that the boy is talking. The author uses the words *I* and *me*. So, I know that this story is told in first-person point of view. The boy is the narrator.

#### Our Turn

*Mornings are always hard, but this one's especially tough* page: Now that we know the boy is telling the story, let's dig in a little further. As we reread this page, I want you to ponder how hearing the boy's words makes you feel. Can you empathize with him?

#### Your Turn

- *Mornings are always hard, but this one's especially tough* page: If you were telling this page from the dad's point of view, how would it sound? How might shifting the point of view change the way the story makes you feel?

- *My dad sees I am sad and pulls me close* page: How about this page? If you were telling this page from the dad's point of view, how would it sound? How might shifting the point of view change the way you react to the story?

### After Reading

#### Nudge Toward Independence

How do you suppose noticing point of view helps you as a reader? What have you learned today that you will use when you are reading and writing your own stories?

**Innovate on Text:** During shared reading, we learned about similes. We are going to write a special kind of simile. We'll call it a simil-ME because it will be about what makes you special and unique. [To prepare for this writing experience, collaboratively brainstorm a list of verbs and comparisons for *like* and/or adjectives and comparisons for *as*.]

Here are the steps:

- Decide whether you want to use *like* or *as*. A simile using *like* will begin with a verb, while one using *as* will start with an adjective. Here are two examples:

| I _____ like (a) _____. | I'm as _____ as (a) _____. |
|---|---|
| I swim like a dolphin. | I'm as quiet as a mouse. |

- If you need help, use the examples and the ideas in the charts we created to write your simil-ME.

- Draw a picture that matches your simile-ME.

**Verb Ideas Chart**

| Verb | Animals/Things |
|---|---|
| run | cheetah, race car |
| sing | canary |
| dance | swan, falling leaves, snowflakes |

**Adjective Ideas Chart**

| Adjective | Animals/Things |
|---|---|
| quiet | mouse, wind |
| slow | sloth, snail |
| clever | fox, book |

## My Favorite Texts and Resources for Social-Emotional Learning Experiences

## Read-Aloud Experience:
## Notice How Relationships Begin

**Book Title:** *Swashby and the Sea* (Ferry, 2020)

**About the Book:** Captain Swashby is enjoying his quiet seaside retirement until a young girl and her granny move in next door. Swashby scratches messages like "No Trespassing" and "Please Go Away" into the sand, but the waves fiddle with his words, changing their meaning. With a little help from his lively new neighbor and his old friend the sea, Swashby realizes that life is more enjoyable when you're in the company of others.

To find a book like this one, look for the following:

- Relationships that develop over the course of a story
- Intergenerational relationships

## Comprehension Conversation

### Before Reading

### Notice the Cover Illustration

The title of this book is *Swashby and the Sea*. Juana Martinez-Neal uses hand-textured paper in her illustrations, which means she created her own paper by adding different items that would give it texture. So, her paper is almost three dimensional. Which character do you think is Swashby? I'm wondering why Beth Ferry chose the title *Swashby and the Sea* instead of *Swashby and the Girl*. [If you are able to remove the paper book jacket, notice and discuss how it is different than the book casing underneath.]

**Set a Purpose:** We're guessing this story is about the two characters on the cover and also the sea. As we read, we'll study and learn about relationships.

### During Reading

- *Captain Swashby loved the sea* page: I'm going to reread this page. Listen to how the author, Beth Ferry, refers to the sea. Did you notice that she uses the word *she*? It's as if the sea is a person. When authors give objects or animals human traits, it is called *personification*. I wonder if this will be important to understanding the rest of the story. Let's keep reading to find out.
- *So when Swashby retired, it was to a small house . . .* page: The word *serene* means quiet, calm, and peaceful. What have we learned about Swashby from the first few pages? [He's friends with the sea; he likes his quiet life.] It looks like his life might be changing. Let's turn the page to find out how!
- *"What now?" she asked* page: Is anyone else noticing a pattern? What keeps happening? Can you predict what will happen on the next page? Tell a neighbor.
- *"PL—AY!" the girl sounded out* page: Remember when the girl was making a starfish wish and Swashby helped? How is he helping on this page? [He's helping her make sand towers.] Has a friend ever helped you when you needed it? How did that make you feel?
- *So the sea decided to meddle more than just a little* page: Uh-oh! What are you thinking?

**Learning Targets:**

- I notice how characters become friends.
- I think, talk, or write about friendship.

## After Reading

- Why do you suppose Swashby thanked the sea? How did the sea help him?

- In the beginning of the story, Swashby thought neighbors were "nosy, a nuisance, annoying." In the end, he saw that they were "fun, and friends, and . . . family." What changed?

## Extend the Experience

- Draw and write about what Swashby was like at the beginning of the story compared to how he was at the end. Record your ideas on the *How Characters Change Reproducible Response Page* found on the companion website (resources.corwin.com/shakeupsharedreading).

---

Meet the Creator!

Book Creator Study: Juana Martinez-Neal

Website: https://juanamartinezneal.com/

Did you know?

- She loves birds.
- She was born and raised in Peru.
- She likes numbering things.

A Few of Her Books:

- *Alma and How She Got Her Name* (Author and Illustrator, 2018)
- *Fry Bread: A Native American Story* (Maillard, Illustrator, 2019)
- *La Princesa and the Pea* (Elya, Illustrator, 2017)
- *Zonia's Rain Forest* (Author and Illustrator, 2021)

---

### Key Vocabulary and Kid-Friendly Definitions:

- *fiddle*: to play around with something

- *meddle*: to mess around without being asked

- *vanish*: to disappear from being seen

View the author talking about *Map Into the World* and reading it aloud at resources.corwin.com/shakeupsharedreading

---

## Similar Titles

 ***Khalil and Mr. Hagerty and the Backyard Treasures* (Springstubb, 2020)**

About the Book: Khalil lives in a noisy apartment above Mr. Hagerty's quiet one. Both neighbors enjoy and share the backyard. Mr. Hagerty helps Khalil read words, while Khalil helps Mr. Hagerty remember them. One summer morning, Mr. Hagerty notices his garden is droopy and Khalil is disappointed that he hasn't found any treasure. That evening, they each secretly plant something for the other to find.

 ***Map Into the World* (Yang, 2019)**

About the Book: Paj Ntaub [BA NDAO] and her family move into a new house. Their neighbors across the street, Bob and Ruth, enjoy being outside on their special bench. Over the winter, Ruth passes away. In the spring, Paj Ntaub uses sidewalk chalk to draw Bob a colorful map to help him find his way back into the world.

---

Name _____

### How Characters Change

| In the beginning . . . | At the end . . . |
|---|---|
| The character | The character |
| | |
| | |

*How Characters Change Reproducible Response Page*

## Short Bursts of Shared Reading:
### *Swashby and the Sea*

#### Focus 1–Match Letters to Sounds:
#### Look for Chunks

### Before Reading

**Set the Stage:** When the sea fiddled with the words Swashby wrote in the sand, it changed them. There were little words and word parts in the big words. As readers, we look for chunks in big words to help us read longer words.

### During Reading

#### Investigate Key Pages

#### My Turn

*Swashby battened down the hatches . . .* page: When I'm trying to figure out a big word, I chunk it into smaller parts. To do that with the word *trespassing*, I break it in chunks that I know: tres-pass-ing.

#### Our Turn

*"What now? she asked* page: Do you see any chunks you know in the word *vanish*? [Van-ish, v-an-ish, va-nish.]

#### Your Turn

There are many other words in this book that you can read using this strategy. It's your turn to try it with a partner. [Write each of the following words on a paper strip or in an electronic document: *whenever, commandeered, umbrellas, scattered, battened, starfish, interrupted, stomping, delivered.* Depending on the number of students you have, you may need to make two sets. In pairs, students identify chunks by underlining or cutting the word apart to show the parts.]

### After Reading

#### Nudge Toward Independence

When you come to a longer word in your reading, remember to break it into smaller chunks. Then look at each chunk and slide through the sounds.

**Innovate on Text:** I thought it might be fun to play around with Beth Ferry's adjective trio idea in our own writing. Think of a word or idea, then write a trio of adjectives to describe that word or idea. [Work with students in a shared writing format to create an adjective trio sentence or perhaps a poem. Then, invite students to try it on their own.]

## Focus 2—Wonder About Words: Adjective Trios

### Before Reading

**Set the Stage:** I'm curious about the words authors use in their writing. Beth Ferry does something really cool that I want you to notice: she uses adjectives in groups of three. Let's reread to see how that sounds.

### During Reading

### Investigate Key Pages

### My Turn

*So when Swashby retired, it was to a small house on a small beach as close to the sea as he could be* page: Listen as I reread to notice how Beth Ferry describes Swashby's life. Yes! Swashby's life was "salty and sandy and serene." Remember the word *serene* means quiet, calm, and peaceful. If I had to pick three adjectives to describe my life, I would use *sunny, quiet,* and *busy*.

### Our Turn

*Swashby battened down the hatches* page: Reread the last three sentences on this page with me. Listen to the three adjectives Swashby uses to describe neighbors [*noisy, a nuisance, annoying*]. Do you think those adjectives show he enjoys having neighbors? Show me with your thumbs—yes or no? If you were going to describe something you did not like, what adjectives would you use?

### Your Turn

*After that, it was easy for Swashby to have tea . . .* page: Remember this page? I'll point while you read the three adjectives that Swashby now uses to describe neighbors. What adjective do you use to describe things you enjoy?

### After Reading

### Nudge Toward Independence

Beth Ferry uses trios or a group of three adjectives to help us understand how Swashby's feelings changed over the course of this book. As a reader, I enjoyed how she repeated this pattern throughout the book. What did you think about it? If you're curious about words, you'll be surprised what you notice!

> ## Adjective Trio Poem
> ## By 1-W
>
> Winter is frigid and flaky and white.
>
> Spring is fresh and flowery and green.
>
> Summer is sunny and sparkly and blue.
>
> Fall is colorful and crunchy and gold.

*Adjective Trio Poem Work Sample*

## Read-Aloud Experience: Notice How Relationships Change

**Book Title:** *The Arabic Quilt: An Immigrant Story* (Khalil, 2020)

**About the Book:** Kanzi and her family emigrated from Egypt to America. On her first day in a new school, Kanzi's classmates laugh when they overhear her mother using an Arabic term of affection, *Habibti*. Seeing Kanzi upset, Mrs. Haugen, her teacher, reassures her that being bilingual is beautiful. To celebrate the asset of being bilingual, Mrs. Haugen invites Kanzi's mom into the classroom to show the children how to write their names in Arabic. Together, the class creates pieces that become a bulletin board quilt with all of their names. Inspired by the Arabic name quilt, the class across the hall makes a Japanese name quilt.

To find a book like this one, look for the following:

- Characters who navigate relationships at school
- Stories that highlight relationship building

## Comprehension Conversation

### Before Reading

#### Notice the Cover Illustration

The title of this book is *The Arabic Quilt*. The subtitle is *An Immigrant Story*. An immigrant is someone who leaves the country in which they were born to move to another country. What do you notice the girl doing on the cover? Notice how the illustrator designed the letters in the title. [They look like they're made out of fabric.] We'll have to read to discover why this book is called *The Arabic Quilt*.

**Set a Purpose:** As we're trying to figure out the meaning of the title, we're also going to focus on the girl in the story. Let's read to hear more about her.

### During Reading

- *In the car, Mama sings along with the songs on the Arabic radio channel* page: We've already learned so much about Kanzi on these first few pages. Share one thing that you learned about her. Can you put yourself in her shoes and imagine how she might be feeling on her first day of school?

- *At lunchtime, Kanzi is surprised when Mama walks through the door* page: Talk about Molly's words and actions on this page. What would you have said or done if you were walking next to Molly? Is this the way we welcome new friends?

- *The next day Molly says . . .* page: Talk about Molly's apology. How did it make you feel? I noticed that Kanzi stood up for herself using her words. Why is it important to stand up for yourself?

- *"That was a really cool project, Kanzi"* page: How does Kanzi and Molly's friendship change on this page? What happens to cause the change?

### Learning Targets:

- I notice how characters' friendships grow and change.

- I think, talk, or write about friendship.

- I use what I've learned about friendship in my own life.

## After Reading

- What a beautiful poem! What words or ideas from Kanzi's poem speak to you?
- Why do you think this story is called *The Arabic Quilt*?

## Extend the Experience

- How did Kanzi's relationship with Molly change over the course of the story?
- Let's create our own class quilt. On this piece of paper [or Google Slide], write your name in the language(s) you speak. Decorate your quilt piece in a way that tells us a little about you.

## Similar Titles

 **The Day You Begin** (Woodson, 2018)

**About the Book:** Based on a poem about her great-grandfather's experience titled "It'll Be Scary Sometimes," Woodson's book shares the heart-wrenching stories of children starting the school year feeling different from their classmates. In the end, when a girl decides to speak up and share her story, she finds that she has something in common with one of her classmates and a friendship begins.

 **The Proudest Blue: The Story of Hijab and Family** (Muhammad & Ali, 2019)

**About the Book:** It's the first day of sixth grade and Asiya's first day of wearing hijab. Her younger sister Faizah, who is the narrator, thinks Asiya looks like a princess in her bright blue hijab. Asiya expresses her faith with strength and pride even when faced with bullies. According to the author's note, Olympic Gold Medalist Ibtihaj Muhammad wrote this story so that readers "can see two sisters taking pride in hijab." Fun fact: The sisters in the story are named after Ibtihaj's sisters.

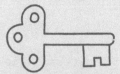

### Key Vocabulary and Kid-Friendly Definitions:

- *awe*: a feeling of wonder
- *bravely*: ready to face danger
- *secretly*: without others seeing or knowing

View the author reading *The Proudest Blue* aloud at resources.corwin.com/shakeupsharedreading

View the book trailer of *The Day You Begin* at resources.corwin.com/shakeupsharedreading

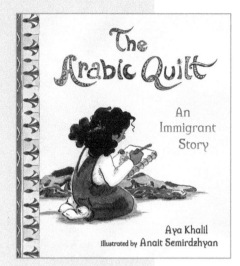

## Short Bursts of Shared Reading:
## *The Arabic Quilt: An Immigrant Story*

### Focus 1—Wonder About Words: Different Ways Authors Write "Says"

### Before Reading

**Set the Stage:** Authors often use the word *Says* to show that characters are talking. Did you know there are other words that are more descriptive and help readers connect with characters? Finding other words for *says* is our purpose for rereading today.

### During Reading

#### Investigate Key Pages

#### My Turn

*At lunchtime, Kanzi is surprised when Mama walks through the door* page: I'm going to reread this page to notice all the different words Aya Khalil uses instead of the word *says*. [Reread and emphasize the words: *snickers, asks,* and *replies.*] Each of those words gives me, as a reader, a different signal. Listen again as I read what each person says as I imagine the author wants me to.

#### Our Turn:

*The next day Kanzi unfolds her quilt in front of the class* page: Reread this page, and think about the difference between writing *says* and writing *shouts*.

#### Your Turn

Now it's your turn. You can either look through a book you're reading to collect other words for *says* or join me as we jot down the words we found in *The Arabic Quilt*. [Collect synonyms for *says* on a reference chart or page in students' notebooks. Here are the ones found in *The Arabic Quilt*: *calls, exclaims, responds, snickers, asks, replies, blurts out, shouts, asks,* and *whispers.*]

### After Reading

#### Nudge Toward Independence

Isn't it amazing how many synonyms there are for the word *says*? Keep noticing and thinking about these words as you read. Try them out when you add talking to the stories you're writing.

## Focus 2—Notice Writer's Craft Moves: Transition Words and Phrases

### Before Reading

**Set the Stage:** In *The Arabic Quilt,* Aya Khalil uses a technique that writers use to move a story through time. Instead of using words like *and* or *and then* over and over, writers use transition words or phrases. Transition words or phrases are like a bridge that gets you from one part of the story to the next.

### During Reading

### Investigate Key Pages

### My Turn

*At lunchtime, Kanzi is surprised when Mama walks through the door* page: Reread the first sentence on this page. On the last page, they were getting started with the day; now it is lunchtime. Instead of having a lot of pages in between, the author uses a transition phrase to move the story through time.

### Our Turn

*The next day Molly says, "Mrs. Haugen said I hurt your feelings"* page: Reread the first sentence on this page. How did this transition help move the story through time?

### Your Turn

[Continue to guide students to notice the transitions and the fact that they are often followed by a comma.]

### After Reading

### Nudge Toward Independence

A *transition* is a word or a group of words that carries the reader from one part of the story to the next. I'm going to write some of the transitions we found on this chart in case you want to use them when you are writing. [On an anchor chart, record phrases like *At lunchtime; That night; Before bed;* and *On Friday.*]

**Innovate on Text:** At the end of the story, Kanzi wrote a special poem for her parents. Draw a picture or write a note to a caregiver telling why they are special to you.

"And a thought occurs to him: Maybe you can't really know anyone just by looking at their face."

—*Milo Imagines the World* by
Matt de la Peña and Christian Robinson

# Converse About Comprehension–Fiction

## Reading Between the Lines and Beyond the Page

In the opening quote of this chapter, Milo ponders, "Maybe you can't really know anyone just by looking at their face." The same is true for a book. Children can't really know a book just by reading the words. Comprehension, deep understanding, lets readers see into the heart of a book. To become skilled at reading between the lines and beyond the page, learners need support and challenge in equal parts. That is why the blend of read-aloud experiences and short bursts of shared reading are a winning combination. During read aloud, you read for pleasure and, through lively conversations, co-create understanding. Shared reading interactions nudge children to dig deeper and reach higher—to make sense of the inner workings of the written word. The book experiences in this chapter will guide your students to get to the heart of books by doing the following:

- Describe and understand characters

- Study story structure

- Engage in illustration study

- Predict using evidence

- Visualize using senses and feelings

- Ponder point of view

- Read between the lines

When you choose to extend the read-aloud experience or provide opportunities for learners to innovate on the text after a shared reading interaction, you nudge them to think beyond the book. Considering the questions, "Where can this book lead me next? What action might I take based on what I've read or heard?" Use the ideas in this chapter as you peer into the hearts of books with your learners. Trust that with each question and silent pause, you are supporting your students in becoming the kind of reader who looks inside themselves and asks, "What does this book mean to me?"

istock.com/TopVectors

## Menu of Shared Reading Interactions

| Book Title | Shared Reading Focus 1 | Shared Reading Focus 2 |
|---|---|---|
| *Catch That Chicken!* (Atinuke, 2020) | Listen for Sounds: Alliteration | Reread for Fluency: Read With Excitement! |
| *Rocket Says Clean Up!* (Bryon, 2020) | Ponder Punctuation: Exclamation Marks = Strong Feelings | Notice Writer's Craft Moves: Blending Fiction and Nonfiction |
| *The Purple Puffy Coat* (Boelts, 2020b) | Wonder About Words: Adjectives | Reread to Boost Comprehension: Notice the Turning Point in a Story |
| *The Pirates Are Coming* (Condon, 2020) | Match Letters to Sounds: Short-*i* Word Families | Reread for Fluency: Join in on Repeated Parts |
| *Simon at the Art Museum* (Soontornvat, 2020) | Reread to Boost Comprehension: Use Pictures and Words to Infer | Notice Writer's Craft Moves: How Dialogue and Inner Thinking Help Readers Understand Characters |
| *Lift* (Lê, 2020) | Reread to Boost Comprehension: Real Versus Make Believe | Notice Illustrator's Craft Moves: Graphic Format Illustrations |
| *Thank You, Omu!* (Mora, 2018) | Wonder About Words: Synonyms | Read to Boost Comprehension: Infer the Big Idea |
| *Harold Loves His Woolly Hat* (Kousky, 2018) | Reread for Fluency: Big and Bold Print | Reread to Boost Comprehension: Identify Character Traits |
| *My Papi Has a Motorcycle* (Quintero, 2019) | Wonder About Words: Onomatopoeia | Notice Writer's Craft Moves: Repetition |
| *Milo Imagines the World* (de la Peña, 2021) | Wonder About Words: Sensory Words and Phrases | Notice Illustrator's Craft Moves: Showing a Character's Inner Thoughts |
| *I'm Sticking With You* (Prasadam-Halls, 2020) | Listen for Sounds: Rhyming Words | Reread for Fluency: Emphasize Italicized Words |
| *We Love Fishing!* (Bernstein, 2021) | Wonder About Words: Contractions | Reread for Fluency: Pay Attention to Punctuation |
| *Outside In* (Underwood, 2020) | Wonder About Words: Compound Words | Reread to Boost Comprehension : Use Pictures and Words to Infer |
| *Big Papa and the Time Machine* (Bernstrom, 2020) | Reread to Boost Comprehension: Understand Point of View | Notice Writer's Craft Moves: Repeated Sentence |

My Favorite Texts and Resources for Comprehension–Fiction

**ATINUKE & ANGELA BROOKSBANK**

**Learning Targets:**

- I learn about characters by noticing their actions.

- I use what I learn to describe characters.

## Read-Aloud Experience: Consider Characters' Actions

**Book Title:** *Catch That Chicken!* (Atinuke, 2020)

**About the Book:** Lami is the speediest chicken catcher in her West African compound. When Lami is in hot pursuit of a feathery foul, the villagers warn her with "Sannu! Sannu!" which means "Take it easy!" Lami, too intent on chicken catching to heed their warning, falls and sprains her ankle. Fortunately, Nana Nadia reminds Lami that she can still be the best chicken catcher by using her wits rather than her speed. Detail-oriented learners will enjoy retracing Lami's path to catch the chicken on the two-page spread of the compound.

To find a book like this one, look for the following:

- Energetic and resilient main characters
- Settings that expand students' worldviews

## Comprehension Conversation

### Before Reading

#### Notice the Cover Illustration

This book cover has clues that will help you predict what might happen in this story. Notice the exclamation mark at the end of the title. Do you suppose the author wants us to read the title like this [read *Catch That Chicken!* aloud with a monotone voice/ no expression] or like this [read *Catch That Chicken!* aloud with excitement]? The picture gives you a hint as to who might be trying to catch the chicken. Share your prediction with a friend.

**Set a Purpose:** Have you ever tried to catch a running animal? Did you catch it? [Listen to a few students' responses.] In this story, we will meet a character who likes to catch chickens. We're going to notice and think about her actions so that we can describe her to people who haven't read the book yet.

### During Reading

- Title page: The author tells us that this story is set, or happens, in West Africa [locate and display West Africa on a digital or physical map or globe]. In this story, when people say the word *sannu* it means "take it easy."

- *And Lami catches her!* page: What have we learned about Lami so far? As we continue reading, notice what Lami does to be the best chicken catcher.

- *One day Lami chases a chicken through the pen* page: Let's talk about Lami's actions—the things she does. What makes her good at catching chickens? [She likes chickens, she doesn't give up, she's speedy, fast, and brave.]

- *She sprains her ankle so badly . . .* page: Oh no! Can you predict what Lami will do now? What would you do if you were in the same situation?

## After Reading

- If you were going to tell someone about Lami, how would you describe her? [Nudge learners to use adjectives rather than retell events in the story. Prompt them to use adjectives by saying, "Lami is . . ."]

- Lami's goal was to catch chickens. What lessons have you learned from Lami that you can use when working toward your goals?

### Extend the Experience

- As we read *Catch That Chicken!* we used Lami's actions to help us identify her personality traits. Let's jot some of Lami's traits on this character trait tree. I will put out copies of character trait trees in case you want to notice a character's traits in other books you're reading. See *Character Trait Tree Response Page* located on the companion website (resources.corwin.com/shakeupsharedreading).

- Be an Observer! Oviparous Animals: Did you know that a chicken is an oviparous animal? In the Observer Center, you'll find books and other sources to help you learn more about oviparous animals. Your challenge is to:

  o Figure out the characteristics of oviparous animals.

  o Choose an oviparous animal that is interesting to you and create a diagram to teach us about that animal.

**Key Vocabulary and Kid-Friendly Definitions:**

- *luckily:* when something happens by a happy chance

- *lunges:* jumps or leaps toward someone or something

- *snatches:* quickly grabs something

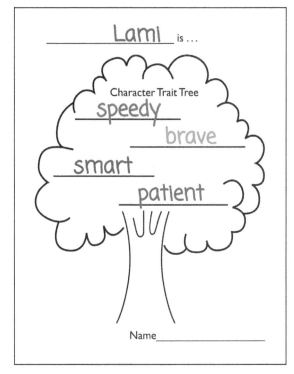

*Character Trait Tree Chart for Lami from* Catch That Chicken!

*Character Trait Tree Reproducible Response Page*

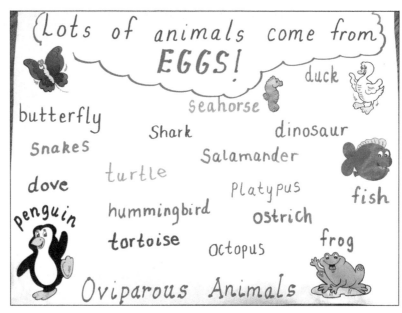

*Oviparous Animals Chart*

......................................................................................................

## Similar Titles

 **Watch Me (Richards, 2021)**

**About the Book:** Based on the true story of Doyin Richards's father, readers meet Joe, who emigrated from Sierra Leone to America in pursuit of his dreams. Whenever Joe encounters doubters or challenges, he persists while saying, "Watch me." In the end, he becomes a doctor. [See book experiences in Chapter 1 on pages 42–45.]

 **Wherever I Go (Copp, 2020)**

**About the Book:** A young girl who calls herself Queen Abia has lived in the Shimelba Refugee Camp in Northern Ethiopia for seven years. Whether pumping water or playing with friends, she approaches life playfully with a blend of imagination and hope. Her positive outlook continues as she is resettled. Readers will love Abia's spirit and energy. Backmatter includes information and resources about refugees and resettlement.

My Favorite Texts and Resources for Studying Characters

_____
_____
_____
_____
_____
_____
_____
_____
_____
_____
_____
_____
_____
_____
_____
_____
_____
_____
_____
_____
_____
_____
_____
_____
_____
_____
_____

ATINUKE & ANGELA BROOKSBANK

## Short Bursts of Shared Reading: *Catch That Chicken!*

### Focus 1—Listen for Sounds: Alliteration

**Before Reading**

**Set the Stage:** As we reread *Catch That Chicken!* we are going to train our ears to listen to the beginning sounds of words.

**During Reading**

**Investigate Key Pages**

**My Turn**

*Lami leans!* page: [Reread page aloud, emphasizing the beginning sounds.] What do you hear? [The beginning sound of each word is /l/.] Listen to how these words sound. When authors repeat the beginning consonant sound, it is called *alliteration*. I think repeated consonant words are fun to say or read.

**Our Turn**

We're going to play a silly sound game. Let's change the first sound in each word to /p/. We'll say the words together to hear what it sounds like when we change the first sound:

Lami leans!  → Pami peans!

Lami lunges! → Pami punges!

Lami leaps!  → Pami peaps!

Now we're going to try it with a different consonant sound! [Continue playing the silly sound game with other consonant sounds that are familiar to your students.]

**Your Turn**

Take turns with your neighbor and change the beginning sound by replacing it with the first sound in your name. [If time and interest permit, repeat the conversation about alliteration on the *But Lami scrambles speedily* page.]

**After Reading**

**Nudge Toward Independence**

Listening to and playing with sounds help grow your reading brains. When you're writing, you can choose words with the same beginning sound, or use alliteration, to make your sentence fun to say.

## Focus 2–Reread for Fluency: Read With Excitement!

### Before Reading

**Set the Stage:** When I read aloud to you, I practice so that I can read as if I am the character talking. This helps me imagine what is happening in the book. Let me show you!

### During Reading

### Investigate Key Pages

### My Turn

*Catch 'am, Lami! Catch, 'am!" shouts Brother Bilal* page: Listen to me read aloud this page. What do you notice? [Discuss the fact that you read it in a cheer-like manner because each sentence ends in an exclamation point.]

### Our Turn

*Catch 'am, Lami! Catch, 'am!" shouts Brother Bilal* page: Now let's reread the same page together. Pay attention to how your words sound. Pretend you are in the compound cheering for Lami to catch the chicken!

### Your Turn

*One day Lami chases a chicken through the pen* page [and the five pages that follow]: Remember this part of the story? This is when everyone is warning Lami to take it easy by shouting, "Sannu! Sannu!" I'm going to point to the words *Sannu! Sannu!* as you read them the way you imagine the villagers would say them. Here we go!

### After Reading

### Nudge Toward Independence

Readers pay attention to the author's signals, like exclamation marks, to help them read with expression. When you notice a character in a story is talking, look at the punctuation marks and remind yourself to read the words like the character would say them.

**Innovate on Text:** *with lots and lots of chickens* page: Remember this two-page spread where we could see all of the places Lami chased the chickens? Think about drawing a scene like this that shows all of the places in one of your stories. Your scene might be real or imagined. You could also draw a picture like this to plan out a story by showing all of the places your character will go.

by **Nathan Bryon** • illustrated by **Dapo Adeola**

**Learning Targets:**

- I learn about characters by noticing their actions.

- I use what I learn to describe characters.

- I connect characters' actions to character traits.

View the author reading *We Are Water Protectors* aloud at resources.corwin.com/shakeupsharedreading

## Read-Aloud Experience: Connect Characters' Actions to Character Traits

**Book Title:** *Rocket Says Clean Up!* (Bryon, 2020)

**About the Book:** In this follow-up to *Rocket Says Look Up!* (Bryon, 2019), Rocket and her family are traveling to a tropical island to visit her grandparents. Rocket's grandparents give whale-watching tours and run an animal sanctuary. When Rocket finds a young turtle tangled in plastic, she enlists the help of fellow beachgoers to clean up the trash. Unlike her brother, who is glued to his cell phone, Rocket's emotions and energy jump off every page.

To find a book like this one, look for the following:

- Characters whose actions clearly reveal their personalities

- Books with an environmental message

## Comprehension Conversation

### Before Reading

#### Notice the Cover Illustration

Do you notice anything out of place on Dapo Adeola's bright, colorful cover? [There's trash in the girl's hand and in the water.] If we combine what you've learned from looking at the cover illustration with the title *Rocket Says Clean Up!* I bet you have some predictions about why Rocket is telling people to clean up. Ask a friend about their prediction.

**Set a Purpose:** While reading to find out if people listen when Rocket tells them to clean up, we're going to look for clues in Rocket's actions that help us learn more about her personality.

### During Reading

- *I can't wait to help!* page: Give me a thumbs up if you would like to work in an animal sanctuary. On this page, I see that Rocket is helping her Grampy. That action shows me that Rocket is *helpful*.

- *I pick her up gently . . .* page: Look at Rocket's face. Can you infer how she is feeling? Why do you suppose she's feeling that way? [Perhaps because she cares about the turtle.] If she's sad because the turtle is hurt, that shows us that Rocket is _____. [Caring, kind.]

- *CLEAN!* page: How has Rocket's mood changed? What caused this change to happen?

- *Theresa's mom makes awesome bins for trash . . .* page: How would you react if something you did ended up in the news? Stand up and show me with your face and body.

### After Reading

- What do you notice in the background on the last page? [A whale's tail.] Why do you think the illustrator included that detail?

- What is something you might do differently after hearing this story?

## Extend the Experience

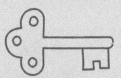

- Character–Trait–Clues: As we were reading, we used Rocket's actions as clues to figure out her character traits. A trait is a characteristic that makes someone or something unique. What are some of Rocket's traits? [Helpful, kind, caring, determined, proud . . .] Let's use the Character–Trait–Clues chart to record what we learned about Rocket's personality. You can use the same chart to record the traits of characters in the books you're reading. See *Character–Trait–Clues Reproducible Response Chart* provided on the companion website (resources .corwin.com/shakeupsharedreading).

**Key Vocabulary and Kid-Friendly Definitions:**

- *release*: to let something go free

- *rescue*: to take away from something unsafe

- *tangled*: twisted or knotted

- Take action! In this story, Rocket takes steps to clean up the beach. After talking to her Grampy about the plastic problem, Rocket does three things. First, she tells people about the dangers of plastic on a beach. Next, she gathers a group of volunteers. Finally, she uses beach-friendly recycling bins that Theresa's mom designed by reusing the plastic. Is there something that you see happening that you want to change? Here are three ways to take action:

  o Inform: Teach others about the issue.

  o Invite: Find others who will join you in the work.

  o Innovate: Think of creative ways to solve the problem.

## Similar Titles

### Stand Up, Speak Up (Joyner, 2020)

**About the Book:** In this story, which is told entirely in two-word sentences ending with the word *up*, we meet a little girl joining a climate change rally. After an uplifting day, she returns home and becomes discouraged when watching environmental disasters on the news. Unable to sleep, she makes a plan. With her parents in tow, she speaks at a town hall meeting and invites her community to join the cause. The final gatefold spread depicts a variety of ways the community members pitch in to help the environment. Backmatter includes brief bios of young people who are supporting the climate change revolution.

### We Are Water Protectors (Lindstrom, 2020)

**About the Book:** This Caldecott Award–winning book depicts a young girl's bravery in standing alongside her community as the "black snake," in the form of an oil pipeline, threatens the water. This call to action from Indigenous author-and-illustrator team Carole Lindstrom and Michaela Goade includes backmatter written by both creators that contextualizes the narrative tale.

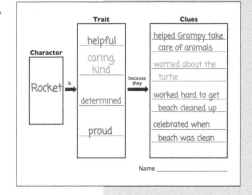

*Character-Trait-Clues Co-Created Chart for Rocket from* Rocket Says Clean Up!

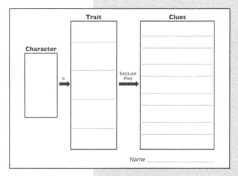

*Character–Trait-Clues Reproducible Response Page*

## Short Bursts of Shared Reading:
### *Rocket Says Clean Up!*

Focus 1–Ponder Punctuation:
Exclamation Marks = Strong Feelings

### Before Reading

**Set the Stage:** [Display an exclamation mark.] Does anyone know what mark this is and what it tells us as readers? Yes! An exclamation mark or exclamation point signals that the person talking has strong feelings. Let's infer how Rocket is feeling and read the sentences that end with exclamation marks the way the Rocket would say them.

### During Reading

#### Investigate Key Pages

**My Turn**

*But first it's time to surf!* page: After looking at Rocket's face and seeing how much fun she's having, I'm inferring she's excited, so I'm going to read the sentences ending with exclamation marks with a lot of energy.

**Our Turn**

*Then Mom and I build a HUGE sandcastle!* page: There are two sentences that end with exclamation marks on this page. How do you suppose Rocket is feeling when they're building the sandcastle? Let's read the sentence together with excitement. Now, look at the words "OH NO!" They also have an exclamation mark after them, but Rocket doesn't look excited, does she? That means we have to read them in a different way. Ready? Pretend you're Rocket and you just found that baby turtle. Read, "OH NO!"

**Your Turn**

*As the day goes on, more and more people join* page: Now it's your turn. I'm going to read the sentence without any emotion, and you have to look at the picture and reread it the way you imagine Rocket would say it. [Read the sentences with exclamation marks on the next few pages in a monotone voice. Invite children to look at pictures to figure out how Rocket is feeling before rereading the sentences with expression. Continue as engagement and time permit.]

### After Reading

#### Nudge Toward Independence

Let's think about what we learned today. What do you know about exclamation marks that you didn't know before? How will what you learned today help you when you're reading and writing?

## Focus 2—Notice Writer's Craft Moves: Blending Fiction and Nonfiction

### Before Reading

**Set the Stage:** Do you remember the difference between fiction and nonfiction texts? Sometimes authors blend the two types of texts together into one book. That's what Nathan Bryon did in *Rocket Says Clean Up!* Let me show you!

### During Reading

#### Investigate Key Pages

#### My Turn

*I'm gonna be* . . . page: In the text, Rocket is talking about all the things she's going to do on vacation. Then, in the speech bubble that reads, "DID YOU KNOW . . ." we learn a fact about Imani Wilmot. I didn't know who she was, and now I want to find out more. For me, reading this fact made my brain think in a different way. It added a little extra to the story.

#### Our Turn

*DID YOU KNOW* . . . page: We're going to tag team read this page. You read *DID YOU KNOW* . . . and I'll read the fact. Notice how adding these facts to the story impacts you as you're reading. What did you learn? Do you like having facts tucked into the middle of the story, or would you prefer them at the end? Talk about that with a friend.

#### Your Turn

If you were going to pick another page to add facts, which page would it be? [Invite a student to choose a page in the story where they might add facts. Turn to the page they've selected. Brainstorm what kind of facts they could add. Write the ideas on sticky notes and place on the page. Continue with a few more learners. Place the book in the classroom library so others can add their ideas and thinking.]

### After Reading

#### Nudge Toward Independence

Sometimes readers think a book has to be either fiction or nonfiction. Today we saw that a book can blend the two together. So, while we were enjoying a story, we also learned some facts. As you're reading other books, notice how authors blend fiction and nonfiction. Think about how that impacts your reading experience. If it makes sense in a story that you're writing, you might add a fact or two.

**Innovate on Text:** In this story, Rocket and the beachgoers work together to clean up the plastic. Cleaning up trash is one way to help our environment. Can you think of other ways? [Collaborate with learners to brainstorm a list that might include ideas like recycle, plant trees, ride your bike, turn off water, and so on.] If you were going to create a book like this one, what would your title be? My title would be *Dr. Walther Says Turn Off the Lights!* Write your title on a sticky note or in your notebook; it might give you an idea for your own story.

Maribeth Boelts  illustrated by Daniel Duncan

## Read-Aloud Experience: Identify Story Elements

**Book Title:** *The Purple Puffy Coat* (Boelts, 2020b)

**About the Book:** Beetle is eager to give Stick Bug a purple puffy coat for his birthday. So eager, in fact, he can't even wait for Stick Bug's big day. Although Beetle believes the coat is "showy and glorious," readers can infer from Stick Bug's expression and actions that he doesn't feel the same way. When Beetle finally comes to the realization that Stick Bug is unhappy with his gift, he gives Stick Bug a new gift—a note stating that he no longer needs to wear the coat.

To find a book like this one, look for the following:

- Straightforward plots with clearly identifiable story elements
- Friendship stories

## Comprehension Conversation

### Before Reading

#### Notice the Cover Illustration

Often the cover gives you a preview about what might happen in the book. What do you see on this book cover? [Two bugs wearing coats and leaves falling around them.] Notice the green bug's face. Can you infer how he is feeling?

#### Back Cover Blurb

If we flip the book over, we can read the back-cover blurb to learn more. [Read the blurb aloud.] After reading the blurb, we know the names of the characters, and we also have a clue as to why Stick Bug has such a sad expression on his face.

**Set a Purpose:** In many stories, the main character has a problem or tries to reach a goal. We've already found some clues that help you predict the possible problem in this story. Let's read to find out if your predictions match what Maribeth Boelts was thinking and to see how the character solves, or fixes, the problem.

#### During Reading

- *Beetle handed Stick Bug a big box* page: Hmmm! What do you suppose is in the box? Notice how looking carefully at the cover led you to make a more accurate prediction!

- *Stick Bug encased himself in a purple puffy coat* page: What is the problem? [Stick Bug doesn't like the coat.] Can you tell how Beetle feels about the coat? What are the clues?

- *"OH, NO!" wailed Beetle* page: What has beetle *finally* figured out? Why do you think it took him so long to realize that Stick Bug didn't like the coat?

- *"I have something for you," said Beetle* page: How did Beetle solve the problem?

### Learning Targets:

- I remember the characters, problem, and solution in a story.
- I talk, write, or draw about the characters, problem, and solution in a story.

## After Reading

- What are some lessons Beetle learned about gift giving and friendship?

- Next time Beetle is going to give someone a gift, what might he do differently?

## Extend the Experience

- As readers, it's important to remember the characters, problem, and solution of a story. To do that, we're going to draw a picture and label those parts of *The Purple Puffy Coat*. Then, for an extra challenge, think about another possible solution and add that to the *Character, Problem, and Solution Reproducible Response Page* located on the companion website (resources.corwin.com/shakeupsharedreading).

- Think about someone special you know. What would you give that person for their birthday? Draw a picture of that gift.

## Similar Titles

 **Frog and Beaver (James, 2017)**

About the Book: Frog and his friends live happily together by the river until Beaver makes a gigantic dam and displaces them. When the dam breaks, Frog saves Beaver's life. Beaver repays Frog's kindness by rebuilding the animals' homes and making a much smaller dam.

 **Something's Wrong! A Bear, A Hare, and Some Underwear (John, 2021)**

About the Book: Jeff, the bear, has a nagging feeling that there is a problem, but he just can't figure out what it is. So he asks his trusted friend, Anders, the rabbit. Anders tells Jeff the truth—he's outside wearing underwear. Anders then stands by Jeff's side when the other animals question his clothing choice.

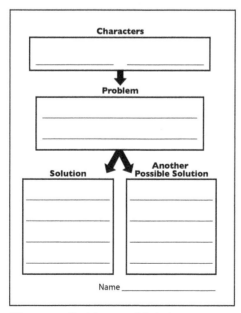

*Character, Problem, and Solution Reproducible Response Page*

### Key Vocabulary and Kid-Friendly Definitions:

- *admiring*: looking at someone or something you really like

- *dashed*: moved fast

- *glumness*: a feeling of sadness

View the book trailer of *Something's Wrong!* at resources.corwin.com/shakeupsharedreading

Maribeth Boelts  illustrated by Daniel Duncan

## Short Bursts of Shared Reading:
### *The Purple Puffy Coat*

### Focus 1–Wonder About Words: Adjectives

#### Before Reading

**Set the Stage:** An adjective is a word that describes a noun (or pronoun). Writers use adjectives to tell what kind (sensory adjectives) or how many (number adjectives). When we read adjectives, we are better able to understand how something looks, sounds, tastes, or smells.

#### During Reading

#### Investigate Key Pages

#### My Turn

*"IT'S A PURPLE PUFFY COAT!" said Beetle* page: As we're rereading these two pages, I'm going to write down the words that Beetle and Stick Bug use to describe the coat. [Jot down *purple, puffy, breathtaking, warm, showy,* and *glorious.*] Remember these words are called *adjectives.*

#### Our Turn

*Beetle and Stick Bug walked the neighborhood* page: Can you find another adjective to describe the coat on this page? [Fancy.] Let's add it to the list.

#### Your Turn

If Stick Bug were to describe the coat, what adjectives might he use? Make a list on your whiteboard, in the chat box, on a digital sticky note, or in the electronic document.

#### After Reading

#### Nudge Toward Independence

Adjectives are everywhere! You'll see them in the books you're reading and hear them in songs on YouTube. When you find them, notice how they help you better understand what kind or how many.

**Innovate on Text:** Draw or print out a photograph of your favorite piece of clothing. Label it with adjectives.

*Favorite Shirt Work Sample*

## Focus 2–Reread to Boost Comprehension: Notice the Turning Point in a Story

### Before Reading

**Set the Stage:** Do you remember when Beetle realized that Stick Bug probably didn't like the purple puffy coat as much as he did? We're going to revisit that part of the story and dig into exactly what happened.

### During Reading

### Investigate Key Pages

### My Turn

*"OH, NO!" wailed Beetle* page: Remember this page? What happened here? [Beetle realized that Stick Bug didn't like the coat.]

An event like this is called the *turning point* of the story. After the turning point, the story "turns" in a new direction. Let's see if we can figure out what that means.

### Our Turn

To better understand how a turning point works in a story, think about how Beetle acted before and after this page. [Flip back to the *While Beetle boasted and bragged . . .* page and reread until the *"I have something for you," said Beetle* page. Stop to jot the difference between Beetle's actions before and after the turning point.]

| Turning Point: Before and After Chart | |
|---|---|
| **Before Turning Point** | **After Turning Point** |
| Beetle gave Stick Bug the purple puffy coat. | Beetle told Stick Bug he didn't have to wear it. |
| Beetle was focused on giving the coat to Stick Bug. | Beetle thought more about how to make Stick Bug happy. |

### Your Turn

Remember how some things in the story stayed the same before and after the turning point? Ask your friend, "What stayed the same?" [Beetle and Stick Bug were friends, Beetle gave Stick Bug a present.]

### After Reading

### Nudge Toward Independence

Today we studied the turning point of a story. Noticing the turning point helps you better understand a character's actions. To use what you learned today, you might mark the turning point in your book with a sticky note. Then, talk about it with a friend to notice the character's actions before and after the turning point.

## Read-Aloud Experience: Use Story Elements to Predict and Retell

**Book Title:** *The Pirates Are Coming!* (Condon, 2020)

**About the Book:** Tom waits at the top of the hill for the pirates to return. Each time a boat approaches, he shouts, "The pirates are coming! The pirates are coming! Quick! Everybody hide!" After repeated false alarms, the villagers ignore him. Your students will gasp when they reach the surprise ending in this swashbuckling *The Boy Who Cried Wolf* reboot.

To find a book like this one, look for the following

- Familiar tales with clearly identifiable story elements
- New twists on traditional tales

## Comprehension Conversation

### Before Reading

#### Notice the Cover Illustration

Look at the boy on the cover. Describe him to someone nearby. Now, let's combine what you've noticed about the boy with the title *The Pirates Are Coming!* What do you predict the boy might do or say in this story? Notice that instead of using one art tool, like paint, as some illustrators do, Matt Hunt chose to combine different art tools including paints, pens, crayons, and digital tools to create the illustrations. I can't wait for you to see his artwork inside the book.

**Set a Purpose:** How would you react if someone screamed, "The pirates are coming!"? What do you predict might happen in this book? Does it remind you of any stories you've read or heard before? Pay attention to what happens in this story so that you can tell your friends about it.

### During Reading

- *And quick as a flash, everybody hid* page: Why do you suppose the villagers are hiding? Take turns with a friend to point out the different places you see hidden villagers. Does this story remind you of any stories you've heard before? [If children are familiar with the fable *The Boy Who Cried Wolf*, discuss how recalling what happened in that story might help them predict the ongoing problem in this story.]

- *And once again (but not quite as quickly this time), everybody hid* page: Why do you suppose the villagers aren't hiding as quickly as they did before? What has changed? What do you predict will happen if Tom shouts "Pirates!" again?

- *"PIRAAAAAAATES!" yelled Tom . . .* page: Hmmm! Did your prediction match the author's thinking? What's next?

- *Meanwhile, the pirate ship sailed silently . . .* page: Uh oh! Make a face to show how you predict the townspeople are going to look on the next page.

### Learning Targets:

- I remember the characters, problem, and solution in the story.

- I use what I've learned about characters, problems, and solutions to help me predict.

- I use story elements to help me retell a story.

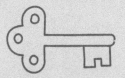
### After Reading

- At the end of this story, there were a few things that surprised me. Did anything surprise you?

- What was the problem in this story? How was it solved? What might Tom do differently next time?

## Extend the Experience

- [Depending on how much experience your students have had with retelling, they can either cocreate the response as a class, engage in partner retelling, or complete an independent response using the *Retell the Story Reproducible Response Page* provided on the companion website (resources.corwin.com/shakeupsharedreading).]

- What was your favorite part of this story? Draw an illustration to show what was happening at that point in the story. Under your illustration, write a caption that explains why you enjoyed that particular event. Start with the sentence stem "I liked this part because . . ."

### Similar Titles

 ### *La Princesa and the Pea* (Elya, 2017)

**About the Book:** In this rhyming, bilingual version of *The Princess and the Pea*, detail-oriented readers will notice that, in addition to the pea his Mamá has placed at the bottom of the mattress stack, the prince tucks a few items of his own between the mattresses.

 ### *Reading Beauty* (Underwood, 2019b)

**About the Book:** Book-loving Princess Lex and her puppy Prince are happy in their kingdom— that is, until Lex turns fifteen. On her birthday, her parents share that a fairy has cursed her with a forever sleep if she gets a papercut. As a cautionary measure, her parents remove all the books from the kingdom. Prince helps Lex sniff the books out so that she can use the information in them to confront the fairy. At the end of the book, readers will be surprised when they learn about the fairy's new job.

| Retell the Story: _____ |
| --- |
| Somebody: _____ wanted _____ |
| but _____ |
| so _____ |
| Finally, _____ |
| In the end _____ |
| Draw a picture of the main character. |
| Name _____ |

Retell the Story: __The Pirates Are Coming!__

Somebody: __Tom__ wanted __to tell everyone when the pirates were coming.__

but __he kept being wrong__

so __the villagers stopped listening.__

Finally, __the pirates came.__

In the end __The pirates were friendly villagers.__

*Retell the Story Reproducible Response Page*

*The Pirates Are Coming! Co-Created Retelling Chart*

## Short Bursts of Shared Reading: *The Pirates Are Coming!*

### Focus 1—Match Letters to Sounds: Short-*i* Word Families

### Before Reading

**Set the Stage:** Word detectives, get ready to tune your ears in to the end of words by looking for rhyming patterns or word families. If you can read and spell one word in the word family, it will help you read and spell all of the other words with the same pattern. We're going to focus on word families that have the short-*i* sound.

### During Reading

### Investigate Key Pages

### My Turn

*Every day, Tom climbed the hill to watch for pirates* page: The word *hill* is from the -ill word family. To decode the word, I will break it into two parts: /h/-/ill/, hill. I'll add the word *hill* to our short-*i* word family chart.

### Our Turn

*a ship!* page: The word *ship* is from the -ip word family. To decode the word, you can break it into two parts: /sh/-/ip/, ship. Try that with me. I'll add the word *ship* to our short-*i* word family chart.

### Your Turn

*"PIRATES!" shouted Tom* page: Can you find a short-*i* word on this page? [Quick.] To decode the word, you can break it into two parts: /qu/-/ick/, quick. Try that with me. I'll add the word *quick* to our short-*i* word family chart.

[Divide the class into three groups, one for each word family. Invite students in each group to work with a partner or on their own to brainstorm and write down as many words as they can think of that have the same spelling pattern. Students may jot words on a whiteboard, Google Jamboard, or piece of paper. Share and write the words on your class word family chart. Chant the words together to listen for the ending sound.]

### Short-*i* Word Family Chart

| -ill Family | -ip Family | -ick Family |
| --- | --- | --- |
| hill | ship | quick |
| | | |

### After Reading

### Nudge Toward Independence

Using the rhyming patterns in words or word families to help you decode and spell words is a smart strategy. If you would like a small copy of the word family chart we made to keep in your notebook, let me know.

## Focus 2–Reread for Fluency: Join in on Repeated Parts

### Before Reading

**Set the Stage:** Have you noticed that when I read aloud, my voice changes? Sometimes I read quietly, and other times I read VERY LOUDLY! When I read with expression, it helps me better comprehend or understand what is happening in the story. Rereading while paying attention to the signals the author gives you will help you be even more fluent readers.

### During Reading

### Investigate Key Pages

### My Turn

*"PIRATES!" shouted Tom* page: This book is fun to read aloud because Tom's warnings are written with such expression. There are big, bold words followed by exclamation marks. As I reread this page, I'm going to pretend I'm Tom shouting to the villagers. I know to read the words in a loud voice because of the signals the author gave me.

### Our Turn

*"PIRATES!" shouted Tom* page: Join me in reading Tom's words. Remember to read loudly without shouting in your friend's ear! How did you know to read the words with a loud voice?

### Your Turn

[Continue chorally reading Tom's warnings throughout the book.]

### After Reading

### Nudge Toward Independence

Fluent readers, like you, notice the clues the authors give them. They use those hints to help them read with expression. Some of those signals might be punctuation marks or big and bold words. As a writer, you can give the same clues to your readers. That way they'll know exactly how you want them to read your words.

**Innovate on Text:** In the fable *The Boy Who Cried Wolf*, the boy is looking out for wolves. In *The Pirates Are Coming!* the boy is on the lookout for pirates. If you were going to write a different version of this tale, what would your main character be watching for? Write the title for your new version, draw a picture to go with it, and put it with your writing ideas. Someday you might choose to write the whole story.

## Read-Aloud Experience: Discover Details in Realistic Texts

**Book Title:** *Simon at the Art Museum* (Soontornvat, 2020)

**About the Book:** Simon and his parents spend their day at the art museum. Simon quickly realizes that he is going to have to find innovative ways to entertain himself. So, among other things, he watches people looking at art. In an unexpected twist, he discovers a piece of art that looks just like him.

To find a book like this one, look for the following:

- Detail-filled illustrations
- Stories set in museums

## Comprehension Conversation

### Before Reading

#### Notice the Cover Illustration

What do you notice about Simon and his parents on the cover? What might his parents be saying? What do you think Simon is saying? Compare Simon's clothes to the words in the title. Do you notice anything interesting? [Simon's clothes are the same colors as the words in the title.] Do you think Christine Davenier did this on purpose?

**Set a Purpose:** Let's join Simon and his family at the art museum. While they are looking at art, we'll be reading, thinking, and talking about the clever details found in the illustrations.

### During Reading

- *Inside the museum, everyone whispered and shuffled . . .* page: Look at Simon in the four illustrations on these two pages. If you were going to put a thinking bubble above his head in each illustration, what would it say? Share ideas with someone nearby.

- *"Is that a swimming pool?"* page: Study the clues in the illustrations. Do you think Simon's parents agree that he is making the art even better? Why or why not?

- *The upstairs gallery was enormous* page: Can you find Simon? What does he mean when he says he's going to "enjoy the art from a new angle"?

- *Some walked right by the art without noticing it at all* page: Look carefully at these two pages. Do you spot anything interesting? [The people and the sculptures look the same. The lady is taking a selfie with a fire extinguisher!]

- *"Whoa," whispered his mom* page: What do you predict Simon spotted? Let's turn the page. Why was his family so surprised?

### After Reading

- What were some of your favorite illustrations in this story? How did the illustrations make this story even better?

- Do you think Simon will want to visit the art museum again? Why or why not?

**Learning Targets:**

- I notice details to learn about characters.
- I notice details in illustrations to enjoy and understand the story.
- I add details to my own illustrations.

## Extend the Experience

- [To prepare for this experience, retrieve a few kid-friendly images from Stefan Draschan's *People Matching Artworks* photo series.] Remember the page where the people looked just like the sculptures they were walking past or the painting that looked like Simon? Did you know that there is a photographer who takes pictures of people looking at art who look like the art? I'm going to show you a few of his images and see if you can see the connections. Write what you notice on your whiteboard.

- Be an Observer! Looking at Art: [Collect kid-friendly art prints to display on a bulletin board, digitally, or in a three-ring binder. Demonstrate how to complete the *Looking at Art Reproducible Response Page* found on the companion website (resources.corwin.com/shakeupsharedreading).] There is so much you can learn when you study a piece of art. Work on your own or with a buddy to see what you notice in a piece of art. Record what you see on the front of the page. Then, flip the paper over and draw your own version of the artwork.

### Key Vocabulary and Kid-Friendly Definitions:

- *enormous*: big, large, huge
- *shuffled:* dragged your feet on the floor while walking
- *unbelievable*: hard to understand that something is true or real

View the author talking about *Parker Looks Up* at resources.corwin.com/shakeupsharedreading

## Similar Titles

 **Explorers (Cordell, 2019) [Wordless]**

About the Book: Before visiting the museum with his family, an orange-shirted boy gets a magical toy from a street salesman. During his visit, he flings the toy around until it ends up in a green-shirted child's hands. When the green-shirted child attempts to return it, the boy rudely grabs it away. Later, the boy's sister flings the toy off a second-floor balcony and the boy gets lost trying to retrieve it. The family of the child with the green shirt helps to reunite the boy with his family, and they all enjoy the butterfly garden together.

 **Parker Looks Up: An Extraordinary Moment (Curry & Curry, 2019)**

About the Book: In 2018, unsuspecting two-year-old Parker Curry stood in awe in front of Amy Sherald's portrait of former First Lady Michelle Obama. A museum visitor snapped a photo, posted it on social media, and the rest is history. This book tells the story of that day and the joy that comes from looking at art.

*Looking at Art Reproducible Response Page*

*Observer Center: Looking at Art*

## Short Bursts of Shared Reading:
### *Simon at the Art Museum*

### Focus 1–Reread to Boost Comprehension: Use Pictures and Words to Infer

### Before Reading

**Set the Stage:** Readers use hints in the words and illustrations along with their schema to infer. Inferring is kind of like being a detective. You use clues to figure out missing information or read between the lines to better understand the author's message.

### During Reading

### Investigate Key Pages

### My Turn

*Simon couldn't see much art from where he was sitting* page: To infer what kind of art the museum guests are viewing, I have to read the words and study the illustrations. When the text reads, "Some of it made people smile," I infer that the art is bright, colorful, and cheerful. [Continue demonstrating your inferring process with the remaining three sentences on this page.]

### Our Turn

*Sometimes people got really close to the art and squinted at it* page: There are two sentences and illustrations on this page. Can you infer what kind of art the folks on this page are viewing? Discuss your inferences with a classmate.

### Your Turn

*Some walked right by the art without noticing it at all* page: Infer what is happening on these two pages. How did the author's words and the illustrator's images work together to make these pages interesting?

### After Reading

### Nudge Toward Independence

To better understand the author's message, readers infer. Inferring takes concentration and persistence. To infer, you have to slow down, reread, think about the words, and look at the pictures. You can do it!

## Focus 2—Notice Writer's Craft Moves: How Dialogue and Inner Thinking Help Readers Understand Characters

### Before Reading

**Set the Stage:** Authors include dialogue and inner thinking so that you can relate to the character. Dialogue is the words that the character speaks, and inner thinking is the thoughts the character has. Let's see how reading dialogue and noticing thoughts helps us get to know Simon.

### During Reading

### Investigate Key Pages

### My Turn

*What IS it with this place? thought Simon* . . . page: Simon's inner thinking shows me that he is a little tired of looking at all of the art in the museum.

### Our Turn

*They passed the museum café* . . . page: On this page, we read Simon's dialogue and his inner thinking. Together they give us a clear picture of what Simon really wants to do. [Eat cheesecake.] Talk it over with a neighbor. Which would you prefer? Looking at art or eating dessert?

### Your Turn

Last page of the book: There are no words on this page. If you were going to add dialogue, what would you have Simon say? What is going on in his mind? Divide your whiteboard or a piece of paper in half. Write down Simon's words and thoughts. Share them with a friend.

### After Reading

### Nudge Toward Independence

Authors want you to feel like you know their characters, like they are your friends. To do this, they let you hear what the characters are saying or thinking. Try adding dialogue and inner thoughts to your own writing. Ask a classmate to read what you've written to see if it helps them get to know your characters.

**Innovate on Text:** When we visited the art museum with Simon, we saw art in all shapes and sizes. Create a piece of your own art. Then, give your masterpiece a name. [Provide students with a variety of art media like construction paper scraps to make collages or paper sculptures, watercolor paints, modeling clay, and so on.]

## Read-Aloud Experience: Discover Details in Imaginative Texts

### Book Title: *Lift* (Lê, 2020)

**About the Book:** There is nothing that cheers up Iris more than pressing the elevator buttons. That is, until her family lets her brother do it instead. While pouting over her loss of button-pushing privileges, Iris finds a discarded elevator button in the trash. Once it's securely taped next to her bedroom closet door, it becomes a portal to other worlds. Told from Iris's point of view in a graphic format, imaginative readers will pour over the details in this book.

To find a book like this one, look for the following:

- Detail-filled illustrations
- Characters taking imaginary journeys

### Comprehension Conversation

**Before Reading**

**Notice the Cover Illustration**

Take a moment to study the cover. Tell a friend one detail that you see. [If you are able to show the book casing underneath the paper book jacket of the hardcover version, the illustrations on the front and back case cover warrant further study and discussion.]

**Set a Purpose:** Just like the illustrations on the cover, the pictures on the inside pages of *Lift* are brimming with important details to help you decide which events in the story are happening in real life and which parts are imaginary.

### During Reading

- Front endpapers: We'll come back to the front endpapers after reading the story to see if they are the same as the back endpapers.
- Title page: Look at where they placed the title of this book. Did you know that the word *lift* has more than one meaning? *Lift* means to pick something up or cheer someone up, and it is another name for an elevator. I'm wondering if understanding the different meanings of the word *lift* is going to be important to the story.
- *Hi, my name is Iris* page: Talk with a friend. Point out the details that appear in this illustration and are important to setting up the action of the story. Who is the main character? When and where is the action happening? What have you learned about Iris?
- *ALL THE BUTTONS!* page: Look at Iris's family's faces. Can you picture what happened when Iris pushed all of the buttons? How is her family feeling about it?
- *When we get back home, I just want to be alone* page: Check out Iris's face when she hears the ding. Where could she be going?
- Back endpapers: Compare the back endpapers to those in the front of the book. How are they similar? How are they different? Why do you suppose the illustrator, Dan Santat, designed them this way?

### Learning Targets:

- I notice details to learn about characters.
- I compare details in illustrations to tell the difference between real and imagined parts of stories.
- I add details to my own illustrations.

## After Reading

- Near the end of the story, Iris says, "After all, everyone can use a lift sometimes." What do you think she means by that?

- So much of this story is told through the illustrations. Think about the real-life and imagined events. Where did the real-life events happen? How about the imagined adventures?

## Extend the Experience

- What is something you can do when a friend or family member needs a lift?

- Glue the door and elevator button found on the *Where Does Your Door Lead? Reproducible Response Page* on the companion website (resources .corwin.com/shakeupsharedreading) to a blank piece of paper. Open the door, and draw where you imagine your door would lead.

## Similar Titles

 **Another (Robinson, 2019) [Wordless]**

About the Book: A girl follows a red-collared cat (who is following a blue-collared cat) through a portal. On the other side, she discovers another world where she meets up with another girl exactly like her.

 **Journey (Becker, 2013) [Wordless]**

About the Book: With a beginning similar to the book *Blackout* (Rocco, 2011), where everyone in her family is too busy to play with her, this wordless picture book follows a girl on an imaginary journey. She uses her red crayon to draw her various modes of transportation.

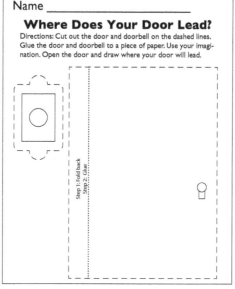

Name _____

### Where Does Your Door Lead?

Directions: Cut out the door and doorbell on the dashed lines. Glue the door and doorbell to a piece of paper. Use your imagination. Open the door and draw where your door will lead.

Step 1: Fold back
Step 2: Glue

*Where Does Your Door Lead? Reproducible Response Page*

**Key Vocabulary and Kid-Friendly Definitions:**

- *betrayal*: when someone does something that lets you down or breaks your trust

- *cheers*: makes you feel happy

- *lift*: to cheer someone up; to pick something up; another word for an elevator [discuss multiple meanings]

View book trailers of *Lift, Another,* and *Journey* at resources.corwin.com/ shakeupsharedreading

## Short Bursts of Shared Reading: *Lift*

### Focus 1–Reread to Boost Comprehension: Real Versus Make Believe

### Before Reading

**Set the Stage:** Did you notice that each place Iris visits when she presses the elevator button is connected to something in her house? Let's jot down the real objects that are linked to the make-believe places.

### During Reading

### Investigate Key Pages

### My Turn

Page with tiger in the jungle: Hmm! I'm wondering. Where have I seen a tiger before? Oh, I remember. Her brother had a stuffed tiger. So, the stuffed tiger is real and the tiger Iris sees when she opens her closet door is imaginary.

### Our Turn

Space station page: Hmm! Let's look back through the illustrations. Are there any objects in Iris's house that might have caused her to imagine traveling through space? [The solar system mobile above her bed and *Out of the World* game that her babysitter brings.]

### Your Turn

Copyright page: Do you remember anything real in the book that is related to this adventure? Let me flip back a few pages to see what you can find. When you spot something, hold your hand up to signal "Stop!" Then, discuss the real-to-make-believe connection.

| Connecting Real and Make-Believe Chart | |
| --- | --- |
| **Real** | **Make-Believe** |
| her brother's stuffed tiger | jungle |
| space board game and mobile | space station |
| Summit book | mountains |

### After Reading

### Nudge Toward Independence:

*Lift* is a blend of real-life action and make-believe adventures. To tie the two together, the adventures were sparked by items in the house. Which parts of the book did you prefer: those that happened in real life or those that were imaginary?

## Focus 2–Notice Illustrator's Craft Moves: Graphic Format Illustrations

### Before Reading

**Set the Stage:** Dan Santat illustrated *Lift* using a graphic format style. On most pages, he used multiple panels with frames around them to show the action. If we study his illustrations, we can find techniques to borrow when we're drawing pictures to go along with our stories.

### During Reading

#### Investigate Key Pages

#### My Turn

*Luckily, that's my job* page: I notice that the panels are labeled with the days of the week. I also see that Iris is wearing different clothes and hairstyles each day. Dan Santat uses multiple panels to illustrate that Iris gets to push the buttons every day. So, if I want to clue readers in to the passage of time in a book, I could draw a separate panel for each day in my story.

#### Our Turn

Two-page spread where worker is fixing elevator: There is a lot of action happening in these six panels. Notice that other than the "Out of Service" sign on the elevator, there is no text in the panels or on the frames around them. Take turns with a friend to tell the story of what you see happening in each panel. How could you use what you learned from this page in your own book?

#### Your Turn

*Ding Dong!* page: Talk about how the onomatopoeia in these panels helps you tell what is happening in Iris's home. [Continue studying Dan Santat's art. Discuss how drawing multiple panels on one page helps move the story along. Notice aloud how sometimes the text is placed inside the panel and other times it is placed on the frames around the panels.]

### After Reading

#### Nudge Toward Independence

When stories are told in a graphic format, it takes time to study the text and illustration in the panels and the text that appears on the frames around the panels to infer what is happening. If graphic format text is something you want to experiment with in your writing, you can continue to study and learn from this book and others like it.

**Innovate on Text:** Where do you think Iris and her brother will go next? Why? Write your prediction on a sticky note, and share it with a friend.

## Read-Aloud Experience: Use Picture Clues to Predict

**Book Title:** *Thank You, Omu!* (Mora, 2018)

**About the Book:** Omu (pronounced AH-moo) is making her thick red stew. When the scent wafts out her window, there is a knock on the door. Omu shares her stew with all of the community members who stop by until it is gone. In the end, the community members repay Omu's kindness by surprising her with dinner.

To find a book like this one, look for the following:

- Plots with suspense and perfect points for predicting
- Text and illustration clues that support predictions

## Comprehension Conversation

### Before Reading

### Notice the Cover Illustration

Oge Mora creates her illustrations in a unique way. Look at the cover. What do you see? She carefully pieces together scraps of colorful paper and clippings from old books to make a unique collage illustration. Wait until you see the pictures inside the book!

**Set a Purpose:** What do you imagine this child is thinking? Which words might the child use to describe what is in the bowl? As we read to find out the answers to these questions, we'll also look for clues that help us predict, or think ahead of our reading.

### During Reading

- *With that, Omu put down her spoon . . .* page: Who do you predict is knocking at her door? Do you see any clues in the pictures to show you who it might be? [Notice the boy in the window playing with his truck.]

  *. . . a little boy* page: Did your prediction match the author's thinking? Let's look back one page. Were there any clues that helped you predict? [Continue this conversation each time someone knocks at Omu's door. Notice that the person who is knocking is pictured on the page that comes before that includes the word "Knock!"]

- *Omu sniffled* page: Look at Omu's face. Can you infer how she is feeling? Who could be knocking at her door now? Whisper your prediction to a friend.

### After Reading

- Share some of the clues that Oge Mora included in the pictures and words that led to your predictions.
- How did predicting help you make sense of what was happening in the story?

**Learning Targets:**

- I use the clues from the words and pictures to help me predict.
- I think about how predicting helps me as a reader.

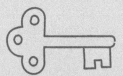

### Extend the Experience

- As we read, we used clues to help us predict. Think about how the story ended. What do you predict Omu will do tomorrow? Draw or write your prediction on this sticky note. Then, we'll share our predictions along with the clues from the story that led to that prediction.

- Compare and Contrast! Multigenre Text Set—Food: Reading about Omu's thick red stew got me thinking about food. So, I started a collection of texts about food and put them in this basket. Read and think about how these texts are the same as or different from *Thank You, Omu!* I'll leave some sticky notes here so you can write down what you notice. If you find other texts about food, please add them to the collection.

**Key Vocabulary and Kid-Friendly Definitions:**

- *evening*: the early part of the night
- *scent*: the way something smells
- *wafted*: when a smell or sound is carried by the wind

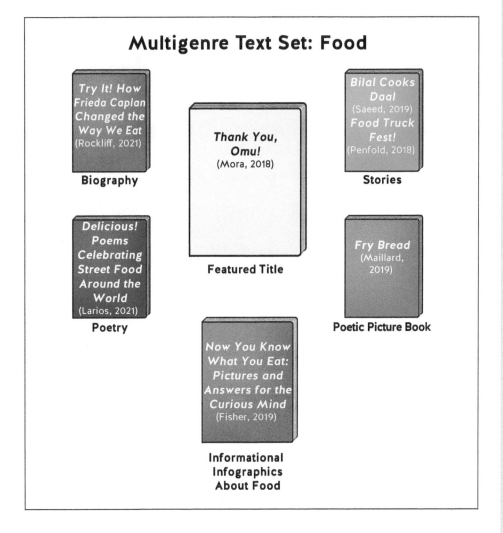

## Multigenre Text Set: Food

*Try It! How Frieda Caplan Changed the Way We Eat* (Rockliff, 2021)
**Biography**

*Thank You, Omu!* (Mora, 2018)
**Featured Title**

*Bilal Cooks Daal* (Saeed, 2019)
*Food Truck Fest!* (Penfold, 2018)
**Stories**

*Delicious! Poems Celebrating Street Food Around the World* (Larios, 2021)
**Poetry**

*Fry Bread* (Maillard, 2019)
**Poetic Picture Book**

*Now You Know What You Eat: Pictures and Answers for the Curious Mind* (Fisher, 2019)
**Informational Infographics About Food**

## Short Bursts of Shared Reading: *Thank You, Omu!*

### Focus 1—Wonder About Words: Synonyms

#### Before Reading

**Set the Stage:** When we read *Thank You, Omu!* the first time, we had so much fun predicting what might happen next. This time we're going to reread to notice all of the different words Oge Mora uses to describe Omu's thick red stew.

#### During Reading

#### Investigate Key Pages

[As you are rereading to find synonyms for *yummy*, invite students to join in on all of the words that appear in capital letters in the story.]

#### My Turn

*With that, Omu put down her spoon . . .* page: Oge Mora uses the word *scrumptious* to describe the stew on this page. I'll write that word down.

#### Our Turn

[Continue to collect synonyms for *yummy* on a whiteboard or chart. They include the following: *yummy, delectable, delicious, scrumptious,* and *tasty*.]

#### Your Turn

Think of one of your favorite foods. Use a word on the chart to describe that food to a friend.

#### After Reading

#### Nudge Toward Independence

When you are reading, think about all the words we learned that mean the same as *yummy*. See if you find any adjectives in your books. You can also challenge yourself to use adjectives when you are writing about your favorite foods.

Thank You, Omu! *Adjective Chart*

## Focus 2–Read to Boost Comprehension: Infer the Big Idea

### Before Reading

**Set the Stage:** When we read this book aloud, we had fun predicting what might happen next. As we made our predictions, we couldn't wait to turn the page. During shared reading, we're going to use our brains in a different way. We are going to infer to figure out any lessons that we can learn from reading this book.

### During Reading

#### Investigate Key Pages

#### My Turn

[Return to the last three pages of the book. Start at the page that begins with . . . *the little boy?*] As I reread the ending of this book, I'm thinking about the big idea or lesson Oge Mora is trying to teach me. To do this, I pay attention to the words the characters say and other clues in the text and illustrations.

#### Our Turn

[Invite students to share and discuss ideas. If you notice that they need extra support, moving beyond literal comprehension toward inferential, help them key into these sentences:

*"Don't worry, Omu. We are not here to ask . . . WE ARE HERE TO GIVE."*

*While Omu's big fat pot of thickened red stew was empty, her heart was full of happiness and love.*]

#### Your Turn

Your challenge today is to use the two-word strategy (Hoyt, 1999, p. 4) to write two separate words that tell what you learned from this book. The two words do not have to go together. [If in person, provide students with two pieces of paper or index cards. If in a distance learning setting, use a digital tool like Jamboard.] Once your words are written, we'll share, compare, and discuss.

### After Reading

#### Nudge Toward Independence

To figure out Oge Mora's big idea, lesson, or moral, we used the characters' dialogue or words along with other clues from the text and illustrations. You can do the same thing when you're reading on your own. If you want to share your big idea thinking with us, write the lesson or moral you learned from the book along with your name on a sticky note. Put the sticky note on the cover of your book, and set it on the sharing chair. Then, you can teach us what you learned.

> **Innovate on Text:** One way to show gratitude is by thanking people who are kind. Let's take a moment to write a thank-you card to a person who has done something nice. It could be a classmate, a person at school, a family member, or someone else. After we're finished, we'll deliver the cards. [Provide students with a blank piece of white paper folded in half like a greeting card.] On the front of your card write, "Thank you, _____!" Inside the card, draw or write to thank the person for their kind act.

HAROLD LOVES HIS WOOLLY HAT

Vern Kousky

**Learning Targets:**

- I use the clues from the words and pictures to help me predict.

- I predict what characters will do.

- I think about how predicting helps me as a reader.

## Read-Aloud Experience: Predict Characters' Actions

**Book Title:** *Harold Loves His Woolly Hat* (Kousky, 2018)

**About the Book:** Harold loves his woolly hat so much that he wears it all the time. Because he believes that his hat makes him special, he can't imagine life without it. One day, a crow swoops down and takes his hat. Harold tries everything to win it back until he discovers the crow is using it to keep its babies warm. This book pairs nicely with *Two Wool Gloves* (Jin, 2019).

To find a book like this one, look for the following:

- Plots with suspense and perfect points for predicting
- Text and illustration clues that support predictions

### Comprehension Conversation

#### Before Reading

**Notice the Cover Illustration**

I'm going to open the book so that you can look at the entire wraparound cover of *Harold Loves His Woolly Hat*. You can probably infer which character is Harold. Do you notice any other animals on the cover? Why do you suppose there are some bees and a crow on the cover? Do you predict the bees and crow will show up in the story?

**Set a Purpose:** Do you have a piece of clothing that you really love? Tell someone nearby about it. It's clear from the title that Harold loves his woolly hat. I'm having a hard time predicting what might happen in this story. How about you? I guess we'll have to start reading to learn more about Harold and his woolly hat.

#### During Reading

- *Then one day, a crow swoops down . . .* page: Ahhhh! Now we know why the crow was on the cover. What's the problem? What do you predict Harold will do next?

- *So Harold tries to make another trade* page: What do you predict? Do you think this trade will work? Whisper your prediction to someone nearby.

- *Once more, the crow only replies, CACAW! CACAW!* page: Oh no! What do you predict Harold will do now?

- *three baby crows!* page: Look at Harold's face! How do you predict this story will end?

#### After Reading

- When you predict, sometimes your prediction matches the author's ideas, and other times, even though you use clues from the story, your thinking is different. That's okay. Your prediction might give you an idea for your own story! Were you surprised by the ending of this book? Why or why not?

- Remember back to when we saw the crow and bees on the wraparound cover? Were they important to the story? What does this tell you about taking time to study the cover illustration?

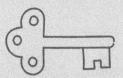

## Extend the Experience

- At the end of the story, the baby crows leave the nest. What do you predict will happen the next day? Write and draw about your prediction.

- Compare and Contrast! Multigenre Text Set—Bears: Reading about Harold the bear got me thinking about other bear texts you might enjoy. So, I started a collection of texts about bears and put them in this basket. Read and think about how these texts are the same as or different from *Harold Loves His Woolly Hat*. I'll leave some sticky notes here so you can write down what you notice. If you find other texts about bears, please add them to the collection.

**Key Vocabulary and Kid-Friendly Definitions:**

- *greedy*: wanting more and more money or things

- *swoop*: to dive down from up high

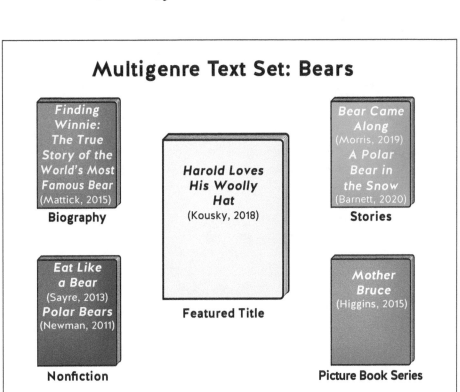

**Multigenre Text Set: Bears**

*Finding Winnie: The True Story of the World's Most Famous Bear* (Mattick, 2015)
**Biography**

*Harold Loves His Woolly Hat* (Kousky, 2018)
**Featured Title**

*Bear Came Along* (Morris, 2019) *A Polar Bear in the Snow* (Barnett, 2020)
**Stories**

*Eat Like a Bear* (Sayre, 2013) *Polar Bears* (Newman, 2011)
**Nonfiction**

*Mother Bruce* (Higgins, 2015)
**Picture Book Series**

## Short Bursts of Shared Reading:
### *Harold Loves His Woolly Hat*

### Focus 1–Reread for Fluency: Big and Bold Print

#### Before Reading

**Set the Stage:** Each time Harold asks the crow to give him his hat back, the text or words change. These changes are signals to help us read the words the way the author wants them to sound.

#### During Reading

#### Investigate Key Pages

#### My Turn

*The crow swoops down and takes the worms . . .* page: On this page, Harold's words look exactly like the rest of the text, so I'm going to read them in a regular voice.

#### Our Turn

*"NOW PLEASE GIVE ME BACK MY WOOLLY HAT!"* page: How does the text on this page look different than the first time Harold asked for his hat back? [The text is larger and written in all capital letters.] Reread the words as if you are Harold.

#### Your Turn

*"NOW WILL YOU GIVE ME BACK MY WOOLLY HAT?!"* page: What do you notice about the words this time? [The words are so big they fill an entire page!] Ready? Read them like Harold.

#### After Reading

#### Nudge Toward Independence

How did Vern Kousky change the words to show Harold was upset or frustrated? [He made them big and bold.] Have you seen big and bold words in other books you've read? Some authors, like Mo Willems, use them a lot. Big and bold words add emotion and make books fun to read!

**Innovate on Text:** *Harold Loves His Woolly Hat* is a make-believe story about a bear who thinks he is special because of his hat. If you were going to write an imaginary story about a character and their favorite item, what would your title be?

_____ Loves Their _____

Write your title for your new version, draw a picture to go with it, and put it with your writing ideas. Someday you might choose to write the whole story.

## Focus 2–Reread to Boost Comprehension: Identify Character Traits

### Before Reading

**Set the Stage:** We learn about characters by noticing their words and actions. We can use what we discover to help us describe the character's traits using adjectives. Let's see what we can find out about Harold.

### During Reading

#### Investigate Key Pages

#### My Turn

*Harold has to win back his woolly hat* page: I know how much Harold loves his hat. When I read Harold's words and pay attention to his actions, I can use what I learn to describe his personality. After reading this page, I'd say in the beginning of the story Harold is hopeful because he thinks the crow will give him his hat back.

#### Our Turn

*"What a greedy little crow," growls Harold* page: Let's reread what Harold says and notice his actions. How would you describe Harold on this page? Use these words to help you: In the middle of the story, Harold is _____ because . . .

#### Your Turn

*Harold tucks the crows in tight . . .* page: Harold's words and actions are much different on this page. What changed? Tell a neighbor what you notice. Use these words to help you: At the end of the story, Harold is _____ because . . .

### After Reading

#### Nudge Toward Independence

Characters' actions and words change throughout a story. After you finish reading, you combine everything you've learned about the character to describe their traits. If you were going to describe Harold to a friend, what would you say: Harold is _____ because . . . To help you to remember how to figure out character traits while you're reading, I made you this strategy chart.

*Character Trait Strategy Chart*

## Read-Aloud Experience: Spot Sensory Language

**Book Title:** *My Papi Has a Motorcycle* (Quintero, 2019)

**About the Book:** When Daisy's papi, a carpenter, gets home from work, they put on their helmets, hop onto his motorcycle, and roar off for an evening spin. On their ride, they savor the sights and sounds of their beloved, changing city. Isabel Quintero tells us in the author's note that this book is "a love letter to both my father, who showed me a different way of experiencing home, and to Corona, California, a city that will always be a part of me." The story is written in first-person point of view from Daisy's perspective.

To find a book like this one, look for the following:

- Sensory language and onomatopoeia
- Stories that celebrate father-daughter relationships

### Comprehension Conversation

#### Before Reading

#### Notice the Cover Illustration

[Launch the conversation before showing the cover.] Imagine you are sitting on the back of a motorcycle riding through your neighborhood. What might you see and hear? How would you feel? Share your ideas with a friend. [Display the cover.] Now take a close look at the cover illustration. What do you see in the background? Can you infer how this girl is feeling?

**Set a Purpose:** An amazing thing about stories is that certain words can help us imagine or visualize that we are right there in the action. Authors do this by using words that describe how something looks, sounds, tastes, smells, or feels. We call these *sensory* words. As we're reading, be on the lookout for words that help you visualize or form a picture in your mind.

#### During Reading

- *Papi revs the engine, and the smell of gasoline hits me . . .* page: Hear the engine? I can picture I'm on the motorcycle with the girl and her papi! The words *rumble* and *growl* help me hear the sound of the motorcycle. Do you see anything in the illustration that helps you imagine you are there? Tell a friend what you see.

- *As we ride on, I feel and hear everyone and everything we pass by* page: What does she hear? How do the onomatopoeias, or the sound words, in the illustrations help you imagine the sounds?

- *Here it is, all of our beautiful city!* page: Why do you suppose the author wrote the colors with no spaces between them? What is she helping us visualize?

#### After Reading

- Wow! What a ride! What feelings or images stayed with you after we closed the book?
- How would you describe this story to a friend?

---

**Learning Targets:**

- I notice sensory words and phrases.
- I pay attention to how they help me imagine a place or experience.

## Extend the Experience

- Visualizing while reading is a strategy that can help you better understand and remember a story. Noticing sensory language and using it as you imagine the places and events in a book will help you visualize.

- Be an Observer! The Sights and Sounds in Our Neighborhood: When Daisy and her papi rode around their neighborhood, they noticed many different people, places, animals, and other scenery. [If possible, take students for a walk around your school building. Snap digital photos along the way. Print and make photos available in a center or on a digital slide. Provide sticky notes to label places or items in illustrations or to add onomatopoeia. Supply construction paper or other building materials so that students can re-create their neighborhood.]

## Similar Titles

 **Eyes That Kiss in the Corners** (Ho, 2021) [Sensory Language]

**About the Book:** An Asian American girl celebrates her "eyes that kiss in the corners and glow like warm tea." This lyrical text exudes warmth and positivity as the young narrator shares her appreciation for the love that is reflected in the eyes of her mama, amah, and younger sister.

 **Hair Love** (Cherry, 2019) [Father-Daughter Relationship]

**About the Book:** It's a big day for Zuri, and she wants her hair to be "perfect." After a few failed attempts, her dad perseveres and, with the help of a YouTube video, styles Zuri's hair into "funky puff buns." She's ready just in time for her mom to come back home from a trip.

---

**Key Vocabulary and Kid-Friendly Definitions:**

- *rebuilds*: builds again

- *soaring*: moving or flying quickly

- *zigzags*: moves back and forth

View book trailer of *Eyes That Kiss in the Corners* at resources.corwin.com/shakeupsharedreading

View short film of *Hair Love* at resources.corwin.com/shakeupsharedreading

## Short Bursts of Shared Reading:
*My Papi Has a Motorcycle*

### Focus 1–Wonder About Words: Onomatopoeia

#### Before Reading

**Set the Stage:** Readers, there are words that describe and imitate a sound. These words are called *onomatopoeia*. When you read these words, they help you imagine the sound you might hear. We're going to reread the pictures in *My Papi Has a Motorcycle* to learn more about these sound words.

#### During Reading

#### Investigate Key Pages

[Project or display the book, "read" the illustrations page by page to read, verbally perform, and discuss the onomatopoetic words.]

#### My Turn

*When I hear his gray truck pull into our driveway, I run outside . . .* page: Look at the words under the girl's shoes: "THUMP! THUMP!" I'm going to say those words the way I think they sound. Then, I'll ask myself, "What does that onomatopoeia tell me about the way she is moving? What other things might make that sound?"

#### Our Turn

[Continue in the same fashion by inviting students to read and chorally "perform" the onomatopoeia included in the illustrations.]

#### Your Turn

[If you wish to collect the words for future reference, jot them on a chart or in an electronic document. Then, invite students to add sound words to this chart.]

#### After Reading

#### Nudge Toward Independence

When book creators include sound words in the illustrations, take the time to notice and read them. Doing this will boost your understanding and enjoyment of the book.

## Focus 2—Notice Writer's Craft Moves: Repetition

### Before Reading

**Set the Stage:** Authors repeat words, phrases, or sentences to catch the reader's attention, create memorable moments, or add rhythm to a story. Let's reread and think about why Isabel Quintero uses repetition in *My Papi Has a Motorcycle*.

### During Reading

#### Investigate Key Pages

#### My Turn

*The shiny blue metal of the motorcycle glows in the sun* page: Rereading this page and hearing the repetition of the word *sun* helps me imagine riding the motorcycle as the bright orange sun is setting.

#### Our Turn

*We ride, ride, ride until the blue glow from the motorcycle begins to dim* . . . page: Talk about how the repetition of the word *ride* adds to your reading experience. Ponder why you think the author used repetition on this page.

#### Your Turn

*I think about my city* . . . page: Reread this page. What is it mostly about? [The changing city.] Do you notice any words that appear more than once? [Changes.] Do you suppose that the author intentionally repeated the word *change*? Turn and talk about that with a friend.

### After Reading

#### Nudge Toward Independence

Isabel Quintero used the repeated words in this book intentionally, or on purpose. She wanted you, as the reader, to take notice. She isn't the only author who uses repetition. As you're reading, notice how authors use repetition to make certain words or big ideas stand out. Think about how you might use repeated words in the stories you are writing.

> **Innovate on Text:** Isabel Quintero wrote this story about a special memory from when she was a kid going on rides with her papi on his motorcycle. What are some special memories that you could turn into a story? Add these memories to your list of writing ideas.

## Read-Aloud Experience: Use Your Imagination

**Book Title:** *Milo Imagines the World* (de la Peña, 2021)

**About the Book:** On a subway ride, Milo draws imagined scenarios about his fellow passengers. He draws one boy as a prince, only to find out he is heading to the same destination as Milo and his sister—to visit their mom, who is incarcerated. Following the realization that "Maybe you can't really know anyone just by looking at their face," Milo reimagines his drawings. After a big family hug, he gives a special drawing to his mom.

To find a book like this one, look for the following:

- Words and images that help readers infer characters' emotions
- Stories that encourage readers to look beyond outward appearances

## Comprehension Conversation

### Before Reading

#### Notice the Cover Illustration

What can you learn about Milo from this picture? The title of this book is *Milo Imagines the World*. Which parts of this illustration look real, and which parts look imaginary? Share your thinking with a classmate. [If possible, notice that the hard cover book casing is different than the paper book jacket. Also, point out the endpapers—notice that they are the same pattern as Milo's hat.]

**Set a Purpose:** In this story, Milo visualizes or imagines, and then he draws what he sees in his notebook. Artists visualize and so do readers. As we're reading, imagine or visualize what it would be like to be Milo, and notice what he sees and hears and how he feels.

### During Reading

- *These monthly Sunday subway rides are never ending . . .* page: Let's reread this page and talk about the different emotions Milo is experiencing. What are you thinking or wondering?
- *Butterflies flood Milo's stomach . . .* page: Have you ever heard the saying "butterflies in your stomach"? What do you think it means? Can you imagine how Milo is feeling as he gets off the train?
- *He's even more surprised when the boy joins . . .* page: I'm going to reread the last line on this two-page spread: "Maybe you can't really know anyone just by looking at their face." Ponder this sentence. What are your thoughts?
- *Milo's chest fills with excitement when he spots his mom . . .* page: Where are they visiting Milo's mom? [Prison.] Think back to the page when we wondered about Milo's mixed emotions. Does that page make more sense now that you know where they were going?

### After Reading

- When you imagine how a character might be feeling, it helps you empathize with the character or put yourself in their shoes. Do you feel like you understand Milo

**Learning Targets:**

- I notice feeling words and phrases.
- I pay attention to how feeling words help me imagine characters' experiences.

a little bit better after reading this book? If you were going to tell a friend about Milo, what would you say?

- What are the big ideas, lessons, or morals that Milo learned?

## Extend the Experience

- [Curate a small collection of images or artwork that include at least one person. You can choose to use the same image with the whole class or different images with small groups.] I'm going to show you an image. Tell a short story about the person in this image. What happens at the beginning, in the middle, and at the end? Listen to a friend's story. How are your stories the same? How are they different? Can you reimagine your story and tell it a different way? Draw a picture to go with your new story.

---

Meet the Creator!

Book Creator Study: Christian Robinson

Website: https://www.theartoffun.com/

---

Did you know?

- Christian was born in Los Angeles, California.
- He once worked at Sesame Street Workshop.

---

A Few of His Books:

- *Another* (Author, 2019) [Wordless Book]
- *Carmela Full of Wishes* (de la Peña, Illustrator, 2018)
- *Last Stop on Market Street* (de la Peña, Illustrator, 2015)
- *Rain!* (Ashman, Illustrator, 2013)
- *School's First Day of School* (Rex, Illustrator, 2016)
- *The Smallest Girl in the Smallest Grade* (Roberts, Illustrator, 2014)
- *You Matter* (Author, 2020)

---

**Key Vocabulary and Kid-Friendly Definitions:**

- *bustling*: busy
- *familiar*: something you've experienced before
- *reimagine*: to think again about something, or think of something differently

View the book trailer and an interview with illustrator Christian Robinson at resources.corwin.com/shakeupsharedreading

## Similar Titles

 ***A House for Every Bird* (Maynor, 2021) [Similar Theme]**

About the Book: A young artist is satisfied that she has drawn birdhouses that perfectly match the appearance of each of her birds. But the birds don't agree. So, the girl steps into her drawings to try to set things straight. After talking and listening to the birds, she realizes, "You can't really tell a bird by its feathers."

 ***Last Stop on Market Street* (de la Peña, 2015) [Similar Plot]**

About the Book: CJ and his grandma are taking the city bus to a soup kitchen on the other side of town, and along the way his grandma teaches CJ some important life lessons. Like *Milo Imagines the World*, the destination of the bus ride is not revealed until the end of the story. You could also invite learners to compare CJ and Milo and discuss the lessons each of the boys learned.

# Short Bursts of Shared Reading:
## *Milo Imagines the World*

### Focus 1—Wonder About Words: Sensory Words and Phrases

#### Before Reading

**Set the Stage:** When we read this book aloud, we focused on visualizing Milo's feelings. We're going to reread some important parts to notice how Matt de la Peña uses special words and phrases to help us imagine we are right there with Milo.

#### During Reading

#### Investigate Key Pages

#### My Turn

*What begins as a slow, distant glow . . .* page: Listen as I reread this page. I'm going to tune into the words that help me use my senses. I use my sense of sight to picture the glow of the subway train lights. To imagine the train clattering down the tracks or the screech of steel, I tune into my sense of hearing. When I read the words "A cool rush of wind," I imagine how that might feel. Taking a moment to visualize helps me picture what it is like to be on a subway platform.

#### Our Turn

*Milo images him trudging through brown mounds of slush* page: Wow! There is so much happening on these two pages. Let's reread and see if we can use our senses to better understand what Milo is imagining. [Discuss the various sensory words and phrases that appear on this page, and invite students to share their visualizations.]

#### Your Turn

*Milo imagines the clop clop clop . . .* page: On this page, Matt de la Peña adds onomatopoeia, or sound words, along with sensory language so you can better see into Milo's imagination. When I point to the sound words, read them the way you imagine they would sound.

#### After Reading

#### Nudge Toward Independence

In picture books like this one, the illustrations help you visualize what is happening, but when you're reading books with no pictures, you have to do that work in your brain. Paying attention to sensory language and imagining yourself into the story will help you comprehend, or understand, the story. It also makes reading a lot more interesting!

Focus 2—Notice Illustrator's Craft Moves:
Showing a Character's Inner Thoughts

### Before Reading

**Set the Stage:** In this book, the illustrator, Christian Robinson, offers us two different points of view in his art. He alternates between what is happening in Milo's real world and what Milo is imagining about the people around him. By peeking inside Milo's notebook, we are able to see what Milo is imagining.

### During Reading

#### Investigate Key Pages

#### My Turn

*Milo tugs his sister's sleeve and holds up the picture* page: On this page, I can read about what's happening in Milo's real world. After Milo's sister ignores him, he goes back to drawing. When I flip to the next page, I see what he is imagining. The pages even look different. I can compare and contrast the two pages to notice the differences.

#### Our Turn

*Milo flips to a fresh page at a bustling Midtown stop* page: What clues let you know that this page is happening in real life? How is the next page different?

#### Your Turn

*The spell is broken when a crew of breakers bounds onto the train* page: When we turn the page to see what Milo imagines, think and talk about why he doesn't really like this picture.

### After Reading

#### Nudge Toward Independence

In this book, you were able to look into Milo's notebook and see the world through his eyes. When looking in his notebook, you could actually see what he was thinking. Christian Robinson gave us a glimpse into Milo's imagination through his artwork. Sometimes writers let us know what characters are thinking by using thought bubbles or by writing the character's inner thoughts. All of these techniques help readers better understand and empathize with a character. Which technique would you like to try in your writing?

**Innovate on Text:** Look around you. Divide a piece of paper in half. On one half, draw something that you see in real life. Then, on the other side, draw an imaginary version of that real-life thing.

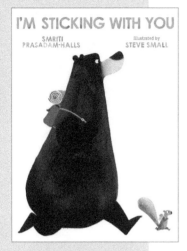

## Read-Aloud Experience: Notice Who's Talking

**Book Title:** *I'm Sticking With You* (Prasadam-Halls, 2020)

**About the Book:** Experience the ups and downs of friendship through the eyes of accident-prone Bear and patient Squirrel who, after needing some space, realizes that his companionship with Bear helps him be his best self. Notice that the font changes thickness to indicate which character is talking.

To find a book like this one, look for the following:

- Books where each character's dialogue is marked in a different way.
- Texts in which characters experience the joys and challenges of friendship.

## Comprehension Conversation

### Before Reading

#### Notice the Cover Illustration

What do you notice about the characters on the cover? [It looks like they are going someplace.] Fun fact! This is the first picture book Steve Small ever illustrated. He made his illustrations by drawing and painting and then put them together using a technology tool called Photoshop. When you tell someone, "I'm sticking with you," what does that mean? [Discuss and/or clarify the meaning of this phrase.]

**Set a Purpose:** Can you predict which character might be saying, "I'm sticking with you"? Sometimes two people, or animals in this case, have different points of view. That means they each see the world in their own way. I'm wondering if that is the case with Bear and Squirrel. There's only one way to find out. Let's read!

### During Reading

- *. . . and bad times, happy or sad* page: Can you figure out who is talking? What are the clues in the words and pictures that help you decide? [You may want to reread the book from the beginning to give learners more clues.]

- *Like peas in a pod, you and I fit* page: Do you think Squirrel is feeling the same way as Bear? Why or why not?

- *We sit by the cliff to* page: Wait! Something changed on this two-page spread. What do you notice? Do you see how the words look different when Squirrel is talking? That helps you know whose point of view we are hearing.

- *Ah! That feels better, each thing in its place* page: What do you suppose the problem is now?

### After Reading

- At first, you were just hearing Bear's point of view, and then you had a chance to listen to Squirrel's thoughts. How did hearing each animal's unique point of view help you understand how they were feeling?

- What lessons did Bear and Squirrel learn about friendship?

### Learning Targets:

- I notice which character is talking.
- I think about how characters' words and actions help me understand their point of view.

### Extend the Experience

- In this book, we learned a lot about friendship. What are some ways that Bear and Squirrel stuck with each other?

*Friends Chart*

### Key Vocabulary and Kid-Friendly Definitions:

- *berserk*: out of control

- *mend*: to fix something

- *tidy*: neat or clean

View the author reading *I'm Sticking With You* aloud at resources.corwin.com/shakeupsharedreading

- Compare and Contrast! Text Set—Lessons About Friendship: Bear and Squirrel learned some important lessons about friendship. After reading and enjoying these books on your own or with a friend, think about the lesson(s) you learned about friendship. Talk about them with a friend or label the book with a sticky note to tell us what you've learned.

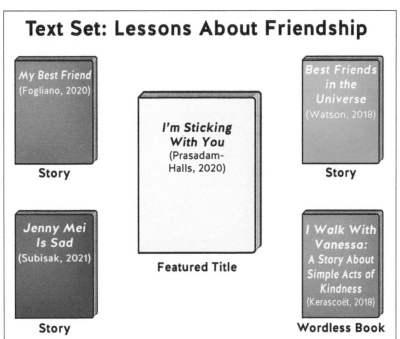

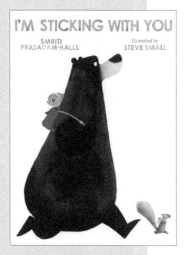

## Short Bursts of Shared Reading: *I'm Sticking With You*

### Focus 1–Listen for Sounds: Rhyming Words

#### Before Reading

**Set the Stage:** Our focus for rereading is to notice how rhyming patterns help us read the words in a text.

#### During Reading

#### Investigate Key Pages

#### My Turn

*Wherever you're going, I'm going too* page: I notice that the rhyming pattern on this page happens at the end of the second and fourth lines. So, I know that the word *you* is going to rhyme with the word *too*. If I say the beginning sound /y/ and think about the rhyme, it helps me read the word *you*.

#### Our Turn

*Whether you're grumpy or silly or mad . . .* page: When I turn the page, I want you to look at the last word. We know it is going to rhyme with *mad* and it begins with the /s/ sound. What word makes sense and has the right sounds? [Sad.]

#### Your Turn

*Ready to be there to help you along . . .* page: Look at the word at the end of this page. It is a tricky one because it begins with a silent *w*. Can you think of a word that rhymes with *along* and begins with an /r/ sound? [Wrong.] Do the sounds match? Does that word make sense? [Continue in the same fashion as you reread a bit more of the book.]

#### After Reading

#### Nudge Toward Independence

A rhyming pattern gives the book rhythm. It also makes it a bit easier to read the words because you know that when words rhyme they will have the same ending sounds.

## Focus 2—Reread for Fluency: Emphasize Italicized Words

**Before Reading**

**Set the Stage:** One way that writers show that a word is important is by using italics. When writers put words in italics, the words look like they are leaning to one side. When readers see italics, that means we need to read the word with more emphasis.

**During Reading**

**Investigate Key Pages**

**My Turn**

*. . . and bad times, happy or sad* page: When I'm reading along and I notice italics like I see in the words *all ears*, I know that I need to read them with more emphasis. Listen to how that sounds. As I keep reading, I see in the next sentence the word *all* is in italics. Listen again as I read that sentence.

**Our Turn**

- *You may think I can't, but I bet you I can* page: Before we reread these two pages, zoom in to see if you can spot the words in italics. Let's reread together and put more emphasis on those words. Why do you think the author chose the words *never* and *you*?

- *We sit by the cliff top* page: When we reread the last sentence on this two-page spread, we see the word *bearly* in italics. This word is in italics because it is a little word joke. The word *barely* is usually spelled b-a-r-e-l-y, but because this story is about a bear, the author spelled it like the animal *bear*. Get it?

**Your Turn**

*Actually . . .* page: The words in italics on this page are like an echo. Get ready to reread them that way!

**After Reading**

**Nudge Toward Independence**

When you see italics in a book you're reading, think about the meaning of the word in the sentence and read it with a little extra oomph.

**Innovate on Text:** In the end, Bear and Squirrel stuck together. Think of a person who you promise to stick by. Divide a piece of paper in half. Draw a picture of you on one side and the person on the other. At the top of the page, complete this sentence: I'll stick by you even when . . .

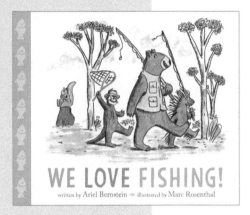

WE LOVE FISHING!
written by Ariel Bernstein • illustrated by Marc Rosenthal

## Read-Aloud Experience:
## Notice Characters' Opinions

**Book Title:** *We Love Fishing!* (Bernstein, 2021)

**About the Book:** Although the narrator states that Bear, Porcupine, Otter, and Squirrel love fishing, it is clear from Squirrel's attitude and comments he does not agree. Readers will giggle as they witness firsthand the differing perspectives of the animals. This book is perfect for reader's theater!

To find a book like this one, look for the following:

- Books where characters' dialogue is marked in different ways
- Characters with differing opinions or perspectives

## Comprehension Conversation

### Before Reading

#### Notice the Cover Illustration

Take a close look at the four animal characters on the cover. Do you think they all feel the same way about fishing? The title of this story is *We Love Fishing!* Talk about that with a friend. [If you are able to remove the book jacket, notice how the book case is different than the book jacket.]

**Set a Purpose:** After looking at the cover, we already have a hint that Squirrel doesn't feel the same way as Otter, Bear, and Porcupine. He might have a different opinion. Let's read to see if we're on the right track.

### During Reading

- *I love fishing* page: Does Squirrel feel the same way about fishing as his friends? What does Squirrel love? [Nuts.]

- *Can we take a taxi?* page: The narrator said that all of the animals love to walk through the woods. After reading this page, do you agree? Notice how Squirrel's words look different than the narrator's words on the next page. Illustrators and book designers change the way words look to help us know who is talking at different points in the story.

- *I don't want to hold it!* page: Uh oh! What do you predict is going to happen on the next page? How do you predict Bear, Porcupine, and Otter will react?

- *Bear, Porcupine, Otter, and Squirrel are done fishing for the day* page: What has changed on this page? Share your thinking with a neighbor.

### After Reading

- What did you think about the ending?
- How did Squirrel's opinion change from the beginning to the end of the book?

**Learning Targets:**

- I notice who is talking.

- I think about how what characters say and do help me understand their point of view.

- I think, talk, and write about point of view.

## Extend the Experience

- Do you think Squirrel will go fishing again? Why or why not?

- Take a survey! Bear, Porcupine, and Otter all thought that everyone loved fishing, but Squirrel had a different opinion. Think of something you love, like pizza, playing tag, or your pet. Survey your friends to find out if they have the same opinion. Ask them, "Do you love _____? Yes or no?" Tally the results on your whiteboard or a piece of paper. Share what you've learned with the class.

**Key Vocabulary and Kid-Friendly Definitions:**

- *peaceful*: quiet and calm

- *refreshing*: something that gives you energy

- *steep*: pointing up; like a big hill or mountain

## Similar Titles

 **Best Day Ever!** (Singer, 2021)

About the Book: This energetic book is told from the perspective of a playful puppy who is thrilled to spend the best day ever with her boy, who uses a wheelchair for mobility. Together they dig, chase, and play frisbee until the pup gets smelly and needs a bath—not the best day ever. Leah Nixon, the illustrator, is a wheelchair user who became paralyzed in an accident at age twenty-nine.

 **Turtle in a Tree** (Hudson, 2021)

About the Book: Two dogs are having a debate. The sweater-wearing dog thinks there's a turtle in the tree, while the tie-wearing dog believes it's a squirrel. They argue back and forth until out pops a squirrel, and then later a turtle. Their dialogue appears in different-colored speech bubbles, making it a perfect book for talking about point of view.

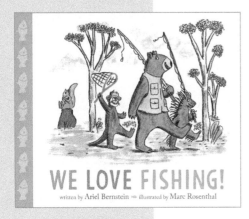

## Short Bursts of Shared Reading:
## *We Love Fishing!*

### Focus 1–Wonder About Words: Contractions

**Before Reading**

**Set the Stage:** When we slow down to investigate, we're going to be on the lookout for a special kind of word called a *contraction*. A contraction is when writers take two words and combine them to make one shortened word, like *does not* becomes *doesn't* or *we will* becomes *we'll*. They replace the missing letter or letters with an apostrophe. Sometimes they do this because it sounds more like talking.

**During Reading**

**Investigate Key Pages**

**My Turn**

*Smell the fresh air* page: As I reread this page, I'm going to notice if there are any contractions. [Point out the words *it's* and *don't*. Read each sentence replacing the contraction with the two words to demonstrate how contractions sound more like natural speech.]

**Our Turn**

*Fishing is so peaceful* page: Let's do the same thing together on this page. We'll reread what Porcupine, Otter, and Squirrel say. First with contractions, and then without to hear the difference. Which do you think sounds more like talking?

**Your Turn**

*I don't want to hold it!* page: This time, I'll reread the sentence aloud. Then you can reread it two times with your partner. The first time read it with the contraction, the second time replace the contraction with the two words that make the contraction. See what you notice. As an extra challenge, would someone be interested in working with a friend to make a chart of all the different contractions that you find in this book? [Show students how to make a two-column chart with the contraction in the left-hand column and the two words it represents in the right-hand column.]

**After Reading**

**Nudge Toward Independence**

Today your brain grew as you noticed and read contractions. I bet you'll notice them in the books you're reading. You might even experiment with them when you're writing.

## Focus 2–Reread for Fluency: Pay Attention to Punctuation

### Before Reading

**Set the Stage:** Readers pay attention to ending marks to help them read as if they are the characters talking. There were so many funny pages in this book. Let's go back and reread a few pages while pretending we are the characters.

### During Reading

#### Investigate Key Pages

#### My Turn

*Let's reel it in!* page: When I look at the sentences on this page, I notice that two of them end with an exclamation mark and the other two with question marks. Those marks give me clues about how the author wants me to read the characters' words. Listen as I read like the characters.

#### Our Turn

*I don't want to hold it!* page: This is one of our favorite pages. Reread Squirrel's words the way you think he would be saying them.

#### Your Turn

*Where's the nearest restaurant?* page: I'm going to divide you into four groups—one for each animal. Then, we'll practice and perform their dialogue on this page. Pay attention to the ending marks and also the facial expressions of the characters to infer how to read their part. After we're done, I'll put this book in a special place and you can do the same thing as you reread the book with your friends.

### After Reading

#### Nudge Toward Independence

Paying attention to punctuation makes reading more enjoyable, especially in funny books like this one. It's kind of like acting. Remember to talk, think, and act like the characters.

**Innovate on Text:** In this book, some of the animals love fishing but Squirrel does not. Think about something you love and something you don't like. Write an opposite book or list poem to tell us more about your likes and dislikes.

I love _____ but I don't like _____.

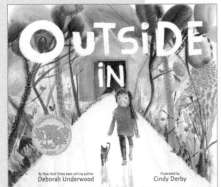

## Read-Aloud Experience: Infer Big Ideas

**Book Title:** *Outside In* (Underwood, 2020)

**About the Book:** Have you ever noticed how a sunny day or birdsong pulls you outside? Cindy Derby's illustrations blend with and enhance Deborah Underwood's carefully chosen words to communicate that even when we're inside, reminders of nature's gifts surround us. Told through the eyes of a young girl, readers learn how nature sneaks in and summons us to venture outside. [If you are able to remove the book jacket, discuss the differences between the book casing and book jacket.]

To find a book like this one, look for the following:

- Themes related to enjoying the natural world
- Characters who are drawn to or prefer being outdoors

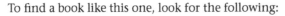

### Comprehension Conversation

**Before Reading**

**Notice the Cover Illustration**

**Learning Targets:**

- I infer the big ideas, lessons, or morals of this story.
- I talk, write, or draw to figure out what those lessons mean to me.

How does Cindy Derby's cover illustration make you feel? Can you tell that she used watercolor paints to create parts of the illustration? Sometimes she used a dried flower stem to draw the lines! If you look closely, you'll see familiar creatures. Tell a friend what creatures you spot. [Notice the owl inside the letter O.]

**Set a Purpose:** Have your clothes ever been turned *inside out*? I wonder why the title of this book is the opposite, *Outside In*. Being a reader is a lot like being a detective. Readers ask questions and then use clues from the title, words, and illustrations to better understand the story. After we enjoy this book, we'll think about what we've learned as both readers and people.

### During Reading

- *We forget Outside is there* page: Does this ever happen to you? Why do you think this happens?
- *with flashes at the window and slow magic tricks* page: Look carefully. What do you see happening outside the windows on these two pages? Does the girl notice?
- *Outside sings to us with chirps and rustles and tap-taps on the roof* page: Compare what is happening outside to what is happening inside. Do you think the girl and her mom hear the birds?
- *I'm here, Outside says* page: What do you predict the girl is going to do on the next page? What are the clues that led you to that prediction?

### After Reading

- Why do you think Deborah Underwood wrote this book? What are the big ideas, lessons, or morals?
- What might you do differently after reading this book?

## Extend the Experience

- Which do you prefer: outside or inside? Share your opinion and the reasons behind it.

- Plants that grow outside give us things we use inside. Here are some examples from the book. Can you add to this list?

### Outside-Inside Chart

| Outside | Inside |
| --- | --- |
| cotton | clothes |
| trees | chairs |
| seeds | bread and berries |

## Similar Titles

 ***Southwest Sunrise* (Grimes, 2020)**

About the Book: Jayden is unhappy that his family is moving from New York City to New Mexico. As they are getting settled, his mother gives him a guidebook and sends him outside. Jayden comes to appreciate the unexpected wonders of the desert landscape. Readers experience the beauty of the Southwest through Jayden's eyes.

 ***Where's Rodney* (Bogan, 2017)**

About the Book: Rodney always wants to be outside, but instead he's stuck inside at school. When Rodney's teacher says they're taking a field trip to the park, Rodney isn't that interested because he thinks they're going to the neighborhood park he's been warned to avoid. Much to his surprise, the class travels by bus to what you can infer is a state or national park, which Rodney finds "magnificent."

**Key Vocabulary and Kid-Friendly Definitions:**

- *beckons*: something is so pretty that you want to see it

- *eager*: when you really want to do or have something

- *steals*: sneaking in

View the author reading *Where's Rodney* at resources.corwin.com/shakeupsharedreading

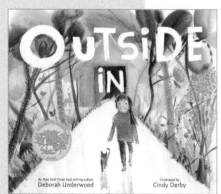

## Short Bursts of Shared Reading: *Outside In*

### Focus 1—Wonder About Words: Compound Words

### Before Reading

**Set the Stage:** Compound words are two separate words joined together. When they are joined together, they make a new word. Sometimes that word has a new meaning. Other times, you can figure out the meaning of the word by using the two small words. Let's listen for and clap the two parts of the compound words in this book.

### During Reading

### Investigate Key Pages

### My Turn

*Now sometimes even when we're outside . . .* page: The word *outside* is made from the words *out* and *side.* I'm going to put my left hand up and say *out,* my right hand up and say *side,* and clap them together to form *outside.*

### Our Turn

*We forget Outside is there* page: There are two compound words on this page. Get ready to say each separate word and clap them together.

### Your Turn

*It sends the sunset and shadows inside to play* page: There are two more compound words on this page. Show me how you would clap *sunset* and *inside.*

### After Reading

### Nudge Toward Independence

Let's review by clapping all of the compound words we found in this book and then thinking about the meaning of the words. Do these words have new meanings, or can we figure out the meaning by using the two small words?

| outside | sometimes | inside |
|---------|-----------|--------|
| sunset  |           |        |

## Focus 2–Reread to Boost Comprehension:
## Use Pictures and Words to Infer

### Before Reading

**Set the Stage:** Readers use clues in the words and illustrations along with their schema to infer. Inferring is kind of like being a detective. You use clues to figure out missing information or read between the lines to better comprehend the author's message.

### During Reading

### Investigate Key Pages

### My Turn

*Outside shows us there is a time to rest . . .* page: On this page, I have to use clues to figure out how outside shows us when it's "a time to rest and a time to start fresh." When I look at the pictures, I see one shows nighttime and the other daytime. So, I can infer the author means that the sun helps us know whether to sleep or wake.

### Our Turn

*Outside steals inside* page: Can you infer what the author means by "outside steals inside"? On this page, the word *steals* means the same as *sneaks*. Tell a friend what you're inferring.

### Your Turn

*Even rivers come inside* page: Hmmm! Be a detective, and use the clues in the pictures and words to figure out what is happening on this page. Are rivers really coming inside?

### After Reading

### Nudge Toward Independence

To better understand the author's message, readers infer. Inferring takes concentration and persistence. To infer, we had to slow down, reread, think about the words, and look at the pictures. You can do it!

**Innovate on Text:** Imagine if creatures and plants from outside came in your home. Draw a picture to show us what might happen.

Story by Daniel Bernstrom    Pictures by Shane W. Evans

**Learning Targets:**

- I infer the big ideas, lessons, or morals of this story.
- I learn lessons from characters.
- I talk, write, or draw to figure out what those lessons mean to me.

## Read-Aloud Experience: Learn Lessons From Characters

**Book Title:** *Big Papa and the Time Machine* (Bernstrom, 2020)

**About the Book:** When a boy is reluctant to go to school, his grandfather takes him back in time to hear family stories and learn some important life lessons.

To find a book like this one, look for the following:

- Characters who impart life lessons
- Multigenerational stories

## Comprehension Conversation

### Before Reading

#### Notice the Cover Illustration

Did you know that on the copyright page it often tells what kind of art tools the illustrator used? I want to read what it says. [Read the note under the ISBN number on the copyright page; appreciate how he added "patience and skill" to the list of tools.] I think Shane Evans's art makes this cover look magical. When you look at the cover, what do you notice or what are you thinking?

**Set a Purpose:** Where are Big Papa and his grandson on the cover? [In a car.] Think about the title of the story *Big Papa and the Time Machine*. As we travel with Big Papa in his time machine, we'll learn about and from these characters.

### During Reading

- *"Do I have to go to school?"* page: Do you remember how you felt on the first day of school or the first time you were away from your family? Show me with your face how you were feeling.

- *"Now, been scared lots of times,"* Big Papa said page: Hmmm. I'm wondering what Big Papa means by "you gotta lose the life you have if you ever gonna find the one you want." Talk with a friend. Start your thinking with *maybe he means . . .* [Scaffold and support students' conversations as needed.]

- *"I couldn't stand to stay on the ground,"* Big Papa said page: Do you have any questions about Big Papa's words on this page? [Guide students as they ask and answer questions to infer Big Papa's message.]

- *"I'm scared you growin' up too fast"* page: What did the boy learn from Big Papa? How did it change how he is feeling about going to school?

### After Reading

- Use the two-word strategy (Hoyt, 1999) to summarize the theme of this story. To do this, think of two words that sum up the big idea. The two words can go together to form a phrase or be two separate ideas.

- To make sense of Big Papa's lessons or messages, we asked questions and talked together. When we question, think, and talk together, it helps us dig deeper into the meaning of a story. Thinking together makes your brain grow!

## Extend the Experience

- In this book, Big Papa showed his grandson what being brave looks like and sounds like. When have you had to be brave? Complete this thought: I am brave when . . .

- Make a timeline: We traveled back in time with Big Papa to memorable events in his life. Ask someone in your family to help you make a timeline of important events in your life. Bring it to school to share with us.

............................................................................................

## Similar Titles

 ### *Maud and Grand-Maud (O'Leary, 2020)*

**About the Book:** Maud looks forward to Saturday sleepovers with her grandmother, Grand-Maud. They wear matching nightgowns, eat breakfast for supper, and watch black-and-white movies. Tucked under Maud's bed is a wooden chest where Grand-Maud collects treasures just for Maud. Some are from a store, some handmade, but the best ones are those that evoke stories from Grand-Maud's childhood.

 ### *Nana Akua Goes to School (Walker, 2020)*

**About the Book:** Zura is worried about Grandparent's Day because Zura's Nana, who is her favorite person in the world, looks different from other grandmas. Nana Akua was raised in Ghana and, following a tradition from her Akan culture, has tribal markings on her face. Concerned that her classmates will be scared of Nana or, worse, make fun of her, Zura is hesitant to bring her to school. Nana Akua knows just what to do. With a quilt made with Adinkra symbols and a bit of face paint, Nana Akua explains what makes her special and invites Zura's classmates (and fellow grandparents) to try out a special symbol of their own.

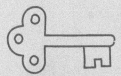

**Key Vocabulary and Kid-Friendly Definitions:**

- *brave*: ready to face danger

- *unexpected*: when something surprises you

View the author reading *Big Papa and the Time Machine* at resources.corwin.com/shakeupsharedreading

story by Daniel Bernstrom    Pictures by Shane W. Evans

## Short Bursts of Shared Reading: *Big Papa and the Time Machine*

### Focus 1—Reread to Boost Comprehension: Understand Point of View

### Before Reading

**Set the Stage:** Authors choose to tell their stories from different points of view. That means that they decide who will be telling the story. Knowing who is telling the story helps us better understand the action. Let's reread to figure out who is telling this story.

### During Reading

#### Investigate Key Pages

#### My Turn

*I won't never forget that September . . .* page: When I read the words and look at the illustrations, I understand that the boy is telling the story. So, I'm going to continue reading, knowing that I will be experiencing the action from his point of view.

#### Our Turn

*We took Big Papa's time machine to a long time ago* page: This page is a little trickier. We are still hearing the story from the boy's point of view, but now we're reading dialogue between the boy and Big Papa. Listen for clues that the boy is telling the story.

#### Your Turn

*"I'm sorry I made you scared"* page: By having the boy tell the story, we can understand how he is feeling as he hears Big Papa's memories. How would the story have been different if it were told from Big Papa's point of view? Do you think you would have found it as interesting? Why or why not?

### After Reading

#### Nudge Toward Independence

How do you suppose noticing point of view helps you as a reader? Do you prefer reading stories told from the main character's point of view? Think about that as you're choosing your books. What have you learned today that you will use when you are writing? Consider how point of view impacts the telling of a story.

## Focus 2—Notice Writer's Craft Moves: Repeated Sentence

### Before Reading

**Set the Stage:** Authors repeat words, phrases, or sentences to emphasize a point, help us remember important parts, or highlight the theme of the story. Let's reread and think about why Daniel Bernstrom chose to include a repeated sentence in *Big Papa and the Time Machine.*

### During Reading

### Investigate Key Pages

### My Turn

*"No, been scared lots of times," Big Papa said* page: This is the first time the sentence "That's called being brave" appears in the story. Big Papa is telling his grandson that sometimes being brave means leaving what's familiar behind and taking a chance on something unknown or new.

### Our Turn

*"I couldn't stand to stay on the ground," Big Papa said* page: Here's the sentence again. What did Big Papa do that was brave?

### Your Turn

[Continue inviting students to notice and discuss the repeated sentence. Emphasize how repetition highlights the theme or big idea of the story.]

### After Reading

### Nudge Toward Independence

Daniel Bernstrom used the repeated sentence in this book intentionally, or on purpose. He wanted you, as the reader, to remember the theme of the story. He isn't the only author who uses repetition. As you're reading, notice how authors use repetition to make certain words or big ideas stand out. Think about how you might use repeated phrases in the stories you are writing.

**Innovate on Text:** If you had a time machine, where would you go—back to the past or into to the future? Write, draw, or video record where you would go and why.

*"OUTSIDE, the world kept growing."*

*Outside, Inside* by LeUyen Pham

# Converse About Comprehension–Nonfiction

## Bringing the Outside Inside

A tray of colorful leaves sits on the table. Kids surround the tray peering through magnifying glasses. Talking. Wondering. "What kind of leaf is that one?" Srikar asks. "Let me check in this book," says Miyah as she flips through the pages, comparing the leaf to photographs. Welcome to the Observer Center, a space (or basket) that brings the outside inside. Here, kids visit to inquire and learn about the concepts and topics brought to light during your book experiences. If you tried the Observer Center ideas offered in Chapter 2, I hope you saw children engaging with texts and with each other while growing their knowledge of the world outside your classroom. There are more Observer Center ideas to come in this chapter and the next.

Another way to bring the outside world into your classroom is by sharing books brimming with fascinating facts. To get you started, I've scoured the shelves to find nonfiction texts that appeal to children and roll off your tongue when read aloud—not always an easy task. When perusing the titles in this chapter, you'll notice that the books are written in a variety of structures and styles. To add to these offerings, I've woven other appealing titles in when suggesting books for text sets and ideas for the Observer Center. The book experiences in this chapter will help learners develop the unique skill set that nonfiction reading requires as they do the following:

- Spot nonfiction text structures
- Integrate information from text and images
- Identify main topics and key details
- Ask and answer questions
- Consider the author's purpose

The world students will grow into will differ vastly from the one they live in today. You can give learners a leg up by tapping into their natural curiosities and offering them engaging learning pathways that stem from interactions with compelling nonfiction texts.

# Menu of Shared Reading Interactions

| Book Title | Shared Reading Focus 1 | Shared Reading Focus 2 |
|---|---|---|
| *Whose House Is That?* (Tekiela, 2021) | Ponder Punctuation: How to Write a Riddle | Notice Writer's Craft Moves: Comparison |
| *My Thoughts Are Clouds* (Heard, 2021) | Ponder Punctuation: Creative Conventions | Notice Writer's Craft Moves: Unique Poetry Techniques |
| *Flying Deep: Climb Inside Deep-Sea Submersible ALVIN* (Cusolito, 2018) | Wonder About Words: Descriptive Language | Notice Writer's Craft Moves: A Day in the Life |
| *Red Rover: Curiosity on Mars* (Ho, 2019) | Reread to Boost Comprehension: Understand Point of View | Notice Writer's Craft Moves: Personification |
| *The Beak Book* (Page, 2021) | Wonder About Words: Verbs | Reread to Boost Comprehension: Learn From Infographics |
| *Star of the Party: The Solar System Celebrates!* (Carr, 2021) | Spotlight High-Frequency Words: Question Words | Notice Writer's Craft Moves: Creative Backmatter |
| *If Bees Disappeared* (Williams, 2021) | Reread to Boost Comprehension: Consider Cause and Effect | Notice Writer's Craft Moves: Adding Diagrams to Explain Details |
| *DROP: An Adventure Through the Water Cycle* (Moon, 2021) | Wonder About Words: Interjections | Reread to Boost Comprehension: Learn From Infographics |
| *Sometimes People March* (Allen, 2020) | Spotlight High-Frequency Words: *People* and *They* | Ponder Punctuation: Make a Statement |
| *Outside, Inside* (Pham, 2021) | Wonder About Words: Compound Words | Notice Writer's Craft Moves: See-Saw Pattern |

My Favorite Texts and Resources for Comprehension–Nonfiction

## Read-Aloud Experience: Notice the Question–Answer Structure

**Book Title:** *Whose House Is That?* (Tekiela, 2021)

**About the Book:** Stan Tekiela, author of *Whose Butt?* (2012), adds to his collection of question-answer structured nonfiction books. This time, animal enthusiasts read clues as they look at a photograph of an animal home. A page turn reveals the animal who inhabits the home along with a paragraph of facts about that particular animal. (If you are interested, see the read-aloud experience featuring *Whose Butt?* on page 224 of *The Ramped-Up Read Aloud*.)

To find a book like this one, look for the following:

- Informational books with a question-answer pattern.
- Structures that children can borrow for their own writing.

## Comprehension Conversation

### Before Reading

#### Notice the Cover Illustration

- I see that the title of this book is written as a question. Perhaps the author is going to ask us questions in this book. What do you notice? Do you think this book is a fiction book or a nonfiction book? What are the reasons behind your thinking?

**Set a Purpose:** As we're reading *Whose House Is That?* pay attention to the pattern that the author uses to organize his ideas. Get ready to learn more about animals' homes.

### During Reading

- *Small and round, this home is constructed of mud and grass* page: Are you starting to detect a pattern? Talk about the pattern with a neighbor.
- *It's an American Robin!* page: Have you ever seen a robin? Did you know they live everywhere in North America? That's news to me!
- *Something amazing happens inside this shiny, bright green house* page: Now that we've read a few more pages, what are you noticing about the pattern in this book? Do you predict it will continue?
- *It's a Monarch Butterfly!* page: Notice how Stan Tekiela helps us pronounce the word *chrysalis*. Adding a pronunciation guide is something that nonfiction authors do.
- [Depending on students' interest and stamina, you might choose to stop here and continue another time. When you continue reading this question-answer book, invite students to share their new learning about the animals they meet.]

**Learning Targets:**

- I notice the question-answer pattern or structure of the text.
- I borrow the structures I learn to create my own texts.

## After Reading

- Explain to a friend how the structure or pattern of this book helps you learn about the different animals and their homes.

- Share your opinion about the question-answer format. Do you find it a helpful way to structure a nonfiction text?

### Extend the Experience

- The question-answer structure is one way to organize a nonfiction book. You might try this approach next time you're writing facts.

- Compare and Contrast! Multigenre Text Set—Books With a Question-Answer Structure: Did you know that authors use the question-answer structure in both fiction and nonfiction texts? I've gathered a few books with the question-answer pattern so that you can compare them to *Whose House Is That?* Notice how they are alike and different. You can also look in the books for ideas that you might use when you're writing your own question-answer text.

**Key Vocabulary and Kid-Friendly Definitions:**

- *cozy*: when something feels warm, safe, or comfortable

- *critter*: a wild animal

- *perched*: seated or resting on a branch or pole

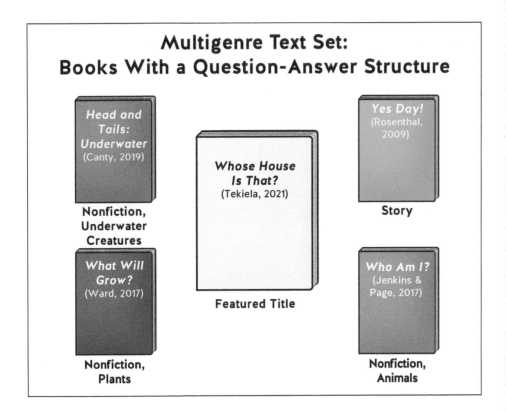

**Multigenre Text Set: Books With a Question-Answer Structure**

*Head and Tails: Underwater* (Canty, 2019) — Nonfiction, Underwater Creatures

*What Will Grow?* (Ward, 2017) — Nonfiction, Plants

*Whose House Is That?* (Tekiela, 2021) — Featured Title

*Yes Day!* (Rosenthal, 2009) — Story

*Who Am I?* (Jenkins & Page, 2017) — Nonfiction, Animals

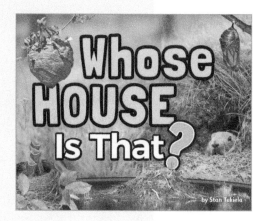

## Short Bursts of Shared Reading:
### *Whose House Is That?*

### Before Reading

**Set the Stage:** On each page, before the author, Stan Tekiela, asks us, "Whose house is that?" he shares some clues to help us guess. When you come up with clues to help someone guess an answer, you are telling or writing a riddle. Let's try to spot the different types of ending marks he uses in his riddles.

### During Reading

### Investigate Key Pages

### My Turn

*This home is usually underground* page: On this page I read three clues. I know this because at the end of each clue there is a period. This tells me that each clue is a statement or a telling sentence. Next comes a question. I know it is an asking sentence because the sentence ends with a question mark. Finally, when I turn the page, I read the answer to the riddle: "It's a Black Bear!" The answer is followed by an exclamation mark, a signal to read the sentence with excitement.

### Our Turn

*This home is strung between tall grasses or twigs and tree branches* page: How many clues are on this page? How can you tell? [Continue for a few pages, noticing how many clues are on each page and pointing out the pattern: clues are telling sentences, the question is an asking sentence, the answer ends with an exclamation mark.]

### Your Turn

Tell your neighbor a riddle. At the end of each clue, draw a period in the air. When you ask the question, draw a question mark. Take turns. When you've both told a riddle, talk about what you learned about the ending marks this author used in his riddles.

### After Reading

### Nudge Toward Independence

Ending marks are signals to readers. In this book, the author uses ending marks to show us which sentences are telling sentences or clues, which sentences are asking sentences, and which sentence is the exciting answer. When you write riddles, remember to add these important ending marks.

## Focus 2—Notice Writer's Craft Moves: Comparison

### Before Reading

**Set the Stage:** Authors use comparisons to help you see how people, places, objects, or animals are the same and different. Comparisons can show how things are related or help you better understand something that might be unfamiliar.

### During Reading

### Investigate Key Pages

### My Turn

*Larger than a football* page: To help me understand the size of this hornet's nest, Stan Tekiela compares the nest to a football. Since I know about how big a football is, I can picture the size of a hornet's nest.

### Our Turn

*This home is wet and sandy and shaped like a shallow dish* page: Think about a plate or dish that you have used. The word *shallow* means the opposite of deep. Like in a kiddie pool there is shallow water so the sides aren't very high, but in a regular pool the sides are higher because the water is deep. Can you picture a shallow dish? Look carefully at the photograph. If you were going to make a comparison to the sunfish's bed, what would you compare it to?

### Your Turn

*This home may be tiny when compared to your home* page: Picture the places you've lived. How do they compare to an anthill? What other comparisons could you make to an anthill? Share your ideas with a neighbor.

### After Reading

### Nudge Toward Independence

How did the comparison in this book help you make sense of the size or shape of the animal homes? Think about ways you might use comparison in your pictures and words. Some of these words and phrases might be helpful when writing comparisons:

- is like
- is bigger than
- is smaller than
- is the same as

If you notice other authors who use comparison, bring their books with you when it's time to share so we can study how they did it.

> **Innovate on Text:** In this book, Stan Tekiela creates riddles about each animal's home. The riddles have clues to help you figure out which animal lived in each home. It's your turn to write a riddle. Instead of writing riddles about animal homes, you can write your riddle about an animal. Find a photo of the animal or visualize it. Think of the animal's characteristics. What does it look like? What does it do? Where does it live? What makes it special? On the front of a piece of paper, write three clues to help us guess the animal. Flip the paper over and write and/or draw a picture of the exciting answer.

## Read-Aloud Experience: Notice Unique Structures

**Book Title:** *My Thoughts Are Clouds: Poems for Mindfulness* (Heard, 2021)

**About the Book:** In this compilation of free-verse poems, Georgia Heard guides children to slow down and attend to their "inner weather report." Each chapter begins with a brief explanation of the mindful practice. The chapters focus on breathing techniques, mindfulness, meditation, and "kindfulness."

To find a book like this one, look for the following:

- Information told through poetry
- Ideas and structures that children can borrow for their own writing

### Comprehension Conversation

#### Before Reading

#### Notice the Cover Illustration

Can you infer what this child is doing? [Looking at the sky, looking at clouds.] The title of this book is *My Thoughts Are Clouds.* Have you ever relaxed on the grass and looked up at the clouds? What did you see? How did you feel? [If you have the hardcover version, notice that the paper book jacket and book casing underneath are designed differently.]

**Set a Purpose:** The subtitle of this book is *Poems for Mindfulness.* This is a unique kind of poetry book. Let's read to figure out why Georgia Heard wrote this book. In other words, what was her purpose? [Georgia Heard makes her purpose clear in "A Note to Readers" on pages 6–7. If you want students to infer her purpose, you might choose to read this note after you've read the poems to confirm what they deduced.]

#### During Reading

- *"There Is a Monkey in My Mind,"* page 10: Can you visualize what Georgia Heard is trying to show us? Do you ever feel like there is a monkey in your mind? What does she suggest you do when you're feeling this way? [Be kind, give it space, lead it to a peaceful place.] What do you infer those suggestions mean? How might you go about calming a monkey in your mind?

- *"My Inner Weather Report,"* page 30: How do you infer the girl is feeling when her inner weather report is stormy? Which emotions do you think of when you hear "sunny with gentle breezes"? What is your inner weather report right now?

- *"Open Your Eyes,"* page 38: What advice is Georgia Heard offering on this page? Is there a suggestion in this poem that might help you be more mindful?

- *"Nature Walk,"* page 40: Which senses are used in this poem? Notice that Georgia Heard added some extra information at the bottom of the page. Let's read the information to learn more about taking a forest bath.

**Learning Targets:**

- I notice unique ways authors share information.

- I borrow ideas and structures I learn to create my own texts.

**After Reading**

- What was Georgia Heard's purpose for writing this book?

- Do you think this book is fiction, nonfiction, or a little bit of both? Share with a neighbor.

## Extend the Experience

- [When your students need to calm down or focus, try the "Butterfly Body Scan" on pages 44–45.]

- Remember the poem on page 30 about our inner weather report? I made this page for you to use when you want to record your inner weather report. I'll put it somewhere handy so you can report on your inner weather. See *My Inner Weather Report Reproducible Response Page* on the companion website (resources.corwin.com/shakeupsharedreading).

**Key Vocabulary and Kid-Friendly Definitions:**

- Will vary based on which poems you choose to read aloud.

**Similar Titles**

 ***The Dirt Book: Poems About Animals That Live Beneath Our Feet*** (Harrison, 2021)

**About the Book:** This collection of poems is about the fascinating underground world. It is ideal for units about bugs and underground creatures. Notice the vertical orientation of each two-page spread highlighting the world that exists above and below the ground.

 ***No Voice Too Small: Fourteen Young Americans Making History*** (Metcalf et al., 2020)

**About the Book:** Budding activists will enjoy learning about the fourteen young people featured in this poetry anthology. Each poem is accompanied by a brief biography of the individual. Backmatter highlights the poetic forms used in the book and the poets whose work is included.

Name _____

### My Inner Weather Report

Today I feel . . .

_____

_____

_____

_____

Sunny     Cloudy     Stormy

*My Inner Weather Report Reproducible Response Page*

## Short Bursts of Shared Reading:
## *My Thoughts Are Clouds: Poems for Mindfulness*

### Focus 1–Ponder Punctuation: Creative Conventions

#### Before Reading

**Set the Stage:** Poets use conventions like spelling punctuation, capitalization, spacing, sentence structure, and so on to communicate meaning. Conventions make writing clear and understandable. Sometimes poets use conventions creatively. Let's see if Georgia Heard creatively used conventions in any of her poems.

#### During Reading

#### Investigate Key Pages

#### My Turn

"*Inside My Mind,*" page 8: I notice that there is something missing before, after, and between the words in this poem. Usually, we capitalize the first word at the beginning of a sentence, leave spaces between words, and add an ending mark at the end—those are the conventions. In this poem, Georgia Heard chose not to use those conventions. I think she did this on purpose so that when I read "Inside My Mind" it sounds like all of my thoughts are jumbled together.

#### Our Turn:

"*Mindfulness Is My Space Bar,*" page 27: Wow! This is such a unique-looking poem. Let's notice the creative ways that Georgia Heard uses conventions. [She leaves out the spaces between the words when writing about not using the space bar and adds large spaces between words when she is writing about using space bar.] How does her choice of conventions make her message clear and understandable?

#### Your Turn

"*Three-Way Loving Kindness Meditation,*" page 52: Talk about the creative conventions that you notice in this poem. [Bold print and italics.] How might you use the techniques you notice as you write your own poetry?

#### After Reading

#### Nudge Toward Independence

As a reader, notice how conventions add to the meaning of the text. When you're writing poetry, let your imagination be your guide as you decide what kinds of conventions you might want to play around with to enhance the meaning of your words.

## Focus 2: Notice Writer's Craft Moves: Unique Poetry Techniques

### Before Reading

**Set the Stage:** In this book of poems, Georgia Heard leads you to understand mindfulness through poetry. Let's notice and name some of the different techniques Georgia Heard uses in her poems.

### During Reading

#### Investigate Key Pages

#### My Turn

*"In and Out Breath,"* page 22: After rereading this poem, I see that Georgia Heard uses opposites to create the poem. Opposites help readers imagine ideas that are alike and different. In this poem, she's telling me to breathe out the negative thoughts and breathe in positivity. That's great advice!

#### Our Turn

*MEDITATION,* page 42: In the description on the opening page of this chapter, Georgia Heard uses a simile to help us better understand meditation. A simile is a comparison using the words *like* or *as*. Imagine a snow globe. Does the image help you visualize meditation? What other objects could you compare to meditation?

#### Your Turn

*"Empowerment Mantra\* Haiku,"* page 48: Notice the symbol after the word *mantra* in the title of this poem. This symbol is called an *asterisk*. An asterisk indicates that there is more information somewhere on the page. Do you see the matching asterisk at the bottom of the page? Let me read that text to you. Now that you know the meaning of mantra, reread the mantras in the hearts and the poem at the bottom of the page with a friend. Notice that Georgia Heard uses a certain poetry structure in the poem at the bottom of the page called *haiku*. Tell a friend what you already know about haiku. [If needed, do a brief demonstration about the structure of haiku poetry.]

### After Reading

#### Nudge Toward Independence

Poets play with words and ideas. I'll leave this book out so that you can review the various techniques Georgia Heard uses in this book. Do any of them appeal to you? If so, give them a try when you're writing a poem.

**Innovate on Text:** On page 48, we read a poem about empowerment mantras. Let me project the poem so that you can study it. On this sticky note, write down your own empowerment mantra and keep it somewhere where you can read it.

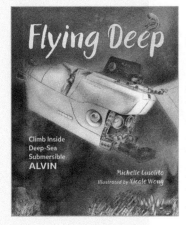

## Read-Aloud Experience: Learn From Illustrations

**Book Title:** *Flying Deep: Climb Inside Deep-Sea Submersible ALVIN* (Cusolito, 2018)

**About the Book:** Michelle Cusolito's debut picture book invites readers to imagine they are the pilot of the submersible Alvin so that they can vicariously experience an eight-hour day exploring the treacherous ocean floor. The mission for the pilot and his two-person crew is to investigate and look for life at the site surrounding underwater volcanoes. According to the author's note, the dive in this book takes place at Nine North, 550 miles off the coast of Acapulco, Mexico. If you're looking for a wordless fiction book to pair with *Flying Deep,* check out *Field Trip to the Ocean Deep* (Hare, 2020).

To find a book like this one, look for the following:

- Engaging illustrations that amplify the text
- Unique techniques used in nonfiction texts

## Comprehension Conversation

### Before Reading

#### Notice the Cover Illustration

Take a moment to study Nicole Wong's illustrations on the cover. In the illustrator's note, she shares that in order to make sure her art was correct, she observed and researched submersibles and deep-sea life. Can you believe she drew this detailed illustration using her iPad? This book has both a title, *Flying Deep,* and a subtitle, *Climb Inside Deep-Sea Submersible ALVIN.* The subtitle adds information about what the book is going to be about. When you hear the subtitle, what does it sound like we're going to do?

**Set a Purpose:** I don't have a lot of schema or background knowledge about submersibles, so I'm excited to read and learn about Alvin. Since Nicole Wong researched her illustrations, I'm guessing they are going to help us understand more about this vehicle. Let's climb inside Alvin and fly through the ocean together.

### During Reading

- Title page: This illustration is called a *cutaway.* It's as if they sliced Alvin in half like an apple so that you can see the inside. What do you notice?

- *Today you'll investigate the site of deadly explosions* page: Look at the illustration. Do you see the white submersible Alvin? Remember the book says it is barely big enough for three. What might you find when you take Alvin into the sea? Do you think you'll find evidence of life? Thumbs up or thumbs down.

- *Lower yourself through Alvin's hatch* page: There are three illustrations on this two-page spread. Each offers a different view or perspective of Alvin. Study each view. What do you see and what can you learn?

- *2:00 p.m.* page: This two-page spread also has three illustrations. What is Nicole Wong trying to teach you? [On the left-hand side we see a close-up of the eelpout,

### Learning Targets:

- I use illustrations to help me better understand the facts.

- I talk, write, or draw about what I've learned.

and on the right-hand side a circle with a close-up of the scientists and a clear picture of the slurp gun.] How do these three illustrations work together to teach you about what is happening on this page?

## After Reading

- How did the illustrations help you to learn about Alvin? Do you think you would have learned as much if I had read you the text without showing the illustrations?

- Why do you think Michelle Cusolito called this book *Flying Deep*? If you were going to give the book a different title, what would it be? Why? [Invite students to write a new title and their rationale for that title on a sticky note, in their notebook, or on a shared electronic document.]

## Extend the Experience

- Draw and label an illustration to show what you've learned from reading this book.

- [Use the Learn More page in the backmatter to locate additional multimodal resources to share with or make available to interested learners.]

## Similar Titles

 ***Otis and Will Discover the Deep: The Record-Setting Dive of the Bathysphere* (Rosenstock, 2018)**

About the Book: Author Barb Rosenstock chronicles the maiden dive of Otis Barton and Will Beebe's Bathysphere in 1930. After learning how the Bathysphere was engineered, suspense builds as readers dive down 100 feet at a time. The repeated phrase *down, down into the deep* ties the book together. Katherine Roy's illustrator's note details the vast amount of research and planning she poured into the illustrations. This book is a bit text-heavy at the beginning, so you might want to read it over the course of a few days.

 ***The Sea Knows* (McGinty & Havis, 2020)**

About the Book: Dive below the surface to meet the creatures that inhabit the undersea world. Told in rhyming couplets enhanced by luminous illustrations, this book will spark curious readers to ask questions. Some of their questions might be answered by reading the additional information provided in the backmatter.

## Key Vocabulary and Kid-Friendly Definitions:

- *eerie*: not easy to explain; mysterious or scary

- *investigate*: to look closely to learn facts

- *thrive*: to grow strong and healthy

View the book trailer of *Otis and Will Discover the Deep* at resources.corwin.com/shakeupsharedreading

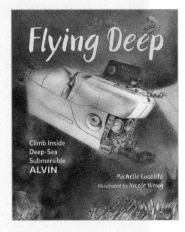

## Short Bursts of Shared Reading: *Flying Deep: Climb Inside Deep-Sea Submersible ALVIN*

### Focus 1—Wonder About Words: Descriptive Language

#### Before Reading

**Set the Stage:** Michelle Cusolito uses descriptive language to support us in visualizing what the scientists are seeing or hearing beneath the sea. Adding descriptive words helps readers learn more about a topic.

#### During Reading

#### Investigate Key Pages

#### My Turn

*Aqua becomes blue-green* page: There are descriptive words on this page that provide clues to guide me in picturing what the scientists are seeing because I can connect them to my experiences. When I read the words *thick blackness,* I visualize it being so dark that you can't see through the water because it's like a *thick* blanket. When the author describes the glowing sea animals like *a natural fireworks show,* I can imagine their lights flashing all around me like they do on the 4th of July.

#### Our Turn

*9:00 a.m.* page: On this page, the author uses onomatopoeia to help us imagine the sounds. Reread the sonar sounds with me. Imagine the sonar pinging until it detects an underwater object. Once it detects an object, it makes a different sound. How about the sound Alvin makes when it's landing on the ocean bottom? Does that sound remind you of any sounds you've heard before?

#### Your Turn

*Cottony fields of bacteria wave in current* page: I'm going to read the descriptions, and I want you to use them to find the organisms in the illustrations. [To check for accuracy, see the backmatter for a glossary with illustrations.]

#### After Reading

#### Nudge Toward Independence

Descriptive language helps readers better imagine what it is like to be in an unfamiliar place like the ocean floor. Visualizing while reading nonfiction books will clue you in to key details that will make it easier to remember the important information that you learn. So, while you're reading, pause and imagine the people, places, animals, or ideas that the author is communicating with images and words. If it helps you to sketch or jot key ideas on a sticky note or in your notebook, that is another smart strategy that readers use.

## Focus 2—Notice Writer's Craft Moves: A Day in the Life

### Before Reading

**Set the Stage:** In this book, we spend an entire day with the scientists inside Alvin. Let's ponder how starting pages with the time of day helps us better understand how time passes while scientists work inside Alvin. [If not too distracting for your learners, provide pairs of students with a moveable clock or use a large display clock to show passage of time.]

### During Reading

#### Investigate Key Pages

#### My Turn

*8:00 a.m.* page: When I see the time of day written at the top of this page, I think about what I'm usually doing at 8:00 in the morning. I know it is morning because the abbreviation *a.m.* is short for a Latin phrase that means before midday. [Share what you're typically doing at 8:00 a.m. on a school day.]

#### Our Turn

*9:00 a.m.* page: Whisper the time written at the top of this page to your neighbor. How does noting the hour of the day help you better understand how time is passing as the scientists embark on their journey? How long did it take to get to the ocean floor? They went two miles in one hour, and the average person walks three to four miles in an hour. Is Alvin moving slowly or quickly?

#### Your Turn

*Noon* page: What does the word *noon* mean? How long have they been underwater? Imagine not being able to use the bathroom for that long. [If students are curious about how the Alvin scientists go to the bathroom, you'll find some humorous facts about this topic in the first paragraph of the Author's Note.]

[Continue rereading, pausing on, and discussing the pages that denote the passage of time. Invite students to determine how much time has passed, what the scientists are doing at that particular time of day, and how the craft technique helps them relate to a typical day for these scientists.]

### After Reading

#### Nudge Toward Independence

Michelle Cusolito wanted you to experience a day in a life of an Alvin scientist, so she included times of day throughout the book. Was this helpful? Can you imagine using this technique in one of your nonfiction books? How might you go about marking the passage of time in a book you're writing? [Brainstorm and share ideas.]

**Innovate on Text:** Use your imagination. Get back into Alvin and dive below the surface. What will you see or do this time? You might start your story this way: The next day, we dove with Alvin again and . . .

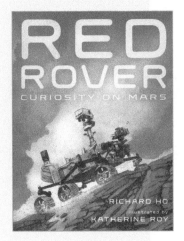

## Read-Aloud Experience: Explore With Illustrations

**Book Title:** *Red Rover: Curiosity on Mars* (Ho, 2019)

**About the Book:** Told from the perspective of the planet Mars, this nonfiction book will interest all readers, particularly your space fans. Katherine Roy's stunningly realistic illustrations paint a picture of the rover's experiences on the surface of the red planet. In Richard Ho's debut picture book, he personifies the Curiosity rover, adding to the appeal of this text.

To find a book like this one, look for the following:

- Engaging illustrations that amplify the text
- Unique techniques used in nonfiction texts

### Comprehension Conversation

#### Before Reading

#### Notice the Cover Illustration

On the front and back covers, we see two different views of the rover Curiosity. Why do you suppose the illustrator, Katherine Roy, chose to show the side view and the back view? What can you learn from studying the two illustrations? [If you are able to display the hard cover book casing underneath the paper book jacket, discuss how the illustration on the book casing makes the rover appear human-like.]

**Set a Purpose:** What do you already think you know about rovers and the planet Mars? [Take a moment to listen to and/or record students' background knowledge.] As nonfiction readers, we learn from the text, or words, and from the illustrations. Travel with me to the red planet to meet a rover named Curiosity. We'll see if the text confirms what you think you know or adds some new learning.

#### During Reading

- *The rover never gets tired* page: What have you learned about the rover so far? [It roams around Mars, it doesn't stop.] How do the illustrations help you imagine what it's like on the surface of Mars?

- *It is curious* page: To understand how the rover works, we have to combine what we read in the words with what we see in the pictures. Notice how the illustrations help you answer these questions. How does Curiosity observe? [With a camera.] What clues tell you this? How does Curiosity collect? [With a shovel.] How did you figure this out?

- *It is not easy to live here* page: Talk with a friend about what you see happening on this page. Turn and ask your friend, "Would you want to live on Mars? Why or why not?" Listen to their answer. Then share your opinion.

#### After Reading

- What do you remember about Curiosity? Turn to a classmate and say, "I remember . . ." (Hoyt, 2002).

**Learning Targets:**

- I use illustrations to help me better understand the facts.

- I talk, write, or draw about what I've learned.

- Do you think there are other rovers headed to Mars? We can learn more about this by reading the backmatter or doing some research. Is anyone interested in working with a team to find out the answer to that question?

## Extend the Experience

- *The Anatomy of Curiosity* page: [If possible, project this page so that children can get a closer look.] Wow! I didn't realize all of the equipment that Curiosity has on it. Notice how Katherine Roy added a key to her diagram. The key explains what all of the abbreviations mean. Point to a part and we'll learn more about it. If you were going to design a rover, what would it look like? Draw a diagram of your rover, and label the parts. Once you're finished, we'll share our rover diagrams with each other.

- Be an Observer! Learn About Space: After reading *Red Rover*, do you have any questions about space? [Jot students' wonderings on a chart.] I've stocked the Observer Center with books and other materials to help you answer your questions. We can't wait to hear what you discover.

## Key Vocabulary and Kid-Friendly Definitions:

- *curious*: asking questions, working to find answers, and wanting to learn new things

- *roam*: to move around without a plan

- *vast*: very large

View the author reading *Mars! Earthlings Welcome* at resources.corwin.com/shakeupsharedreading

## Similar Titles

 **Mars! Earthlings Welcome (McAnulty, 2021b)**

**About the Book:** Mars is personified and inviting Earthlings to visit. Mars, the "party planet," entices visitors by comparing itself to its sister planet, Earth. This engaging nonfiction book is the fifth installment in Stacy McAnulty's Our Universe picture book series.

 **Mars' First Friends: Come on Over, Rovers! (Hill, 2020)**

**About the Book:** Mars is bored, lonely, and looking for someone who will play with him. After giving up on his solar siblings for companionship, Mars is surprised by the arrival of Spirit and Opportunity. These puppy-like rovers make the perfect pets. Backmatter is packed with details about the solar system, Mars, and the rovers.

*Observer Center: Space*

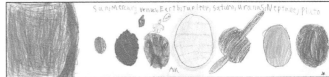

*Observer Center: Space Work Sample*

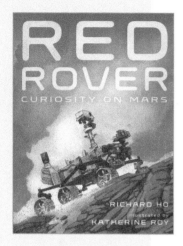

## Short Bursts of Shared Reading: *Red Rover: Curiosity on Mars*

### Focus 1–Reread to Boost Comprehension: Understand Point of View

#### Before Reading

**Set the Stage:** Authors write from different points of view. That means they decide who will narrate the story or share the facts. Richard Ho chose to write *Red Rover* from an interesting point of view. As we reread, we'll work together to identify the point of view from which *Red Rover* is told.

#### During Reading

#### Investigate Key Pages

#### My Turn

*They call me Mars* page: I remember when I got to this page, I was surprised that Mars was the one who was telling the story. I realized Mars was the narrator when I saw that the author was using the words *me* and *I*. The words *me* and *I* are clues that the book is written in first-person point of view. I didn't notice that it was written in first-person point of view until I got to this page. Let's go back in the book to see if there were other clues that we might have missed.

#### Our Turn

*They sailed across a sea of space and landed on unfamiliar ground* page: Let's reread this page and focus on the last sentence. Is there a clue in the sentence that tells you that Mars is talking? [. . . it is like *here*.] If someone else was narrating the book, the words would have read, "It tells them what it is like *on Mars*." Instead they read, "It tells them what it is like *here*." Talk about the difference with a neighbor.

#### Your Turn

*I am cold* page: Read the first word in every sentence, and see what you notice. [All but one of the sentences begin with the word *I*.] Remember, when an author is writing in first-person (or first-planet!) point of view, they use the word *I*. The use of the word *I* is another clue that Mars is the one who is sharing the facts—the book is told from the planet's point of view. Why do you suppose Richard Ho chose to write this book as if he were Mars?

#### After Reading

#### Nudge Toward Independence

When you are reading, notice the point of view in nonfiction books. This helps you know who is narrating.

## Focus 2—Notice Writer's Craft Moves: Personification

**Before Reading**

**Set the Stage:** Personification is when a writer gives an animal or object human traits. It's like they bring that creature or object to life. Notice the little word *person* in the big word *personification*. As we reread, ponder how and why Richard Ho personified the rover, Curiosity.

**During Reading**

**Investigate Key Pages**

**My Turn**

*The tracks play hide-and-seek . . .* page: Do you ever play hide-and-seek? Hide-and-seek is a game that people play, isn't it? That's a clue that Richard Ho is trying to personify Curiosity, to make it like a human.

**Our Turn**

*It is curious* page: Reread this page to see if we can find more clues that Curiosity is behaving in a human-like manner. [It observes, measures, collects, and is thirsty.] Do you do any of these activities? Are you ever thirsty? Can you imagine what it would be like to be Curiosity?

**Your Turn**

*The rover seems lonely, roaming by itself* page: Reread this page with me, then talk to your neighbor about the clues that help you know Curiosity is personified. [It's lonely and it has friends.] Do you ever feel lonely? Does a vehicle like a rover really have feelings?

**After Reading**

**Nudge Toward Independence**

Authors often use personification in books with animal characters—where the animals act like people. Look in your book box [or wherever your students keep their independent reading books] and see if you can find another book where animal characters do human things.

**Innovate on Text:** Think of a nonliving object you have at school or at home. [Brainstorm items like pencil, toothbrush, backpack, pillow, and so on.] Write from that object's point of view. Here are some ideas to get you started:

My name is _____.

I like to _____.

I live _____.

When no one is looking, I _____.

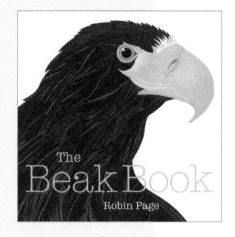

## Read-Aloud Experience: Discover Details—Expository Nonfiction

**Book Title:** *The Beak Book* **(Page, 2021)**

**About the Book:** Bird beaks come in many shapes, sizes, and have a multitude of purposes. Robin Page's eye-catching bird profiles will draw readers in. Her concise explanations are ideal for highlighting the concept of main idea and key details. To allow time for rich conversations, you might consider spending two sittings on the interactive read-aloud experience.

To find a book like this one, look for the following:

- Clear, straightforward facts coupled with supportive illustrations
- Informational text about a specific aspect of a topic

### Comprehension Conversation

**Before Reading**

**Notice the Cover Illustration**

Wow! Robin Page's cover illustration really catches my eye. I can't stop looking at it. Did you know that she creates her artwork by layering different textures and colors together using digital tools? To make each image look realistic, she collects and studies photographs of the animal. What kind of bird do you think this is? Let's see if we can find this bird inside the book to confirm we've correctly identified it.

**Set a Purpose:** What are all of the different actions your hands can do? [Listen to students' responses.] I wonder if birds can do as many things with their beaks as we can with do with our hands. I bet you can tell from the title *The Beak Book* that we're going to learn more about birds' beaks. Get ready to become beak experts!

**During Reading**

- *This beak is for straining* page: Do any of you have a strainer in your kitchen? [If needed, display an image of a strainer.] Can you picture what this duck's bill is doing? I didn't know a duck's bill strained or filtered out its food from the mud. That's new learning for me.

- *This beak is for sniffing page:* Point to your nostrils. Now, aim your finger at the book page to where the kiwi's nostrils are located. Tell your neighbor what the kiwi does with its nostrils. [As you read the next few pages, continue defining words that might pose a challenge to your learners and relating the bird's behavior to familiar objects or human behaviors. If you are planning to stop halfway, read up to the *This beak is for stabbing* page.]

- *This beak is for ripping* page: Do you recognize this bird? [It's the bird that we saw on the cover.] Now that we've read and learned about many different uses for birds' beaks, let's take a moment to notice how Robin Page organizes her information. What does she tell you first? [What the bird uses the beak for.] That's the main idea of the page. What do the rest of the words on the page tell

**Learning Targets:**

- I understand what the book is mainly about.
- I remember key details about the topic.

you? [Details.] How do the details and illustrations work together to help you better understand each main idea?

## After Reading

- What do you know about bird beaks that you didn't know before?
- Which bird(s) did you find the most interesting?

## Extend the Experience

- Divide a piece of paper in half. Write down two facts you remember from this book.

  Be an Observer! Investigate Animal Parts: [To prepare for this extension, gather assorted animal books, images, and multimodal resources along with mentor texts like these:

  o *Eye to Eye* (Jenkins, 2014)

  o *Feathers: Not Just for Flying* (Stewart, 2014)

  o *What Do You Do With a Tail Like This?* (Jenkins, 2003)]

Reading *The Beak Book* got me thinking. I know how much you love studying animals, so I thought you would enjoy writing your own animal parts book. If you're interested, I put everything you might need in the Observer Center. While you're there you can work on your own or with a friend to . . .

o Pick an animal part like eyes, ears, nose, mouth, and so on.

o Research to find out what that part does on three different animals.

o Write and illustrate, design a Google Slide, or record a short video to share what you learned.

## Similar Titles

 ***Crossings: Extraordinary Structures for Extraordinary Animals* (Duffield, 2020)**

**About the Book:** Find out about the structures that humans have designed and built to allow wildlife to cross busy highways. The repeated refrain *over, under, across, and through* carries readers through this engaging STEM-meets-nature picture book.

 ***Play in the Wild: How Baby Animals Like to Have Fun* (Judge, 2020)**

**About the Book:** Kids will discover a lot of similarities between their play and that of the creatures in this book. Each two-page spread begins with a topic sentence and, after a page turn, is followed by another two-page spread with kid-friendly details. Informative backmatter includes a glossary and more specifics about each animal.

---

**Key Vocabulary and Kid-Friendly Definitions:**

- *impressive*: unusual or not ordinary
- *powerful*: having a lot of strength
- *unusual*: not usual or ordinary

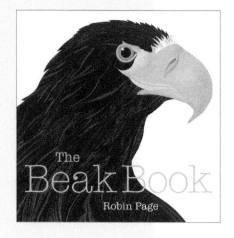

## Short Bursts of Shared Reading: *The Beak Book*

### Focus 1–Wonder About Words: Verbs

#### Before Reading

**Set the Stage:** Did anyone notice that Robin Page uses the same kind of words when explaining what birds do with their beaks? She uses verbs, or action words. I wonder if it was a challenge for her to come up with all of those verbs. Let's tune into the verbs by rereading only the main idea sentences. As we read each page, we're going to each act out the action in our own way.

#### During Reading

#### Investigate Key Pages

#### My Turn

- *This beak is for straining* page: To visualize this action, I might pretend my fingers are a strainer and I'm pouring water through them.
- *This beak is for sniffing* page: Here I'm going act like I'm sniffing a flower.

#### Our Turn

[Reread the remaining pages, inviting students to act out each verb.]

#### Your Turn

Now, you're going to imitate Robin Page's pattern and, using verbs, tell a friend three actions you do with your feet. It will sound like this: These feet are for _____.

#### After Reading

#### Nudge Toward Independence

In this book, Robin Page uses action verbs or words that tell what the animal does with its beak. As readers, verbs help us visualize or imagine the character's or creature's actions. Writers choose their verbs carefully, just like Robin Page does in this book. When you're writing about a character or animal, choose a verb that clearly describes the action. Try to be specific. For instance, there are many synonyms for the verb *run* like *dash, race, rush, jog, scamper, scurry,* or *trot*. Which verb would you pick to describe how a horse runs? How would you describe a running rabbit? [Continue exploring synonyms for other verbs your students might use in writing.]

**Innovate on Text:** After reading *The Beak Book*, I started thinking about all the different actions humans do with their body parts. What do you do with your hands, eyes, brain, heart, feet, fingers, toes, or nose? It's your turn to write your own nonfiction book to teach us. You can borrow the pattern Robin Page uses in her book: A [body part] is for _____. [Provide students with a stapled-together booklet made out of blank copy paper. I suggest a cover and three or four inside pages, but you can adjust the length and size of the book based on the needs of your students.]

## Focus 2–Reread to Boost Comprehension: Learn From Infographics

### Before Reading

**Set the Stage:** [If possible, project the infographic. You may also want to have a world map or globe nearby.] Often, in nonfiction books, writers include backmatter. Listen to the word *backmatter*. *Matter* is a fancy word for *stuff*, and since it is found in the back of the book, it's called backmatter. You can read the backmatter to learn even more about the topic. In *The Beak Book*, Robin Page designed an infographic to add information that wasn't already included in the book.

### During Reading

#### Investigate Key Pages

#### My Turn

When I'm gathering facts from an infographic, I start by reading the title. The title of this infographic is *Where the birds live and what they eat.* The title helps my brain tune in to the kind of information I'll be looking for in the words and images. I also see this silhouette of a human next to all of the birds. I'm going to read the caption because I bet it explains why it's here. [Discuss the concept of relative size and how using an adult human as a comparison makes it easier to imagine the size of each bird.]

#### Our Turn

I want to learn more about the scarlet ibis. First, I'll find it on the infographic. Now, I can learn these three facts:

- Its relative size or how big it is compared to a human
- What it eats
- Where it lives

Which bird did you find interesting? [Repeat the process using birds selected by students.]

#### Your Turn

Work with a partner. Pick a bird that we haven't learned about yet. Learn more about its size, diet, and habitat. To challenge yourself, find two birds to compare. Notice how their size, diet, and habitat are alike and different.

### After Reading

#### Nudge Toward Independence

Infographics are helpful when learning about a topic. When studying an infographic, remember to read the title and any captions, labels, or keys. Then, read the words inside and outside the infographic. Ask yourself, "What is this infographic teaching me?" Determine the main idea or message that you take away from the image.

# STAR OF THE PARTY
### The Solar System Celebrates!

Written by Jan Carr  Illustrated by Juana Medina

**Book Title:** *Star of the Party: The Solar System Celebrates!* (Carr, 2021)

**About the Book:** Get ready to party! In this clever narrative nonfiction book, the planets work together to throw the sun a birthday party. Readers learn key details about the solar system from the planets' banter while they plan the guest list, make place cards, and decide on a present. The frontmatter includes a one-paragraph description of the sun and each of the eight planets written from their point of view. In the engaging backmatter, online resources are followed by additional facts presented in a graphic format featuring the planets' dialogue in speech bubbles.

To find a book like this one, look for the following:

- Facts woven throughout a narrative nonfiction text
- Narrative nonfiction texts about space

## Learning Targets:

- I understand what the book is mainly about.
- I remember key details about the topic.

## Comprehension Conversation

### Before Reading

### Notice the Cover Illustration

I'm opening the book so that you can enjoy the entire wraparound cover. What do you notice about Juana Medina's illustrations? [The planets look realistic, and she's added faces, arms, and party hats.] Who do you suppose will be the "star of the party"? Look at the unique back cover blurb—it's an invitation to the party!

**Set a Purpose:** Now that we have a pretty good idea about what might happen in *Star of the Party*, I have a question for you. Do you think this book tells a story, helps us learn facts, or is a little of both? There's only one way to find out—let's join the party!

### During Reading

- *Who's invited?* page: Jan Carr has included a description about the sun and each of the planets. As readers, you can decide whether you want to read these descriptions before or after the rest of the book. For today, we're going to skip these descriptions.

- *Mercury started a guest list* page: Did you learn any facts on this page? What were those facts mainly about? [Pluto.]

- *What about the moons?* page: Back to the question I asked before we started reading. What do you think—is this book fiction, nonfiction, or a little of both? [A little of both.] I agree! This book is called a *narrative nonfiction* book because it has characters [the planets], a setting [the solar system], a goal [to throw a party for Sun], and a resolution or ending [the party was a success] while at the same time sharing facts about the planets.

- *Then came the task of thinking of a birthday present* page: Jan Carr helps us learn about the planets by organizing the pages. Most of the pages have a main topic and then some key details. Tell a friend the main topic of this page. [Belts.]

- *Suddenly, there was another voice* page: Talk about this page with a neighbor. Discuss what it is mainly about.

- *All the planets looked at Sun* page: Think about the words Sun uses to describe her party. What do they all have in common? [Discuss the words *beaming, radiant,* and *glowing* and why the author chose to use these multimeaning words.]

### After Reading

- Jan Carr chose to write about the planets by blending facts into a story. What's your opinion about this approach? Did you enjoy and learn from this book? Why or why not?

- Did you learn anything new about space? Share your new learning with a friend.

### Extend the Experience

- Narrative nonfiction texts tell us a story while teaching us facts. So, when telling someone about this book, you can either retell the story or recount the facts. Choose which one you prefer, and complete that side of the *Retell or Recount Reproducible Response Page* found on the companion website (resources.corwin.com/shakeupsharedreading).

- Compare and Contrast! Multigenre Text Set—Solar System: As a reader and a learner, do you prefer to learn facts by reading expository nonfiction, narrative nonfiction, or other types of texts? To help you compare and contrast the different types of texts, I've started this basket.

**Key Vocabulary and Kid-Friendly Definitions:**

- *bragging*: talking too proudly about something you have or can do

- *cozy*: warm, safe, comfortable

- *task*: work to do

online resources

View the book trailer for the Our Universe Series by Stacy McAnulty at resources.corwin.com/shakeupsharedreading

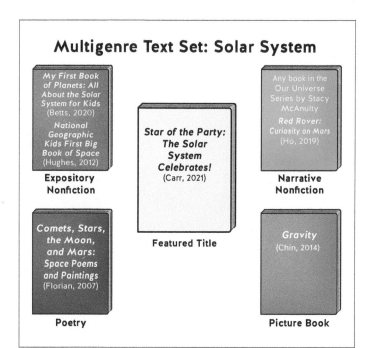

## Multigenre Text Set: Solar System

My First Book of Planets: All About the Solar System for Kids (Betts, 2020)

National Geographic Kids First Big Book of Space (Hughes, 2012)

**Expository Nonfiction**

*Star of the Party: The Solar System Celebrates!* (Carr, 2021)

**Featured Title**

Any book in the Our Universe Series by Stacy McAnulty

Red Rover: Curiosity on Mars (Ho, 2019)

**Narrative Nonfiction**

Comets, Stars, the Moon, and Mars: Space Poems and Paintings (Florian, 2007)

**Poetry**

*Gravity* (Chin, 2014)

**Picture Book**

Name _____

**Retell or Recount**

| Retell the Story | Recount the Facts |
| --- | --- |
| | Three Fascinating Facts |
| In the beginning _____ | 1. _____ |
| In the middle _____ | 2. _____ |
| At the end _____ | 3. _____ |

*Retell or Recount Reproducible Response Page*

## Short Bursts of Shared Reading:
## *Star of the Party: The Solar System Celebrates!*

### Focus 1–Spotlight High-Frequency Words: Question Words

### Before Reading

**Set the Stage:** There are words that you will read in a lot of books. These are called *high-frequency words*. As we reread, we are going to find and study question words.

### During Reading

### Investigate Key Pages

### My Turn

*"Let's plan the Sun's party!" said Jupiter* page: I'm going to reread this page and stop when I hear a question word. Here is the question word *why*. The word *why* makes two sounds wh = /w/ and y = /i/. I'm going to write that word on my whiteboard while saying the sounds: /w/-/i/, why.

### Our Turn

*What about the moons?* page: Do you see a question word on this page? Here is the question word *what*. That word makes two sounds wh = /w/ and at = /ut/. Let's write that word on our whiteboards while saying the sounds: /w/-/ut/, what.

### Your Turn

Now, let's flip to the back cover blurb. First, we'll say the words and their sounds together. Then, you can write them on your whiteboard:

    who = /hoo/

    what = /w/-/ut/

    where = /w/-/air/

    when = /w/-/en/

For an extra challenge, write a question or two about the planets. Start with a question word. Ask a friend to see if they can answer your question.

### After Reading

### Nudge Toward Independence

You are going to come across question words in the books you read and use them when you write. Thinking about what they look like and sound like will help you do both!

**Innovate on Text:** Imagine you are throwing a birthday party for a creature or other object found in nature. Create an invitation like the one found on the back cover of the book. Let's try one together. To complete one on your own, use the *Invitation Reproducible Response Page* found on the companion website (resources.corwin .com/shakeupsharedreading).

## Focus 2—Notice Writer's Craft Moves: Creative Backmatter

### Before Reading

**Set the Stage:** Writers add backmatter to texts for many reasons. Information found in the backmatter might give you more background information, expand on the facts in the book, and/or explain more about how the writer or illustrator completed the book. In *Star of the Party,* Jan Carr designed the backmatter in a graphic format, like a graphic novel or comic strip. Let's take a look!

### During Reading

### Investigate Key Pages

### My Turn

*Why do we orbit Sun?* section: The planets are talking and joking, but they are also sharing some facts. So, I have to read the dialogue and pull out the important facts. In this section, I learned that the planets orbit the sun because of gravity.

### Our Turn

*So if Sun's pulling us, why don't we get pulled straight in?* section: What facts can you learn from reading the dialogue between Venus and Mars? Tell someone nearby a fact you learned from this comic.

### Your Turn

*Ta-da!* section: As we reread this section, your challenge is to sort the facts from the jokes and other dialogue. [If possible, underline or mark the facts in some way.] I will put this book in the classroom library so that you can continue exploring the rest of the informational comic strips.

### After Reading

### Nudge Toward Independence

The backmatter in this book added information to the facts we learned in the book in creative ways. Be on the lookout for other nonfiction books with creative backmatter. Share them with us so we can use them as mentor texts for our own writing.

A _____ Party

for _____

Who? _____

What? _____

Where? _____

When? _____

Name _____

*Invitation Reproducible Response Page*

A  Thank-You  Party

for Tree

Who? All the birds

What? Celebrate you being our home

Where? In the forest

When? On a sunny spring day

Name _____

*Invitation Co-Created Chart*

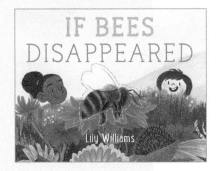

## Read-Aloud Experience: Wonder Before, During, and After Reading

**Book Title:** *If Bees Disappeared* (Williams, 2021)

**About the Book:** Travel to Kent, England, with a young girl as your guide to learn what would happen to the ecosystem if bees disappeared. Lily Williams clearly describes the cause-and-effect consequences of bee extinction. In the end, she leaves readers with a sense of optimism about the growing awareness of the importance of bees. The backmatter includes a list of ways to help save bees. If your students like this book, read aloud the others in the series, including *If Sharks Disappeared* (Williams, 2017), *If Polar Bears Disappeared* (Williams, 2018), and *If Elephants Disappeared* (Williams, 2019). (Refer to the Read-Aloud Experience using *If Sharks Disappeared* on page 260 in *The Ramped-Up Read Aloud*.)

To find a book like this one, look for the following:

- Informational books about topics that appeal to kids
- Books that lead to more questions

## Comprehension Conversation

### Before Reading

#### Notice the Cover Illustration

When I open the wraparound cover so that you can see both sides, what do you notice? [The bee on the cover has a dashed line around it.] Why do you suppose Lily Williams drew a dashed line around the bee on the cover?

**Set a Purpose:** The title of this book is *If Bees Disappeared.* What do you think would happen if bees became extinct? Is there anything you are wondering about? As we read to learn more about bees, we'll see if the book answers your before-reading questions and if you have any other questions along the way.

### During Reading

- *Bees are keystone species . . .* page: When I first read this page, I wondered what the term *keystone species* meant. Then, I noticed how Lily Williams explains terms in the text. [Point out how she defines *keystone species* and *pollinators* in the text.] Are there any other words that you're wondering about?

- *Bees are considered a superorganism* page: Again, we can see how Lily Williams helps us understand key words. [Point out how she defines *superorganism* in the text.] We've learned a few important facts about bees. Turn to a friend and tell them something you remember from the first few pages. What are you still wondering?

- *there would be no natural pest control* page: Wow! A lot would happen if honeybees disappeared. Explain what the diagram on this page is teaching you. Do you have any questions?

- *Thankfully, the news about bees is buzzing* page: Are you wondering about any of the words or ideas on this page? [If children are unfamiliar with the term *urban farm initiative*, explain that it is an action plan to grow crops in towns and cities.]

**Learning Targets:**

- I wonder and ask questions before, during, and after reading.

- I figure out ways to answer my own questions.

## After Reading

- As readers, we wondered about many things as we learned about bees. Sometimes nonfiction books leave us with some unanswered questions. Do you have any after-reading questions? How could you go about answering them?

- What did you learn from reading this book that could help you when you are writing a nonfiction text?

### Extend the Experience

- Work with a partner to make a Google Slide or poster to teach the people in our school one way that they can help save bees. Once your posters or slides are finished, we'll post or project them.

- Compare and Contrast! Multigenre Text Set—Bees: Lily Williams wrote this book about bees to help us understand how important they are to the ecosystem. Other authors have written books about bees for different purposes. I've collected some bee books in this *Buzzing About Bees* basket. After reading and enjoying these books on your own or with a friend, think about the lesson(s) you learned from reading each book or the reason why you think the author wrote the book. Talk about it with a friend, or label the book with a sticky note to tell us what you've learned.

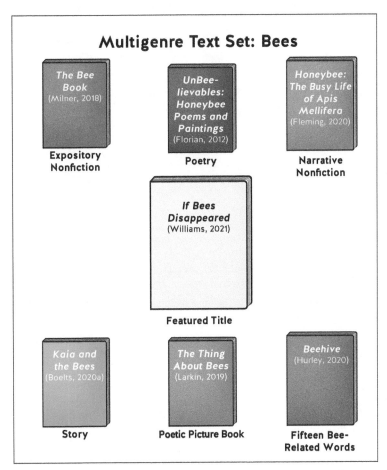

**Multigenre Text Set: Bees**

| | | |
|---|---|---|
| *The Bee Book* (Milner, 2018) | *UnBee-lievables: Honeybee Poems and Paintings* (Florian, 2012) | *Honeybee: The Busy Life of Apis Mellifera* (Fleming, 2020) |
| **Expository Nonfiction** | **Poetry** | **Narrative Nonfiction** |

*If Bees Disappeared* (Williams, 2021)

**Featured Title**

| | | |
|---|---|---|
| *Kaia and the Bees* (Boelts, 2020a) | *The Thing About Bees* (Larkin, 2019) | *Beehive* (Hurley, 2020) |
| **Story** | **Poetic Picture Book** | **Fifteen Bee-Related Words** |

## Key Vocabulary and Kid-Friendly Definitions:

- *disrupting*: stopping something that is happening

- *survive*: to keep living or growing

- *threatened*: not having a good chance of living or growing; in danger

View *The Thing About Bees* book trailer at resources.corwin.com/shakeupsharedreading

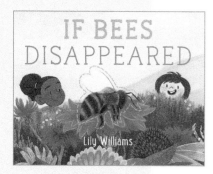

## Short Bursts of Shared Reading:
*If Bees Disappeared*

### Focus 1—Reread to Boost Comprehension: Consider Cause and Effect

**Before Reading**

**Set the Stage:** In this book, Lily Williams describes what will happen if honeybees disappear. She tells us the cause, or why they might disappear, and then the effect, or what will happen if they do.

**During Reading**

**Investigate Key Pages**

**My Turn**

*Unfortunately, today honeybees are threatened by environmental and man-made causes . . .* page: Here we learn one of the reasons, or causes, that honeybees might disappear. When I turn the page, I learn one effect. I'm going to record my learning on a cause-and-effect chart.

**Our Turn**

*If honeybee pollination disappeared . . .* page: On the next page, you're going to find out the effect of honeybee pollination disappearing. I'll turn the page so that you can read and ponder the effect. What should I write on the chart?

**Your Turn**

As we continue reading, you can share what you think we should add to the cause-and-effect chart.

**After Reading**

**Nudge Toward Independence**

Writers use cause and effect to help us see connections between events. As readers, noticing those connections helps us better understand the information.

| *If Bees Disappeared* by Lily Williams | |
|---|---|
| **If . . .** | Then . . . |
| honeybees disappeared | the plants they pollinate would disappear |
| honeybee pollination disappeared | birds would disappear |
| lots of fruits disappeared | birds would disappear |
| birds disappeared | some of our favorite foods would disappear |
| **Cause** | Effect |

If Bees Disappeared *Cocreated Cause and Effect Chart*

## Focus 2—Notice Writer's Craft Moves: Adding Diagrams to Explain Details

### Before Reading

**Set the Stage:** Nonfiction writers include diagrams to help readers visualize and understand details. Let's look back to see how Lily Williams uses the nonfiction text feature of a diagram.

### During Reading

### Investigate Key Pages

### My Turn

*Bees are keystone species . . .* page: This diagram shows different species of bees. I notice that they are divided into sections by color, and each section is labeled. I don't know exactly what the labels mean, but I can infer that the bees in blue live together in hives because *social* means being with others and the bees in green live alone because that is what *solitary* means. I didn't realize that some bees didn't live in a hive. I learned something new from reading this diagram!

### Our Turn

*Honeybees are considered a superorganism* page: Use the diagram along with the words on the page to identify which type of bee is flying away from the hive.

### Your Turn

*so would most of the plants they pollinate* page: The diagram on this page compares honeybee pollination to wind pollination. Explain in words what is shown in the diagram.

### After Reading

### Nudge Toward Independence

Reading diagrams adds to your learning. Including diagrams in the nonfiction texts that you are writing will help your readers better understand the information.

**Innovate on Text:** Imagine about what might happen if other things in our world disappeared. The ideas you write about don't have to be living creatures. What if items like pencils, vehicles, or books disappeared? Use your imagination to write and draw about what might happen. This sentence stem might be helpful: If _____ disappeared then _____.

## Read-Aloud Experience: Wonder as You Learn

**Book Title:** *DROP: An Adventure Through the Water Cycle* (Moon, 2021)

**About the Book:** I've read a lot of books about the water cycle, but this one floats above the rest. The facts are told from the expressive point of view of a personified drop of water who has been around for 4.5 billion years and experienced every aspect of the water cycle. Front and back endpapers present infographics about the states of water and the water cycle, respectively.

To find a book like this one, look for the following:

- Innovative informational books about the water cycle
- Books that lead to inquiry

## Comprehension Conversation

### Before Reading

#### Notice the Cover Illustration

Notice the drops of water on the cover. Can you tell how Emily Kate Moon created them? [Listen to students' thoughts.] She used real water mixed with India ink and dropped the dyed water onto the page. Sometimes she used a dropper. Have you ever seen one of those? [Display an image of or show a real eye dropper.]

**Set a Purpose:** You can tell from the subtitle, *An Adventure Through the Water Cycle,* that this book is going to be about the water cycle. What do you already think you know about the water cycle? Is there anything you're wondering about this book or about water before we begin?

### During Reading

- *She has lounged in every lake and soaked in every sea* page: Drop has been around a while, hasn't she? Let me reread when Drop says: "So much sea to see!" The author uses a homophone to make a word joke. Homophones like *sea* and *see* are words that sound the same but have different meanings or spellings. *Sea* is another word for the ocean, and you *see* with your eyes. Does the joke make sense now?

- *The sun fills Drop with energy* page: Do you have any questions about what is happening to Drop right now? What are you wondering?

- *A crowded cloud can be quite an event!* page: There is a lot happening in this cloud. Turn and ask a neighbor if they have any questions.

- *If she freezes into snow or ice, she may be stuck . . .* page: I have a question. When she was in the glacier, why did Drop ask, "Are we there yet?" What are your thoughts?

### After Reading

- On a sticky note [real or virtual], write any lingering questions you have about this book. Once we have your after-reading questions, think about what you

**Learning Targets:**

- I wonder and ask questions before, during, and after reading.
- I notice how the author shares information.
- I figure out ways to answer my own questions.

could do to answer those questions. Then, we can work together to find the best way to answer your specific questions.

- Emily Kate Moon chose to teach you about the water cycle from the point of view of a drop of water. What did you think of this technique?

## Find Answers to After-Reading Questions

- Reread or relisten to all or parts of the book.
- Talk about your questions with another reader.
- Read or listen to someone read the front flap, back flap, back cover blurb, and/or backmatter to gather more information.
- Research to discover more about the topic.
- Write or draw about what you learned from the book.
- Find more information online about the author's purpose by searching for the author's website, interviews with the author, or other multimedia information.

## Extend the Experience

- Create an infographic to show what you learned about the water cycle. [Display key water cycle vocabulary to support students as they label their infographic.]
- [Gather the following supplies so that students can make their own Drop story: eye droppers, water mixed with food coloring, and heavy-weight white drawing paper.] Use the eye dropper to drop water onto your paper. Let your drops dry. Once they are dry, add details to tell your own story about Drop.

## Similar Titles

 ***Blue Floats Away* (Jonker, 2021)**

About the Book: Little Blue, an iceberg, is separated from his parents. He floats away and sees new things. Eventually, the sun melts Blue and he evaporates. In the end, Blue returns to his home as a snow-producing cloud.

 ***Fairy Science: Solid, Liquid, Gassy* (Spires, 2020)**

About the Book: In the follow-up to *Fairy Science* (Spires, 2019), Esther, the science-loving fairy, is joined by her friends Clove and Fig to debunk the magical myths their fellow sprites believe. When their pond disappears, the team observes, asks questions, forms a hypothesis, conducts experiments, and examines the results. Backmatter includes a simple rainy day experiment kids can do at home.

**Key Vocabulary and Kid-Friendly Definitions:**

- *adventure*: an exciting or dangerous trip or experience
- *lounged*: spent time relaxing
- *surface*: the outside of something

View the book trailer of *DROP* at resources.corwin.com/shakeupsharedreading

## Short Bursts of Shared Reading: *DROP: An Adventure Through the Water Cycle*

### Focus 1—Wonder About Words: Interjections

### Before Reading

**Set the Stage:** Writers add interjections to the text or pictures to express how someone is feeling. Interjections can show positive or negative feelings like surprise, disgust, joy, disappointment, or excitement.

### During Reading

### Investigate Key Pages

### My Turn

*Drop spends most of her time in the ocean* page: There are two interjections on this page: *Woo-hoo!* and *Sweeeet.* When I read these interjections, I know that Drop is excited about being in the ocean.

### Our Turn

*Because that's when Drop gets to be . . . RAIN* page: Do you see the interjection on this page? Read the interjection the way you think Drop would say it.

### Your Turn

*a whole new adventure begins!* page: There is one interjection on this page and one on the next. Read each interjection, and then tell a friend how you think Drop is feeling.

### After Reading

### Nudge Toward Independence

Yippee! We've read and learned about more interjections. I've listed all of the interjections we found in the book *DROP* on this chart. Notice how interjections help authors express a character's feelings. If you find any interjections in the books you're reading, add them to the chart. Ponder how you might use an interjection on this chart to show a character's feelings when you're writing.

*Interjection Chart*

## Focus 2–Reread to Boost Comprehension: Learn From Infographics

### Before Reading

**Set the Stage:** To teach us more about the water cycle, Emily Kate Moon adds infographics to the front and back endpapers. An infographic is a chart, diagram, or picture that communicates information. Infographics, as the word implies, present information graphically, or through images.

### During Reading

### Investigate Key Pages

### My Turn

Back endpapers: I'll start by reading the title of this infographic. The title will explain what I should be learning by studying this infographic. Next, I'm going to look at what is happening in the picture. I see arrows pointing around a circle. The arrows are symbols to show me the path that water follows as it moves around the planet. Of course, you can't really see a line and arrows in real life. They are on this image to represent the water cycle.

### Our Turn

Back endpapers: Drop says that these are her favorite big words. I'll read each word, and then you can look at the images to see if you can figure out what the word means. If we need more information, we can read the definitions that appear next to the infographic.

### Your Turn

Front endpapers: Begin by reading the title of this infographic. Next, look carefully at the words and images. Ask yourself, "What is this infographic teaching me?" [The three states of water.] Turn to someone nearby to think and talk about what you see and what you can learn from reading this infographic. Remember to use words, images, and symbols to help you comprehend the image.

### After Reading

### Nudge Toward Independence

What did you learn from the infographics that you didn't learn from reading the book? Do you prefer reading the infographics or reading the text? What strategies did you use when reading the infographic that will help you the next time you read one?

**Innovate on Text:** [Gather infographics from online sources, or find books like *Animals by the Numbers: A Book of Animal Infographics* (Jenkins, 2016) or *Me and the World: An Infographic Exploration* (Trius, 2020).] Create an infographic about a topic of interest. Use these infographics to spark ideas.

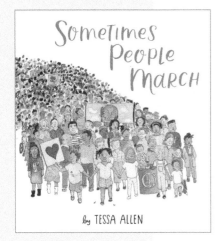

by TESSA ALLEN

## Read-Aloud Experience: Take Action

**Book Title:** *Sometimes People March* (Allen, 2020)

**About the Book:** To ground the book in something familiar to young learners, Tessa Allen begins with marching ants and marching bands. She then continues with straightforward, carefully crafted facts about the variety of reasons people engage in political protests. The illustrations include contemporary as well as historical marches. The backmatter labeled "Movements, Marches, and Key Figures in the Art" provides a brief synopsis along with corresponding page numbers of the events found in the illustrations.

To find a book like this one, look for the following:

- Narrative nonfiction about peaceful protests
- Accounts that are realistic and optimistic

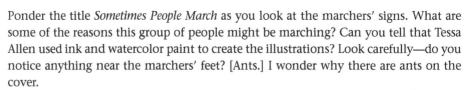

### Comprehension Conversation

#### Before Reading

#### Notice the Cover Illustration

Ponder the title *Sometimes People March* as you look at the marchers' signs. What are some of the reasons this group of people might be marching? Can you tell that Tessa Allen used ink and watercolor paint to create the illustrations? Look carefully—do you notice anything near the marchers' feet? [Ants.] I wonder why there are ants on the cover.

**Set a Purpose:** Authors write books for different reasons. While we're reading *Sometimes People March*, ask yourself, "Why did Tessa Allen write this book?" Afterward, we'll talk about your answers to that question.

### During Reading

- *Marching is something people do together . . .* page: Before we discuss this page, I'm going to define two of the words. The word *resist* means to work to change something, and the word *injustice* means that something is wrong because it isn't fair or equal. In your own words, tell your neighbor why people march. Now, use the picture clues on the opposite side of the page to see if you can figure out what needs to change.

- *Sometimes people carry signs . . .* page: We've learned many reasons that people march. Have you ever been in or heard about a march? What were people marching to change?

- *People resist with meetings* page: Marching is one way to resist, but there are other ways. Tell a friend another way that people resist.

- *People are more powerful together* page: Why do you suppose people are more powerful when they march or resist together?

**Learning Targets:**

- I ponder the author's purpose for writing this text.
- I notice interesting ways authors share information.

### After Reading

- What do you know about marching now that you didn't know before we read this book?

- In this book, we learned about a lot of different reasons people march and other ways people resist injustice. Have you ever seen something happening at school or in your community that made you want to march?

## Extend the Experience

- To identify the author's purpose, think to yourself, "What was the *main* reason Tessa Allen wrote this book?" Here are three reasons authors write:

  o inform: teach you about the topic

  o persuade: talk you into doing something using reasons or arguments

  o entertain: make you smile, laugh, or keep you interested

On a piece of paper or in your notebook, complete these sentence stems to share your thinking: The author wrote this book mostly to _____. I think that because _____.

- Sometimes when people march, they carry signs. If you were going to march, what would you march for? What would your sign read?

••••••••••••••••••••••••••••••••••••••••••••••••••••••••••••••••••••••••••••••

### Similar Titles

 **Love Is Powerful (Brewer, 2020)**

**About the Book:** Mari and Mama are making a sign. When Mari questions the reason for the sign, Mama explains that it is "a message for the world." Mari then wonders how the world will be able to see her sign, and Mama explains, "Because love is powerful." During the march, when Mari yells her message, the crowd calls back. In the backmatter, the author includes a photo of and note from Mari about her experience at the 2017 Women's March in New York City.

 **We March (Evans, 2012)**

**About the Book:** A family joins the March on Washington on August 28, 1963. Evans shares the story with few words and simple yet compelling illustrations. It would be helpful if children had a bit of background knowledge about the march to fully appreciate this powerful text.

**Key Vocabulary and Kid-Friendly Definitions:**

- *courage*: ability to face fear or danger

- *powerful*: strong, full of energy

- *resist*: to work to change something

View the creators talking about *Love Is Powerful* at resources.corwin.com/shakeupsharedreading

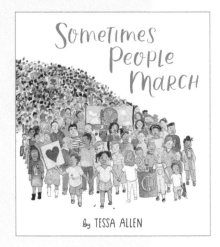

## Short Bursts of Shared Reading:
### *Sometimes People March*

Focus 1—Spotlight High-Frequency Words:
*People* and *They*

### Before Reading

**Set the Stage:** There are two high-frequency words in this book that you have to learn by heart because the letters and sounds don't match. The words are *people* and *they*. Let's write these words together. [Assist children, as needed, as they spell and write the word *people* on one piece of paper (or index card) and the word *they* on another. Children will place the words on the floor (or desk) in front of them.] During shared reading, we are going to listen for these two words.

### During Reading

### Investigate Key Pages

### My Turn

*Sometimes people march* page: When I read the word *people,* I'm going to point to the card that reads *people.*

### Our Turn

*Marching is something people do together . . .* page: Let's read this page together. When you read the word *people,* point to the word *people,* and when you read the word *they,* point to the word *they.*

### Your Turn

[Continue in the same fashion for as long as students are engaged.]

### After Reading

### Nudge Toward Independence

Look at the words: How do you spell the word *people*? How do you spell the word *they*? Now, turn the word cards over. Tell a friend how to spell each word. Ask a friend to do the same with each word.

## Focus 2–Ponder Punctuation: Make a Statement

### Before Reading

**Set the Stage:** I noticed something interesting about this book the first time we read it—Tessa Allen used only one type of ending punctuation because all of the sentences in this book are statements, or telling sentences.

### During Reading

### Investigate Key Pages

### My Turn

*Sometimes ants march* page: I see that this sentence begins with a capital and ends with a period. This sentence is a statement. It is telling me that ants march. To signal that it is a telling sentence, Tessa Allen placed a period at the end.

### Our Turn

*Sometimes bands march* page: Reread the two sentences here. What kind of sentences are they? What mark do you see at the end of each sentence?

### Your Turn

*People march for many reasons* page: What is different about the two sentences on these pages? [One is short and one is long, but they are still both statements and end with a period.]

[Continue rereading and pointing out that each statement in this book ends with a period.]

### After Reading

### Nudge Toward Independence

Why do you suppose Tessa Allen chose to write an entire book of statements? Writers add a period at the end of a sentence that tells or states something. A sentence that makes a statement is called a *declarative sentence*. When you are writing statements or telling sentences, don't forget to add a period!

---

**Innovate on Text:** The title of this book is *Sometimes People March*, and in it we learned many reasons why people march. Marching is an action. What are some other actions that people do? [Make a list with your students that might include actions like read, write, play, run, swim, and so on.] Write an action that people do. Then list a few reasons why people do that action. Use these sentence stems to get started:

Sometimes people _____. They _____ to _____.

Examples:

Sometimes people play. They play to have fun. They play to use their imagination.

Sometimes people run. They run to get exercise. They run to catch the bus.

---

**Learning Targets:**

- I ponder the author's purpose for writing this text.

- I notice interesting ways authors share information.

- I think about how the book made me feel.

## Read-Aloud Experience: Understand Important Events

**Book Title:** *Outside, Inside* (Pham, 2021)

**About the Book:** LeUyen (LAY-Win) Pham chronicles the coronavirus pandemic in a way that celebrates essential workers and showcases resilience, hope, and the human spirit. In her words, "This book is a time capsule of our moment in history, when all the world came together as one to do the right thing" (Author's Note). Take the time to read the rest of the Author's Note as it is very moving. You may choose to read part or all of it to your students. If you want to read the paragraphs that focus on LeUyen Pham's process for creating this text, read the two that begin with *In those first weeks of quarantine, I started sketching moments from each day,* and *Nearly every face painted in this book is inspired by a real person, from people in the news to family.*

To find a book like this one, look for the following:

- Nonfiction about historical events
- Accounts that are realistic and optimistic

## Comprehension Conversation

### Before Reading

#### Notice the Cover Illustration

Let me open the book so that you can see all of the details that LeUyen Pham digitally painted on this wraparound cover. Tell a friend something you see and something you're thinking. Ask them what they see and think. Where do you think this cover takes place? [In the kitchen.] What are your clues?

**Set a Purpose:** I'm excited to share *Outside, Inside* with you. There is so much to talk and learn about in this book. As we're enjoying the words and illustrations, let's ponder when this book takes place and see if we can figure out LeUyen Pham's purpose for writing it.

### During Reading

- *. . . went INSIDE* page: Do you remember or have you heard about a time when everyone had to stay inside? [Listen to students' recollections.] This book takes place in 2020 during the coronavirus pandemic. Let's continue reading to see what the author shows us about that time in history.

- *Well, almost everyone* page: Who do you see in this illustration? [Paramedics, firefighters, trash collectors, mail carriers, delivery people, grocery workers.] These folks are all essential workers. They were brave and kept working during the pandemic.

- *OUTSIDE, there were fences both real and pretend* page: There is so much to look at and think about on this page. What do you notice? What are you wondering? [Discuss students' observations and questions.]

- *INSIDE, we waited . . .* page: Let's pause again on this page. What do you notice? What are you wondering? [Discuss students' observations and questions.]

- *But on the INSIDE, we are all the same* page: Think quietly for a minute about what this page means to you.

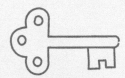
## After Reading

- How did the ending make you feel? [Happy, hopeful.] Do you think LeUyen Pham did that on purpose?

- Why do you think LeUyen Pham wrote this book? What did she want us to remember about this time in history? How would you finish this sentence: LeUyen Pham wrote *Outside, Inside* to help me understand _____.

### Extend the Experience

- Time capsule: In the Author's Note, LeUyen Pham calls this book a *time capsule* of a moment in history. Time capsules can be filled with real items or, like this book, drawings of memories. Using the *Time Capsule Reproducible Response Page* found on the companion website (resources.corwin.com/shakeupsharedreading), draw pictures of memories from your year in [insert grade level here] grade so far.

**Key Vocabulary and Kid-Friendly Definitions:**

- *lonely*: feeling sad when you are by yourself

- *pretend*: something that is not true or real; make-believe

- *unremarkable*: plain or ordinary

online resources

View the book trailer of *Outside, Inside* at resources.corwin.com/shakeupsharedreading

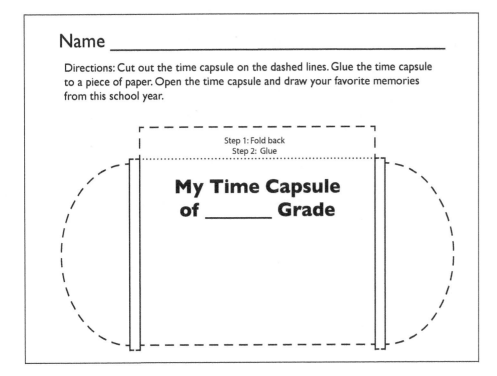

Name _____

Directions: Cut out the time capsule on the dashed lines. Glue the time capsule to a piece of paper. Open the time capsule and draw your favorite memories from this school year.

Step 1: Fold back
Step 2: Glue

**My Time Capsule of _____ Grade**

*Time Capsule Reproducible Response Page*

<table>
<tr><td colspan="2" align="center">Meet the Creator!</td></tr>
<tr><td colspan="2" align="center">Book Creator Study: LeUyen Pham</td></tr>
</table>

**Did you know?**

- She was born in Vietnam. She and her family fled Vietnam in the last days of the Vietnam War.
- She worked as a layout artist for DreamWorks Feature Animation.
- She has a cat named Sardine and a gecko name Kumquat.

**A Few of Her Books:**

- *Bear Came Along* (Morris, Illustrator, 2019)
- *The Bear Who Wasn't There* (Author, 2016)
- *Freckleface Strawberry* (Moore, Illustrator, 2007)
- *Grace Goes to Washington* (DiPucchio, Illustrator, 2019)
- *The Princess in Black* (Hale & Hale, Illustrator, 2014) [Series Book]
- *Love Is Powerful* (Brewer, Illustrator, 2020)

## Similar Titles

 ### *The All-Together Quilt* (Rockwell, 2020)

**About the Book:** Since 2008, author Lizzy Rockwell has been creating community quilts with an organization called Peace by Piece, and this book is their heartwarming story. Readers meet the members of a diverse group of intergenerational quilters as they get an insider's look into how a quilt is designed and stitched together. Backmatter includes more information about Peace by Piece and quilting.

 ### *Keeping the City Going* (Floca, 2021)

**About the Book:** In the spring of 2020, Brian Floca found himself drawing the vehicles that were still out on the quiet streets of New York City. His drawings became this book of gratitude to the essential workers who keep the city healthy and safe. They are "the people on the streets driving this and that, heading from here to there." [See the Author's Note for more details.]

## My Favorite Informational Texts and Resources

## Short Bursts of Shared Reading: *Outside, Inside*

### Focus 1—Wonder About Words: Compound Words

#### Before Reading

**Set the Stage:** Compound words are two separate words joined together. When they are put together, they make a new word. Sometimes that word has a new meaning. Other times you can figure out the meaning of the word by using the two small words. Let's listen for and clap the two parts of the compound words we find in this book.

#### During Reading

#### Investigate Key Pages

#### My Turn

*Everybody who was OUTSIDE . . .* page: The word *outside* is made from the words *out* and *side*. I'm going to put my left hand up and say *out,* my right hand up and say *side,* and clap them together to form *outside*.

#### Our Turn

*Everyone* page: Both of the words on this page are compound words. Get ready to say each separate word and clap them together.

#### Your Turn

*Well, almost everyone* page: Here's another compound word. Show me how you would clap *everyone*. [Continue in the same fashion, pausing to clap compound words. If you want to give students more practice clapping compound words, below you are additional words with the same endings as those in the book.]

Compound words ending with *side: hillside, fireside, poolside, seaside, bedside, beside*

Compound words ending with *where: elsewhere, somewhere, anywhere, nowhere*

#### After Reading

#### Nudge Toward Independence

Let's review by clapping all of the compound words we found in this book and then thinking about the meaning of the words. Do these words have new meanings, or can we figure out the meaning by using the two small words?

| something | everybody | outside |
| --- | --- | --- |
| inside | everyone | everywhere |
| birthdays | without | |

## Focus 2–Notice Writer's Craft Moves: See-Saw Pattern

**Before Reading**

**Set the Stage:** When we read this book the first time, we focused on understanding the meaning of the words. This time, I want you to ponder the way the author arranges the words to see if they form a pattern.

**During Reading**

**Investigate Key Pages**

**My Turn**

*Everybody who was OUTSIDE* . . . page: When I look at the word *outside* on this page and the word *inside* on the next, I notice some ways that LeUyen Pham made them stand out: They appear in all capital letters. The word *outside* is blue. The word *inside* is red. I wonder why she did that.

**Our Turn**

*OUTSIDE, the sky was quiet* page: Hmmm! What do you notice about the words *outside* and *inside* on this page and the next? When the same words appear in the same order, that is called a *pattern*. This pattern has a special name—it's called a *see-saw pattern* because the words repeat back and forth: *outside, inside, outside, inside.* [As you reread, continue to notice the pattern.]

**Your Turn**

*INSIDE* . . . Wait! Something changes on this gatefold page. Why do you think the author changed the pattern? Talk about that with your friend.

**After Reading**

**Nudge Toward Independence**

Noticing patterns helps you predict what might come next. I bet you are going to find a pattern in a lot of the books you are reading.

> **Innovate on Text:** Inside and outside are opposites. Do you know any other pairs of opposites? [Create a list of opposite pairs to get students started, such as happy-sad, night-day, up-down, big-small.] Think about how you could use a pair of opposite words along with a see-saw pattern to create your own book.

"Hey, Dad, you broke my concentration!

It's my turn to tell the story tonight.

May I please finish now?"

*Octopus Stew* by Eric Velasquez

# Inspire Writers!

## Sharing Our Stories

I still remember the day I read *Octopus Stew* for the first time. I had been frantically searching for books with male main characters, after realizing that I had selected many texts featuring girls for the book experiences in this professional resource. Tired of hearing me complain, my husband joined the search and, thankfully, found *Octopus Stew*. I won't give anything away about this story except to say that I've shared it far and wide. Finding mentor texts for writers is an ongoing quest, one that I take quite seriously. Why? Because I believe in the power of writing, especially for our youngest learners. Like Ramsey in *Octopus Stew*, children have stories to tell and worlds to create out of their words. Use the books in this chapter as mentors while you and your learners explore how writers do the following:

- Uncover ideas
- Tell a story
- Play with patterns
- Try out a text structure
- Collect words
- Pen a poem

When cooking up a writing stew, gather your students around and start with the main ingredient of a compelling mentor text. Next, stir in a heaping spoonful of conversation. Give writers time to simmer. Spice it up with scaffolding and support. Watch the pot carefully as stories will soon bubble up. (By the way, you can jump to page 218 for book experiences centered on *Octopus Stew*!)

istock.com/TopVectors

# Menu of Shared Reading Interactions

| Book Title | Shared Reading Focus 1 | Shared Reading Focus 2 |
|---|---|---|
| *In a Jar* (Marcero, 2020) | Ponder Punctuation: Commas in a Series | Notice Writer's Craft Moves: Speeding Up Time |
| *Ten Beautiful Things* (Griffin, 2021) | Spotlight High-Frequency Words: Number Word Sort | Reread for Fluency: Emphasize Italicized Words |
| *Sunrise Summer* (Swanson, 2020) | Reread to Boost Comprehension: Read Backmatter to Enhance Understanding | Notice Writer's Craft Moves: Comparison |
| *Octopus Stew* (Velasquez, 2019) | Wonder About Words: Onomatopoeia | Notice Writer's Craft Moves: Choose Precise Words in Dialogue |
| *A New Green Day* (Portis, 2020) | Ponder Punctuation: Quotation Marks | Reread for Fluency: Tag-Team Reading |
| *I Want to Ride the Tap Tap* (Joseph, 2020) | Match Letters to Sounds: Word Families *-ap* and *-op* | Reread to Boost Comprehension: Notice Characters' Reactions |
| *How to Find a Bird* (Ward, 2020) | Spotlight High-Frequency Words: Word Hunt | Reread to Boost Comprehension: Look at Labels |
| *13 Ways to Eat a Fly* (Heavenrich, 2021) | Match Letters to Sounds: *-ed* Ending | Notice Writer's Craft Moves: Creative Backmatter |
| *Hello, Rain* (Maclear, 2021) | Wonder About Words: Onomatopoeia | Notice Writer's Craft Moves: Using Figurative Language |
| *Over and Under the Rainforest* (Messner, 2020b) | Wonder About Words: Prepositions | Reread to Boost Comprehension: Read Backmatter to Learn Even More |
| *Write! Write! Write!* (VanDerwater, 2020) | Reread for Fluency: Reader's Theater | Notice Writer's Craft Moves: List Poems |
| *The Last Straw: Kids vs. Plastics* (Hood, 2021) | Reread for Fluency: Reader's Theater | Notice Writer's Craft Moves: Concrete or Shape Poems |

My Favorite Texts and Resources for Inspiring Writers

## Read-Aloud Experience: Write About Memories

**Book Title:** *In a Jar* **(Marcero, 2020)**

**About the Book:** Llewellyn and Evelyn collect everything imaginable. Throughout the seasons, they fill their jars with memorable moments and much more. When Evelyn tells Llewellyn she is moving away, his jar feels empty. Fortunately, the two collectors figure out a way to share their new experiences across the miles.

To find a book like this one, look for the following:

- Plots that encourage readers to gather ideas or memories
- Characters who find inspiration outdoors

### Comprehension Conversation

**Before Reading**

**Notice the Cover Illustration**

Have you ever found something and put it in a jar? [Listen to a few of your students' responses.] What do the bunnies on the cover have inside their jars? [If you are able to show the book casing found under the book jacket of the hardcover version, marvel at all of the jars.]

**Set a Purpose:** We're going to read *In a Jar* from a writer's point of view and see what we can learn from this story that might help us when we are writing. I can't wait to find out what else the bunnies put in their jars.

**During Reading**

- *When he held a jar and peered inside . . .* page: What happens when Llewellyn looks inside the jar? [He remembers what he's seen and done.] Do you think Llewellyn could write about what's inside his jar?

- *Llewellyn scooped that cherry light into his jars* page: Talk with a neighbor about what Llewellyn put inside the jar this time. What are your thoughts? Can you really put a sunset in a jar?

- *Over time, their jars filled the walls of Llewellyn's house* page: This is one of my favorite pages! I'll put this book in the classroom library so you can enjoy looking inside all of the jars. Notice what Llewellyn and Evelyn are doing. [Drawing.] I wonder if they are writing about one of the memories they are keeping inside a jar. What do you think?

- *With Evelyn gone, Llewellyn's heart felt like an empty jar* page: This page is so different from the rest. What do you notice? How does it make you feel?

- *The next day, he prepared a package* page: What are other ways that you share experiences and memories with your friends?

**Learning Targets:**

- I notice how characters collect memories.
- I think about my memories.
- I use my own memories when I'm writing.

View the author read aloud at resources.corwin.com/shakeupsharedreading

## After Reading

- At the beginning of the story, it said that Llewellyn was a collector. What did he collect? Are any of you collectors? What do you collect? Tell a friend about your collection. Ask them about theirs.

- How might collecting ideas and memories help you as a writer?

### Extend the Experience

- Draw an outline of your own unique jar. Inside the jar, draw and label ideas or memories that you might write about someday.

- Be an Observer! Dig Into Rocks: [To prepare for this extension, curate a rock collection and some informational resources about rocks.] Llewellyn and Evelyn are collectors. People collect many different things. In the Observer Center, I've placed a rock collection and some information about rocks. Here are some activities you might do as you explore the rock collection:

  o Collectors Examine: Look at the rocks with a magnifying glass. What do you notice? Draw a diagram of the rock.

  o Collectors Compare and Sort: Pick out a few rocks. Make categories on a piece of paper or whiteboard. Sort the rocks according to the categories. Talk with a friend about how the rocks are alike and what makes them different.

  o Collectors Identify: Which rock is your favorite? Why? What is its name? Search in a book or online to identify the rock.

**Key Vocabulary and Kid-Friendly Definitions:**

- *ordinary*: something you might usually do or see

- *peered*: looked closely at something

- *ventured*: bravely moved or traveled around

## Similar Titles

 ***The Night Walk* (Dorléans, 2020)**

**About the Book:** It's the middle of the night as Mama and Papa wake their two children for a night-time adventure. On their trek, the indigo darkness is punctuated by warm light gleaming from various sources. When the family makes their final climb to the top of a ridge, they are rewarded with "the light of a new day." Discuss how the small moments the kids had on their nighttime walk could turn into ideas for writing. This book would also be ideal for a science lesson on sources of light.

 ***Wonder Walkers* (Archer, 2021)**

**About the Book:** The book begins with one child asking, "Wonder walk?" and the other replying, "Sure." As they walk through fields and forests, the curious pair voice their questions about the natural world. Read this book to inspire inquiry and spark writing ideas, and then take a wonder walk with your class.

*Observer Center: Rocks*

## Short Bursts of Shared Reading: *In a Jar*

### Focus 1—Ponder Punctuation: Commas in a Series

#### Before Reading

**Set the Stage:** Today we're going to search for and learn about commas. A comma looks like a period with a tail on it. Let's study the commas in this book to see what we can find out.

#### During Reading

#### Investigate Key Pages

#### My Turn

*He collected small, ordinary things . . .* page: Here is a list of all of the items that Llewellyn collects. I notice that each phrase is followed by a comma. A comma is a signal to rest or pause. Listen to how that sounds. [Reread the page aloud.] Writers use commas to separate a list of three or more things.

#### Our Turn

*From then on, Llewellyn and Evelyn collected things together* page: On this page there is a list of natural occurrences that are hard to hold. What do you notice after each item on the list? [A comma.] Let's reread the list together using what we just learned about commas.

#### Your Turn

*Evelyn knew just what to do* page: Here is another list of things that Evelyn collected in the city. I'll read it first, and then you can echo after. Notice the comma after each of the things Evelyn collected.

#### After Reading

#### Nudge Toward Independence

What did you learn about commas? [Listen to answers to gauge students' understanding.] When writers use commas between items in a list, it is called *commas in a series*. I bet you'll start noticing commas between items in a list in the books you're reading. Remember that a comma is a signal to pause while you're reading. Next time you're writing a list, add a comma between each item to remind your readers to pause.

## Focus 2–Notice Writer's Craft Moves: Speeding Up Time

**Before Reading**

**Set the Stage:** Our goal while rereading is to pay attention to how time passes in the story. See what you can learn from Deborah Marcero that might be helpful when you're writing your own stories.

**During Reading**

**Investigate Key Pages**

**My Turn**

*Llewellyn was a collector* page: When I look at this page, I notice that the story begins in autumn, or fall. I know this because of the colorful leaves that Llewellyn is collecting.

**Our Turn**

*They collected the wonders of winter . . .* page: Which season is it now? [Reread the next two pages together. Discuss how Deborah Marcero speeds up time by including one page about each season—winter, spring, and summer.]

**Your Turn**

*And so, when the golden leaves of autumn began to fall once again* page: How much time passed during the story? [A year.] Did it feel like it took a year? Why or why not? Talk about what you learned with a friend.

**After Reading**

**Nudge Toward Independence**

Sometimes writers speed up time in the middle of their story. In this story, Deborah Marcero wrote one page about each season so that the story could start and end in the fall. She did this to move the story along, keep our interest, and include all the important parts. You might try this technique when you are writing a story.

> **Innovate on Text:** Tell, write, or draw about a favorite memory. Think back to that time. What did you see, hear, taste, touch, or smell? How does that memory make you feel?

## Read-Aloud Experience: Write About Observations

**Book Title:** *Ten Beautiful Things* (Griffin, 2021)

**About the Book:** Lily, who has encountered some kind of life-changing event, journeys with her grandmother to their new home. During their car ride to Iowa, Lily's Gram encourages her to find ten beautiful things. Though skeptical at first, Lily begins to enjoy the game and takes comfort knowing she's going to be living with her grandmother.

To find a book like this one, look for the following:

- Plots that encourage readers to gather ideas or memories
- Multigenerational stories

## Comprehension Conversation

### Before Reading

### Notice the Cover Illustration

Maribel Lechuga used a combination of digital tools and other art tools to create the landscape you see on the wraparound cover of this book. Take a moment to enjoy the illustration, and then tell someone nearby what you notice. Do you see any beautiful things on the cover?

**Set a Purpose:** You can probably infer from the title *Ten Beautiful Things* that somewhere in this book we're going to hear about ten things that are beautiful. There is also something happening in this book that is implied—that means we have to read, notice, and think to figure it out. Put on your seatbelt, and let's go for a drive!

### During Reading

- Title page: Talk with someone about what you notice and what you're thinking. Where do you suppose the girl is going?

- *Lily ran her finger across the Iowa map* page: Okay, readers. There are some big clues on this page. We now know where Lily is going and who is going with her. Why do you suppose she is going to a new home? [Discuss possible reasons a child might go to live with their grandparents.]

- *Fence posts rushed past* page: Can you infer how Lily is feeling on these pages? Why do you suppose Gram is trying to get her to look for ten beautiful things?

- *Later Gram signaled and turned the car onto a smaller road* page: What do you think the author means when she writes, "but food didn't fill up her hollow places?" Remember the word *hollow* means empty on the inside.

**Learning Targets:**

- I notice where people find ideas.
- I think about places I can find ideas.
- I use my own ideas when I'm writing.

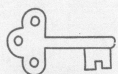
- *At a rest area Lily bounced out of the car . . .* page: Gram and Lily have found beautiful things with their eyes and ears. What sense are they using now? Do you think Lily's feelings are changing? Are there any clues on this page that help you know that?

- *"Nope. Ten, easy."* page: What has Lily learned on her car trip with Gram?

## After Reading

- Would you agree that this book is about a lot more than ten beautiful things? Why or why not? What are some ideas or feelings that you took away from this story?

- If you were going to write about one of the ten beautiful things in the story, which would it be and why?

## Extend the Experience

- Lily's Gram used the ten beautiful things game to help her focus on the world around her instead of what was making her feel sad. We can use the idea of ten beautiful things in another way. Fold a piece of paper into fourths. In each rectangle, draw and label something you find beautiful. Then, choose one of those beautiful things and write more about it.

- Be an Observer! Geography: [To prepare for this extension, collect any/all of the following: a children's atlas, assorted maps, a globe, devices to access Google Earth, and any other geography-related books or resources.] In the beginning of the book, Lily was looking at a map of Iowa to see where they were going. Maps are images of Earth's surface that show us where things are. I've collected some different kinds of maps. Pick a place you would like to visit. Find it on a map, globe, or Google Earth. Use your finger to trace the path from where you live to that location. Is the place close or far away? What mode of transportation could you use to get there? What are some beautiful things you might find along the way?

## Similar Titles

 ***In-Between Things* (Tey, 2018)**

About the Book: In her debut picture book, Priscilla Tey uses rhyming text and engaging illustrations to explore things in the middle, both real and imagined. This unique book could lead to conversations and writing about in-between objects, animals, and much more.

 ***Ten Ways to Hear Snow* (Camper, 2020)**

About the Book: It's the morning after a blizzard and also "grape leaf day." Lina is anxious to get to her grandma's place to check on her, help her cook, and tell her about the snow. Aware that Sitti is losing her eyesight, Lina notices different sounds that snow makes as she walks through her neighborhood.

### Key Vocabulary and Kid-Friendly Definitions:

- *complaints*: what you say about something you're not happy with

- *hollow*: empty on the inside

- *gleamed*: shined or glowed

View the book trailer of *Ten Beautiful Things* at resources.corwin.com/shakeupsharedreading

## Short Bursts of Shared Reading: *Ten Beautiful Things*

### Focus 1–Spotlight High-Frequency Words: Number Word Sort

#### Before Reading

**Set the Stage:** Number words appear in many books we read. Today we're going to find the number words and sort them to see if their letters do or do not match the sounds. [Show children how to set up their whiteboards or a piece of paper like the comparison chart.]

#### During Reading

#### Investigate Key Pages

#### My Turn

*Lily gasped* page: As I'm rereading, I see the number word *one*. That is a tricky word because it's spelled o-n-e but it sounds like this /w/-/un/. The letters and sounds don't match, so I'm going to write that on the *don't match* side of my comparison chart.

#### Our Turn

*Lily felt the complaints starting in her belly again* . . . page: Let's reread this page together. Do you see a number word? You're right! Here's the number word *two*. This word is also a tricky word because it's spelled t-w-o but it sounds like this /t/-/ew/. The letters and sounds don't match, so let's all write *two* on the *don't match* side of my comparison chart.

#### Your Turn

Let's continue rereading while searching for number words to add to your comparison chart. [Note: The number word *five* does not appear in the text.]

#### After Reading

#### Nudge Toward Independence

Some of the number words have a predictable letter-sound match, so you can use your phonics skills to decode and spell those words. In the other number words, the letters and sounds don't exactly match, so you have to use the sounds that do match and work to remember what they look like when you're reading and how they are spelled when you're writing.

| Letter-Sounds Match | | Letter-Sounds Don't Match | |
|---|---|---|---|
| three | 3 | one | 1 |
| five | 5 | two | 2 |
| six | 6 | four | 4 |
| seven | 7 | eight | 8 |
| nine | 9 | | |
| ten | 10 | | |

*Number Word Sort Comparison Chart*

## Focus 2–Reread for Fluency: Emphasize Italicized Words

### Before Reading

**Set the Stage:** One way that writers show a word is important is by using italics. When writers put words in italics, the words look like they are leaning to one side. When readers see italics, that means we need to read the word with more emphasis.

### During Reading

#### Investigate Key Pages

#### My Turn

*"We're not looking for pretty"* page: When I'm reading along and I notice italics like I see in the word *beautiful*, I know that I need to read that word with more emphasis because Gram is telling Lily something doesn't have to be pretty to be beautiful. Listen to how that sounds as I reread this page.

#### Our Turn

*When they'd been almost there for a long time* page: Before we reread this page, zoom in to see if you can spot the word in italics. Let's reread together and put more emphasis on the word *almost*. Why do you think the author chose to put the word *almost* in italics?

#### Your Turn

*"We're ten," Gram said* page: There are two words printed in italics on this page. I'll reread each sentence as if there weren't italics, and you echo me reading the words with extra oomph.

### After Reading

#### Nudge Toward Independence

When you see italics in a book you're reading, think about the meaning of the word in the sentence and read it with a little extra oomph. Since it's a challenge to write in italics, you can simply underline words you want readers to emphasize in the pieces you're writing.

> **Innovate on Text:** In this book, Lily and Gram notice ten beautiful things on their drive. Think about another list of things you could make by filling in the blank: Ten _____ Things. [Collaborate with your students to brainstorm a list of possible ideas. Here's a few to get you started: Ten School Things, Ten Cold Things, Ten Hot Things, Ten Fun Things, Ten Furry Things, Ten Green Things, and so on.]

## Learning Targets:

- I notice how authors add interesting details to a story.

- I use what I've learned to write my own real-life stories.

### Read-Aloud Experience: Tell a Real-Life Story

**Book Title:** *Sunrise Summer* (Swanson, 2020)

**About the Book:** Imagine traveling with your family to a remote part of Alaska every summer to fish for salmon. That is exactly what illustrator Robbi Behr has done since she was a little girl. Now, Robbi, her husband Matthew (author), and their family spend their summers in Coffee Point, Alaska, running a commercial salmon fishing business. *Sunrise Summer* is told from their daughter's point of view about her first experience on the fishing crew. The book includes four pages of backmatter that take you behind the scenes.

To find a book like this one, look for the following:

- Narrative tales told in first person
- Real-life stories

### Comprehension Conversation

#### Before Reading

#### Notice the Cover Illustration

- What are the people on the cover doing? Is this something you would like to do?

- The illustrator Robbi Behr used pen, ink, and gouache to create the characters. Gouache (GWASH) is a paint that is not see-through, or transparent, like watercolor paint. Then, she made the backgrounds using digital collages. I think her illustrations are beautiful. We'll see if you agree. [If you have the hardcover version, notice that the paper book jacket and hardcover book casing are different.]

**Set a Purpose:** We're going to read *Sunrise Summer* like a writer to notice the details the author and illustrator added to help us enjoy the story.

#### During Reading

- *It's summer again, my favorite time of the year* page: Who do you suppose is telling us the story? What time of year is the story happening?

- *Our trip takes two days and four flights and four thousand miles* page: When writing a story, it is helpful if readers know the *when* and *where* or the setting of the story. Where is the family going? [To help your students picture where this story is set, locate and display Alaska on a map or globe.]

- *Last summer, I picked tundra berries and made forts . . .* page: Now we know what she is going to be doing this summer. How would you feel about joining the fishing crew?

- *Until they come, we keep busy* page: Look at the girl's face. Can you infer how she is feeling?

- *We keep an eye out for grizzlies . . .* page: Yikes! Talk with a friend about what's happening on this page.

- *They're heavy and they're slimy . . .* page: What are some differences you notice between Alaska and where you live?

## After Reading

- What parts of the story stuck with you? What details do you remember?

- Do you think you and your family would enjoy going to Coffee Point, Alaska, for the summer? Why or why not?

## Extend the Experience

- This family travels to Alaska for the summer. What do you enjoy doing during the summer? Draw and label a picture or record a video to tell us about it.

- If you were going to write a story about a memorable event, what would your event be?

## Similar Titles

 **The Camping Trip (Mann, 2020)**

**About the Book:** Ernestine got a new sleeping bag, stuffed her duffle bag full of supplies, and made some trail mix with her dad. She's ready for her first camping trip with Aunt Jackie and cousin Samantha. Once at the campsite, Ernestine quickly realizes that camping is a bit more challenging than expected. In the end, she discovers the hidden joys of spending time outdoors. Like *Sunrise Summer*, the author compares camping to city life. This first-person narrative is told in a graphic format, with speech bubbles sprinkled throughout.

 **Fatima's Great Outdoors (Tariq, 2021)**

**About the Book:** The Khazi family is going on their first camping trip. After a long, unpleasant week at school, Fatima is ready. At the campsite, she learns how to pitch a tent and build a fire. The feeling of accomplishment and pride in her newfound "superpowers" carries with her when she returns to school. This book is based on Ambreen Tariq's childhood experiences growing up as an Indian immigrant and her family camping trips. Tariq founded an online community called Brown People Camping.

### Key Vocabulary and Kid-Friendly Definitions:

- *crew*: a group of people who work together

- *fetch*: to go get something and bring it back

- *mending*: fixing

View the author talking about *Fatima's Great Outdoors* at resources.corwin.com/shakeupsharedreading

## Short Bursts of Shared Reading: *Sunrise Summer*

### Before Reading

**Set the Stage:** This story is based on true events. While reading, we could picture what it would be like to spend the summer fishing in Alaska. To give us the behind-the-scenes story, the author and illustrator added backmatter. Let's read the backmatter together and ponder how we might add a few interesting after-story details to enhance our books.

### During Reading

#### Investigate Key Pages

#### My Turn

*Hello, I'm Robbi* page: [Read the first three paragraphs on this page.] I find it so interesting to hear that Robbi and her family have been going to Coffee Point since she was a little girl. Knowing that *Sunrise Summer* is based on true events makes me like it even more. In this section, we found out a little more about the characters' real lives. That's something you could share with readers in your backmatter.

#### Our Turn

*Our part of Alaska is very remote* page: [Read the next three paragraphs to learn more about Coffee Point, Alaska.] What was surprising to you about Coffee Point? Here we learned about the setting of the story. You might add a detailed picture of the setting in the backmatter of your book.

#### Your Turn

[To provide access for all of your learners to the rest of the information in the backmatter, consider audio or video recording yourself reading it aloud. Then, place the recording in an area where students can listen and learn more.] I'm going to put this book in the classroom library so you can learn more about the story behind *Sunrise Summer* on your own or with friends.

### After Reading

#### Nudge Toward Independence

Authors include backmatter in a fiction book to add background information to the story by telling more about the ideas, characters, or setting. Taking the time to read or listen to the backmatter deepens your understanding of the story. Think back to what you learned from reading the backmatter in this book. Plan how you might add some background information at the end of one of your stories. We can't wait to see what you add!

## Focus 2–Notice Writer's Craft Moves: Comparison

**Before Reading**

**Set the Stage:** Authors use comparisons to help you see how things are the same and different. Comparisons can show how things are related or help you better understand something that might be unfamiliar. We can learn more about comparisons by rereading a few pages of *Sunrise Summer*.

**During Reading**

**Investigate Key Pages**

**My Turn**

*Some families pack swimsuits and sandals when they go on vacation* page: To help us understand the difference between a summer vacation somewhere warm and their summer in Alaska, Matthew, the author, compares what someone might pack for a beach vacation to what they pack to go to Alaska.

**Our Turn**

*Some beaches have boardwalks and lifeguards and smooth white sand* page: What is the author comparing on this page? Which beach would you rather visit?

**Your Turn**

*While my brothers chase lemmings on the tundra* page: Here is another comparison page. What is the author comparing this time? [The differences between what the girl and her brothers are doing.] Talk to a neighbor. Which activities would you prefer?

**After Reading**

**Nudge Toward Independence**

How did the comparison in this book help you better understand what it is like to fish in Alaska? What are some ways you might use comparison when you are trying to explain something in your writing? Remember, you can compare things using either pictures or words. If you notice other authors who use comparison, bring their books with you when it's time to share. If you try comparison as a writer, let us know so we can learn from you.

**Innovate on Text:** In *Sunrise Summer*, the girl tells about her first time on the fishing crew. Do you remember the first time you learned to do something? Write or draw about that special time.

### Read-Aloud Experience: Tell a Make-Believe Story

**Book Title:** *Octopus Stew* (Velasquez, 2019)

**About the Book:** Ramsey's painting of Super Octo inspires his grandma to make *pulpo guisado*, or octopus stew. While at the store buying the ingredients, Ramsey receives a warning about octopuses on his phone. Ignoring Ramsey and his phone alert, Grandma prepares the octopus and an adventure begins. In a surprising mid-book twist, readers discover Ramsey is telling this tall tale to his family, which leads to a classroom conversation about the connection between storytelling and writing. Velasquez sprinkles in the nonstandard Spanish his family spoke and includes a pronunciation key and definitions for those who do not speak Spanish fluently.

To find a book like this one, look for the following:

- Narrative tales told in first person
- People sharing make-believe stories

### Comprehension Conversation

#### Before Reading

#### Notice the Cover Illustration

Do you see the looks on the characters' faces? What do you suppose is happening? [Listen to students' ideas and predictions.] Notice how Eric Velasquez's oil-paint illustrations are so realistic they look almost like photographs. What do you notice in the background? [The shadows of octopus tentacles.]

**Set a Purpose:** As we enjoy the book *Octopus Stew* together, pay attention to how this story is told. See what you learn from Eric Velasquez that you can use when you're writing your stories.

#### During Reading

- *At the store I saw lots of cool-looking fish* page: Who is telling this story? [The boy.] How can you tell? Remember, when a writer uses the words *I* or *my*, they are writing from a first-person point of view. Do you agree with the boy's opinion about the octopus? Do you have any thoughts or predictions?

- *I decided to do some web surfing when a warning popped up . . .* page: Trade ideas with your neighbor. What do you guess the phone warning said?

- *Then Grandma came to sit with me while I did my homework* page: Whoa! What do you predict is going on? Let's turn the page and find out!

- *Dad interrupted* page: Wait a minute! This isn't part of the story. Let's talk about what we learn on this page.

#### Learning Targets:

- I notice how authors add suspense to the story.
- I use what I've learned to write my own make-believe stories.

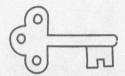

## After Reading

- Share your opinion about the ending.

- If you were telling this story to your family, how would it end?

### Extend the Experience

- Sometimes writers give us hints about what might happen later in a story. This is called *foreshadowing*. Foreshadowing adds suspense to the story and makes you want to turn the page to find out what will happen next. [Point out the tentacle shadows on the cover, the phone warning, and the look on the characters' faces when they hear noises coming from the kitchen.] Have you noticed foreshadowing in books you've read or shows you've watched?

- The boy told an imaginary story to his family. Think of a make-believe story with a beginning, middle, and end. Tell or write the story.

## Similar Titles

 ***The Paper Kingdom* (Ku Rhee, 2020)**

**About the Book:** Daniel is so sleepy when he has to go with his parents to their nighttime job. To keep Daniel entertained as they clean an office building, Mama and Papa weave a magical tale of the Paper Kingdom. In the Author's Note, you learn that this book was inspired by Helena Ku Rhee's hardworking parents.

 ***A Pizza With Everything on It* (Scheele, 2021)**

**About the Book:** The son of a pizza shop owner requests a pizza with everything on it. When his dad obliges, they go on an imaginary pizza adventure complete with pizza black holes and a swirling pizza vortex. This story is sure to fire up readers' imaginations!

**Key Vocabulary and Kid-Friendly Definitions:**

- *feared*: felt like there is expected danger

- *hollered*: yelled or shouted

- *warning*: a signal or sign that there could be trouble or danger

## Short Bursts of Shared Reading: *Octopus Stew*

### Focus 1–Wonder About Words: Onomatopoeia

#### Before Reading

**Set the Stage:** When Ramsey and Grandma were drawn to the kitchen, it was the onomatopoeia, or sound words, that alerted them that something was going on. Adding onomatopoeia to your story helps readers imagine the sounds.

#### During Reading

#### Investigate Key Pages

#### My Turn

*Then Grandma came to sit with me . . .* page: I notice that the onomatopoeia on this page follow a repetitive pattern. Do you hear it? Why do you suppose the author wrote the words that way? Perhaps you could try the same technique in your writing.

#### Our Turn

*The sounds got louder* page: Let's reread this page together and listen to the onomatopoeia. What do you notice? [All the of words begin with the letter B, and they're written in a repeating pattern.]

#### Your Turn

Two-page spread with the octopus coming out of the pot: This time the sound words are placed all over the page. They are part of the illustration. It's your turn to read them. How do the placement and size of the words impact their meaning and the way that you read them aloud?

#### After Reading

#### Nudge Toward Independence

Once you're on the lookout for onomatopoeia, I bet you'll notice them in a lot of the books you're reading. [Invite students to record their favorite onomatopoetic words on a class chart or in their notebooks.] When you're adding onomatopoeia to your writing, try the techniques we learned from Eric Velasquez—repeating the words and/or adding them to your illustrations.

## Focus 2–Notice Writer's Craft Moves:
## Choose Precise Words in Dialogue

### Before Reading

**Set the Stage:** We noticed that Ramsey was telling the story. To make the characters come alive, Eric Velasquez added dialogue—he made his characters talk. This is something you can do in your stories. I want to show you different ways you can choose a precise word to mark your dialogue so readers will know how to read it.

### During Reading

### Investigate Key Pages

### My Turn

*When Grandma saw my painting . . .* page: On this page, instead of using the words *Grandma said,* the author wrote *Grandma snapped at me.* When someone snaps at you, that means they say the words like they are upset. Listen to me read Grandma's words.

### Our Turn

*The octopus got so big it blew the lid off the pot* page: Let's look at how the talking is marked on this page. [Discuss the use of the phrases *I warned* and *Grandma hollered* and how they are more descriptive than using the word *said.* Invite students to reread the dialogue with those words in mind.]

### Your Turn

*I put on my Super Ram cape and marched into the kitchen* page: On this page, Ramsey *yelled.* Can you think of other words you could us in place of *yelled*? [Invite students to brainstorm a list of possibilities. If needed, provide access and guidance in using a thesaurus. Some options include *shouted, called out, screamed,* or *shrieked.*]

### After Reading

### Nudge Toward Independence

When you add talking to make your characters come to life, think about the words you use to tell your reader how to read the characters' words.

> **Innovate on Text:** In the beginning of the story, the boy was painting Super Octo. Invent your own superhero. Divide a paper into fourths. Write a short comic about your superhero.

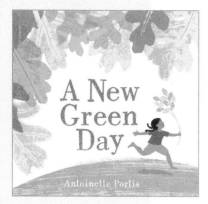

## Read-Aloud Experience: Riddles

**Book Title:** *A New Green Day* (Portis, 2020)

**About the Book:** Poetic riddles invite readers to guess the creatures that inhabit and events that take place in our natural world.

To find a book like this one, look for the following:

- Structures that children can borrow for their own writing
- Books about the natural world

### Comprehension Conversation

**Before Reading**

**Notice the Cover Illustration**

Antoinette Portis created the illustrations for this book using a variety of art tools. She made the leaves look realistic by using leaf prints and the letters with hand stamps. That means instead of typing the letters, she pressed each letter stamp into ink and stamped it onto the page. I'm guessing that took a lot of time and patience. What do you think?

**Set a Purpose:** *A New Green Day* is a unique book. As we read, see if you can figure out the structure or pattern. Get ready to do some guessing!

### During Reading

- *"Morning lays me on your pillow"* page: Before I turn to the next page, use the clues on this page to try to guess who or what is talking. Put your head together with a friend to figure it out.

- *"I'm a map of my own green home"* page: Are you noticing a pattern in this book? Can you guess what is talking to you on this page?

- *"I'm a mountain that moves"* page: Hmmm! Any possible answers to this riddle? Trade ideas with someone nearby.

- *"I race up the hill while lying at your feet"* page: What could be talking to you now? What would wave at you when you wave at it?

### After Reading

- Share your opinion about the pattern of this text. Did the riddle-like structure keep you interested?

- Why do you suppose the author wrote this book? What did you learn from reading it?

**Learning Targets:**

- I notice patterns or structures in a text.
- I borrow structures to create my own texts.

## Extend the Experience

- Write your own nature riddle from the point of view of the creature or natural event. Use the word *I* in your clues. Write three clues on the front of the page. Draw your answer on the back. See if your readers can guess. See *Riddle Reproducible Response Page* found on the companion website (resources.corwin.com/shakeupsharedreading).

- If you were going to give this book a different title, what would it be and why?

**Key Vocabulary and Kid-Friendly Definitions:**

- *chorus:* when a group of people sing together or animals make noise together

- *rumble:* a long, low sound

- *thrum:* to play a tune by strumming or plucking a string instrument

· · · · · · · · · · · · · · · · · · · · · · · · · · · · · · · · · · · · · · · · · · · · · ·

## Similar Titles

 **Can an Aardvark Bark? (Stewart, 2017)**

**About the Book:** In this question-answer structured text, readers learn the different ways that animals use sounds to communicate. Be ready, because you'll be hearing grunts, growls, bellows, barks, and squeals long after you close this book.

 **Lion of the Sky: Haiku for All Seasons (Salas, 2019)**

**About the Book:** Readers guess their way through season-themed poems that Laura Purdie Salas calls "riddle-ku." In the backmatter, she provides a brief explanation of how she invented "riddle-ku" and offers an invitation to students to try writing their own.

---

Name _____

### My Riddle

1. _____

_____

2. _____

_____

3. _____

_____

What is it?

It is a . . .

⇨

*Riddle Reproducible Response Page*

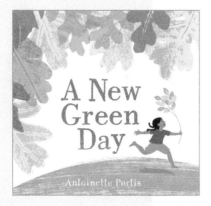

## Short Bursts of Shared Reading: *A New Green Day*

### Focus 1–Ponder Punctuation: Quotation Marks

#### Before Reading

**Set the Stage:** Antoinette Portis created this riddle book in a unique way. She wrote the clues as if the creature or natural event was talking. To show us we are reading the exact words of the speaker, she uses quotation marks. Quotation marks always come in pairs and are placed before and after the speaker's words.

#### During Reading

#### Investigate Key Pages

#### My Turn

*"I scribble on the walk in glistening ink"* page: I see the quotation marks before and after the snail's words. This helps me know that the snail is talking (even though snails don't really talk). When authors make animals or other nonhuman things talk, it is called *personification*.

#### Our Turn

*"When I move, I measure"* page: Aim a finger at the beginning quotation mark. Aim your other finger at the ending quotation mark. Tell a friend who is talking on this page. [Inchworm.]

#### Your Turn

*"I slash the sky with my bright fangs"* page: What are the marks at the beginning and end of this page called? What is their purpose?

#### After Reading

#### Nudge Toward Independence

When a character in a book is talking, authors use quotation marks. Quotation marks surround the exact words of the speaker. When you're writing and a character is talking, see if you can add quotation marks before and after the words they say.

## Focus 2–Reread for Fluency: Tag-Team Reading

### Before Reading

**Set the Stage:** Let's read the book tag-team style. I'll read the words in quotation marks, and you read who is saying them. Imagine the creature or natural event who is talking. Read their name in a voice that you think sounds like theirs.

### During Reading

### Investigate Key Pages

### My Turn

*"Morning lays me on your pillow"* page: Let me demonstrate how tag-team reading works. I'll read the words in quotation marks on this page. Now it's your turn. You read the words that tell who is talking on the next page.

### Our Turn

We'll continue to take turns—my turn, your turn.

### Your Turn

[Continue tag-team reading as long as time and interest permit. You may not be able to complete the entire book.]

### After Reading

### Nudge Toward Independence

Reading in a tag-team style—where you alternate by each person reading a page—is fun to do with a friend, family member, or caregiver. It's a smart way to practice reading smoothly and with expression. You also can reread the pieces you've written in a tag-team style. When you read your own writing aloud, you'll often notice words and ideas that you want to fix or change.

**Innovate on Text:** There were four animals in this book. A snail, an inchworm, a tadpole, and a cricket. Create one of these creatures out of materials from around our classroom. See if your friends can guess which one you built.

## Read-Aloud Experience: Days of the Week Pattern

**Book Title:** *I Want to Ride the Tap Tap* (Joseph, 2020)

**About the Book:** Monday through Friday (Lendi through Vandredi in Haitian Creole), Claude accompanies his dad to the tap tap stop. Claude wishes he could ride along with his dad, but he has to go to school. Finally, on Sunday (Dimanch), Claude's parents take him to the beachfront, where they meet up with all of the people that they met at the tap tap stop during the week. With Haitian Creole sprinkled throughout, non-Creole-speaking readers will have to infer the meaning of the words or consult the glossary in the back of the book.

To find a book like this one, look for the following:

- Structures that children can borrow for their own writing
- Stories about vehicles

### Comprehension Conversation

#### Before Reading

#### Notice the Cover Illustration

As you look at this colorful cover illustration, notice the setting. This story takes place in Haiti. [Locate Haiti on a map or globe.] In Haiti, they have vehicles called tap taps. A tap tap is kind of like an Uber or Lyft but can be big like a school bus. When you want to get off at your stop, you tap the window. That's why it's called a tap tap.

**Set a Purpose:** From the title, you can already infer that someone in the story wants to ride the tap tap. As we read to figure out who wants to ride and why, pay attention to any patterns you notice in the story. Noticing patterns can help us predict what might happen next.

#### During Reading

- *On Madi, the tap tap rolled down the mountain* page: Let's see. The first page happened on Monday, and this page happens on Tuesday. Are you noticing a pattern? Can you predict what day it will be on the next page?

- *On Vandredi, a man banged on a steel drum* page: You were right about the days of the week pattern. Are you noticing any other patterns? [Each day, Claude meets someone new at the tap tap stop.] Do you remember who Claude met? [Mango seller, fisher, hat weaver, painter.] Tomorrow is Saturday. Any predictions? Share with a neighbor.

- *On Samdi, Claude woke up early* page: How does Claude feel on this page? What clues besides his face help you know his mood?

## Learning Targets:

- I notice patterns or structures in a text.
- I borrow structures to create my own texts.

- *The tap tap clanked to a halt* page: Finally! Claude gets to ride the tap tap. Where do you suppose he and his family are going? Whisper to a friend.

- *Claude hurried off the tap tap and ran to the beachfront* page: Look! The mango lady is at the beachfront. Think about the patterns in this story. Who else might Claude meet at the beach?

## After Reading

- Did we find the answers to our questions? *Who* wanted to ride the tap tap? [Claude.] *Why* did he want to ride it? [Invite children to share their thinking.]

- When authors use patterns like the ones in this story, some people call it a *predictable book*. Would you agree or disagree with that term? Did the pattern make this book more predictable? Why or why not?

## Extend the Experience

- When Claude finally gets to the beachfront, he is able to eat a mango, reel in a fish, weave a straw hat, paint with an artist, and dance to the beat of the drum. Which of those activities would you want to do? Work with a partner. Act out your preferred activity. See if your partner can guess which one it is. Then switch.

- Which is your favorite day of the week? Why? Write, draw, or record a video to explain your reasons.

## Similar Titles

 ***Bunnies on the Bus*** (Ardagh, 2019) [Repetitive refrain]

**About the Book:** Kids will join in on the repetitive refrain "Bunnies on the bus! Bunnies on the bus! No wonder there's a fuss about bunnies on the bus!" as you read this detail-filled rollicking romp on the Sunny Town bus. After the read-aloud experience, go back to study the ongoing storylines in the illustrations. Notice the escaped masked bandits, a bear preparing for a date, and so much more!

 ***The Old Truck*** (Pumphrey, 2020) [Circular pattern]

**About the Book:** In this story with a circular text structure, a farm family owns a red truck. As the truck ages, so does the daughter. After many years, the daughter becomes the farmer, rebuilds the truck, and gets it running again. In the end, she and her young daughter use the truck to help with their farm chores.

### Key Vocabulary and Kid-Friendly Definitions:

- *dashed*: moved fast or raced

- *halt*: stop

- *pleaded*: asked or begged for something

View the authors reading *The Old Truck* at resources.corwin.com/shakeupsharedreading

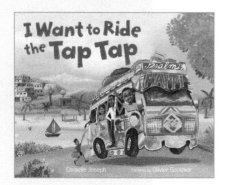

## Short Bursts of Shared Reading:
### *I Want to Ride the Tap Tap*

#### Focus 1—Match Letters to Sounds:
#### Word Families -*ap* and -*op*

### Before Reading

**Set the Stage:** Word detectives, get ready to tune your ears in to the end of words by looking for rhyming patterns or word families. If you can read and spell one word in the word family, it will help you read and spell all of the other words with the same pattern.

### During Reading

#### Investigate Key Pages

#### My Turn

*On Lendi morning, Claude and Manman walked Papa to the tap tap stop* page: I notice that the words *tap* and *stop* both end with the letter p, but they have a different middle vowel sound. The words *tap* and *stop* are in different word families. I'm going to write them on a word family chart so that you can see the spelling pattern at the end of the word. Say the words *tap* and *stop*. Listen to the ending sounds.

#### Our Turn

Can you think of another word that rhymes with *tap*? Can you think of another word that rhymes with *stop*?

#### Your Turn

[Divide the class into two groups, one for the -*ap* word family and one for the -*op* word family. Invite students in each group to work with a partner or on their own to brainstorm and write down as many words as they can think of that have the same spelling pattern. Students may jot words on a whiteboard, Google Jamboard, or piece of paper. Share and add the words to your class word family chart. Chant the words together to listen for the ending sounds.]

| Word Family Chart | |
|---|---|
| -*ap* Family | -*op* Family |
| tap | stop |

### After Reading

#### Nudge Toward Independence

Using the rhyming patterns in words or word families to help you decode and spell words is a smart strategy. If you would like a small copy of the word family chart we made to keep in your notebook, let me know.

## Focus 2–Reread to Boost Comprehension:
## Notice Characters' Reactions

### Before Reading

**Set the Stage:** Characters react to events and challenges differently. When we notice how the character responds to situations, we learn more about that character. How did Claude respond to disappointment? Let's reread to find out.

### During Reading

**Investigate Key Pages**

**My Turn**

*On Lendi morning, Claude and Manman walked Papa to the tap tap stop* page: When Claude couldn't go to the market, he reacted by dreaming of mangoes. He thought about how delicious they would taste. Dreaming about mangoes probably helped him feel a bit less disappointed. I'm going to pause and dream about mangoes. I'll imagine how they smell and taste.

**Our Turn**

*On Madi, the tap tap rolled down the mountain* page: Notice Claude's reaction after he found out he couldn't go fishing. What did he do? [He imagined he was fishing.] Stand up and show me what he looked like when he was pretending to fish. Do you think acting like he was fishing changed his mood?

**Your Turn**

*On Vandredi, a man banged on a steel drum* page: Tell a friend about Claude's reaction. How do you suppose it made him feel? Now, stand up and act out his reaction. Do you feel better after banging on the drums?

### After Reading

**Nudge Toward Independence**

Putting yourselves in the character's shoes by drawing or acting out what they are doing may be helpful when understanding characters' reactions. You can try this out while you're reading. If you choose to act out the characters' reactions, you'll want to make sure that you are doing it in a way that won't disturb the learning of others. As a writer, think about how your character might react to other characters or events. You can show readers a character's reaction by adding details to your pictures like the illustrator did in this book.

**Innovate on Text:** [Make blank books that have a cover and seven pages, one for each day of the week.] If you are interested in writing your own days-of-the-week story, I've made these blank books for you. I've also collected some other books with a days-of-the-week pattern to use as mentor texts:

*Cookie's Week* (Ward, 1988)

*Perfect Square* (Hall, 2011)

*Pigs to the Rescue* (Himmelman, 2010)

*Zero Local: Next Stop Kindness* (Murrow & Murrow, 2020) [Wordless]

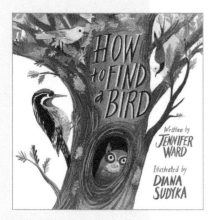

## Read-Aloud Experience: Explain How To

**Book Title:** *How to Find a Bird* (Ward, 2020)

**About the Book:** A boy and girl are out bird watching. Walk along with them and discover the secrets to finding these feathered friends. Bird species are labeled throughout the book. Backmatter includes resources and ideas for bird watching and identification.

To find a book like this one, look for the following:

- Innovative procedural text structures
- Structures and ideas children can borrow for their own writing

## Comprehension Conversation

### Before Reading

#### Notice the Cover Illustration

Can you see the variety of birds on this wraparound cover? What different colors do you see in their feathers? Noticing the colors of a bird's feathers is one way to identify birds. Which other body parts might help you identify a bird? Diana Sudyka's realistic paintings will help us learn about a lot of different kinds of birds.

**Set a Purpose:** Birds are such interesting creatures, and no matter where you live, you can usually spot them around. In *How to Find a Bird*, Jennifer Ward is going to give us some tips about bird watching. Read with your writer's eye, and notice how she shares these tips. As we read, I'll write down the tips so we can remember them and use them when we're looking for birds.

### During Reading

- *To find a bird, first you'll want to blend in* page: We've already learned two ways to find a bird. What should you do if you want to find a bird? [Jot *blend in* and *move slowly* on a chart, whiteboard, or electronic document.]

- *Don't just look up to find a bird* page: What other tips can we add to our list? [Jot *be quiet* and *look up and down* on a chart, whiteboard, or electronic document.]

- *So don't just look up to find a bird* page: We've learned about looking up and down. Now we see there is one more place to look. Where is it? [*Look straight ahead.*]

- *And if you feed them, they will come* page: I didn't think about this way to find birds! Let's add it to our list. Have you ever seen birds at a bird feeder?

### After Reading

- Do you feel like you'll be better at finding birds after reading this book?

- Let's reread everything on the list that we made from the book. Is there anything else we should add to the list?

**Learning Targets:**

- I notice how-to structures in texts.

- I borrow how-to structures to create my own texts.

### Extend the Experience

- Pick something that you know how to do. Write a text that tells us the steps or tips for doing that activity.
- Compare the bird songs found on the two-page spread near the end of the book to the real bird songs website found on the Learning Target Chart (resources.corwin.com/shakeupsharedreading). Discuss why the author chose the words and onomatopoeia found on this page to describe the bird songs.

**Key Vocabulary and Kid-Friendly Definitions:**

- *clever*: smart; a good problem solver
- *seeking*: looking for or trying to find something
- *stealthy*: sneaky, quiet

### Similar Titles

 ***How to Make a Bird*** **(McKinlay, 2021)**

**About the Book:** In a teetering structure at the edge of the sea, a little girl uses bones, feathers, and found objects to create a bird. Once complete, she magically sets it free. This is a whimsical twist on how-to writing.

 ***How to Solve a Problem: The Rise (and Falls) of a Rock-Climbing Champion*** **(Shiraishi, 2020)**

**About the Book:** Teenage rock climbing phenom Ashima Shiraishi approaches every boulder she climbs as a problem to be solved. She learns from each fall and uses the knowledge she's gained to plan and execute each small move needed to make it to the top. This inspirational book is a social-emotional learning lesson in itself. Be sure to check out a video clip of Ashima climbing—she's amazing!

*How to Find a Bird List*

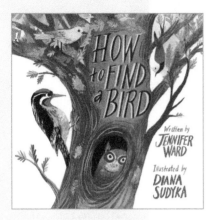

## Short Bursts of Shared Reading: *How to Find a Bird*

### Focus 1–Spotlight High-Frequency Words: Word Hunt

#### Before Reading

**Set the Stage:** When you can quickly read and write high-frequency words, or those words that you read and spell a lot, it saves room in your brain to sound out or spell more challenging words. We're going to review some of the high-frequency words you already know by finding them in the book *How to Find a Bird*.

#### During Reading

#### Investigate Key Pages

#### My Turn

[Display the following high-frequency words: *down, find, have, look, some, your, when, where*. Adjust the words based on your students' needs. This activity is designed to reinforce known words through repeated exposure, not to introduce or teach new words.]

#### Our Turn

Choose a high-frequency word from this list. Write it on the top of your whiteboard. Slide through the sounds and say the word to yourself. Today as we reread this book, we are going to hunt for high-frequency words. When you see and hear the word that's at the top of your whiteboard in the text, write it again somewhere else on your whiteboard.

#### Your Turn

How many times did you write the word? What does this tell you about high-frequency words?

#### After Reading

#### Nudge Toward Independence

Hunting for high-frequency words is something you can do on your own or with a friend. It is one way to review and practice these important words so you can start using them in your own writing.

## Focus 2—Reread to Boost Comprehension: Looking at Labels

### Before Reading

**Set the Stage:** Labels help readers identify the object or creature that is pictured on the page. Reading the labels helps you understand more about both the images and add to the meaning of the text. Writers use labels in many different ways. Let's check out how the creators use labels in *How to Find a Bird.*

### During Reading

### Investigate Key Pages

### My Turn

*Quiet is good too* page. I can learn from the label under this bird that it is a Tundra Swan. I don't know much about Tundra Swans. Now that I read the label and know its name, I can research to find out more.

### Our Turn

*Of course you can always look up to find a bird too!* page: Wow! There are a lot of labels on this page. Do you see any birds you recognize? As we're reading the labels together, notice how some of the birds' names match their appearance. [Point out the Scissor-tailed Flycatcher and Goldfinch.]

### Your Turn

*And if you feed them, they will come* page: You might have seen some of the birds on this page in your neighborhood. Do you recognize any of them? Ask your neighbor if they do. Then, we'll read the labels.

### After Reading

### Nudge Toward Independence

How did the labels in this book help you as a reader? When you are writing a non-fiction book, what are some different places where you could add labels? [Discuss the possibility of labeling individual animals or objects or parts of an animal or object.]

**Innovate on Text:** You learned a lot of different ways to find a bird. Make a poster or Google Slide with the title *How to Find a Bird* to show your friends in the building one way they might try if they are looking for birds.

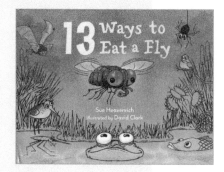

## Read-Aloud Experience: Share Facts in Creative Ways

**Book Title:** *13 Ways to Eat a Fly* (Heavenrich, 2021)

**About the Book:** If your students like gross facts, they will gobble up every page of this inventive book! A swarm consisting of thirteen different species of fly zips across the page. One by one, the flies are devoured in various ways. This book is factual, creative, and a treat to read aloud.

To find a book like this one, look for the following:

- Innovative nonfiction text structures
- Structures and ideas children can borrow for their own writing

## Comprehension Conversation

### Before Reading

#### Notice the Cover Illustration

What creatures do you see on the cover? Would any of these creatures like to eat that fly? After I read the back cover blurb, let's count the flies on the back cover. How many flies are there? Do you have any predictions about what might happen in this nonfiction book?

**Set a Purpose:** As writers, we have a lot of decisions to make. One decision is how to organize or structure our text. As we're reading *13 Ways to Eat a Fly,* notice how Sue Heavenrich organizes this book.

### During Reading

- *13 Zapped* page: Wait! What? Did you hear the fact I just read? Let me reread it. Did you know that a frog uses its eyeballs to push the fly down its throat? What is your reaction to that fact? Talk to a friend about it.

- *12 Wrapped* page: The author uses comparison on this page to help us understand how a spider rolls a fly in its silk. Can you picture what this looks like? Do you notice anything about the flies on this page? [There are only 12 and there used to be 13.]

- *7 Midflight* page: The prefix *mid-* means the middle part, point, time, or position. There are two words with that prefix on this page. How does knowing the meaning of the prefix help you better understand this fact?

- *2 Zombified* page: Oh, now this page is really gross. Tell a neighbor what you learned!

### After Reading

- Which fact was the most memorable? Why?
- How did Sue Heavenrich organize the facts? Could you use this structure in your own writing?

**Learning Targets:**

- I notice unique structures in nonfiction texts.
- I borrow unique structures to create my own nonfiction texts.

## Extend the Experience

- 3-2-1 Strategy (Zygouris-Coe et al., 2004/2005). Write down three discoveries you made while listening to this book. Then, write down two facts that stood out or were interesting to you. Finally, jot down a lingering question. See *3-2-1 Strategy Reproducible Response Page* found on the companion website (resources.corwin.com/shakeupsharedreading).

  o  3 things I discovered

  o  2 interesting facts

  o  1 question I still have

**Key Vocabulary and Kid-Friendly Definitions:**

- *devour*: to quickly eat or swallow something; to gobble it up

- *munch*: to chew noisily; to crunch

- *snatches*: quickly grabs something

## Similar Titles

 **The Bug Club** (Gravel, 2021)

About the Book: Part journal, part informational book. Elise Gravel writes about her fascination with bugs in general and shares facts about some of her favorite bugs. Her enthusiasm for the topic will encourage readers to join "The Bug Club."

 **Butterflies Are Pretty Gross!** (Mosco, 2021)

About the Book: Did you know that some butterflies have butts that look like heads while others eat poop? Your students will delight in hearing these and other lesser-known facts from a monarch butterfly narrator. This book is the first installment in the Nature's Top Secret Series. The next is *Flowers Are Pretty Weird* (Mosco, 2022).

---

Name _____

### 3-2-1

**Three** Things I Discovered:

_____

_____

_____

**Two** Interesting Facts:

_____

_____

**One** Question I Still Have:

_____

_____

---

*3-2-1 Reproducible Response Page*

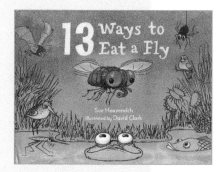

## Short Bursts of Shared Reading: *13 Ways to Eat a Fly*

### Focus 1–Match Letters to Sounds: *-ed* Ending

#### Before Reading

**Set the Stage:** As we reread the rhyming word pairs in this book, we're going to study the suffix *-ed*. When the *-ed* ending is added to verbs, it changes the verb from present tense to past tense. The *-ed* ending makes three different sounds: /ed/, /d/, and /t/.

#### During Reading

#### Investigate Key Pages

#### My Turn

*13 Zapped* page: When I read the rhyming verb pair on these two pages, I'm going to focus on the *-ed* ending and listen carefully to the sound it makes. In both *Zapped* and *Wrapped,* the *-ed* ending stands for the /t/ sound. That's one of the sounds the suffix *-ed* makes.

#### Our Turn

*9 Snatched* page: Reread the rhyming word pair with me. [Snatched, hatched.] Listen to the *-ed* ending. What sound do you hear at the end of each word?

#### Your Turn

*3 Liquefied* page: Reread the rhyming word pair on this page and the next one. [Liquefied, zombified.] What is different about the *-ed* ending sound in these two words? [The *-ed* ending stands for the /d/ sound instead of the /t/ sound.]

#### After Reading

#### Nudge Toward Independence

When we read and write words with the suffix *-ed,* it's helpful to remember that it is spelled *-ed* but doesn't always make the /ed/ sound. The words in this book with the *-ed* ending make the /t/ and /d/ sound. Can you find words in your books where the *-ed* ending makes the *-ed* sound? Remember, when you add the suffix *-ed* to words, add the letters *-ed* rather than just a *t* or *d*.

**Innovate on Text:** In this nonfiction book, the author teaches us 13 different ways to eat a fly. Since I'm guessing you don't want to eat a fly, think about your favorite food. What are three different ways you can eat that food? I'm going to write about three ways to eat an apple.

## Focus 2–Notice Writer's Craft Moves: Creative Backmatter

**Before Reading**

**Set the Stage:** Writers add backmatter to texts for many reasons. Information found in the backmatter might give you more background information, expand on the facts in the book, and/or explain more about how the writer or illustrator completed the book. Sue Heavenrich chose some interesting approaches in her backmatter. Let's check them out.

**During Reading**

**Investigate Key Pages**

**My Turn**

*The Non-Human Insectivore's Guide to Fine Dining* page: This section cracks me up. The author wrote it as if we were going to eat flies. [Read aloud while highlighting innovative ways the author wove facts into this guide.]

**Our Turn**

*Nutrition Fact Label*: Where have you seen a label like this before? [On food packages.] Have you ever seen one in a book before? I think it was a clever idea to add it here. What's your opinion?

**Your Turn**

*Edible parts of a fly* page: What can you learn from reading this diagram? Notice the comments after each fly body part. Talk with someone nearby about why you think the author added those details.

**After Reading**

**Nudge Toward Independence**

The backmatter in this book added information in creative ways to the facts we learned in the book. Be on the lookout for other nonfiction books with creative backmatter. Share them with us so we can use them as mentor texts for our own writing.

3 Ways to Eat an Apple
- Fresh
- Baked (in pie)
- Covered with caramel

*Three Ways to Eat an Apple Demonstration Text*

## Read-Aloud Experience: Point Out Playful Language

**Book Title:** *Hello, Rain!* (Maclear, 2021)

**About the Book:** A little girl and her dog dash outside to frolic in a rainstorm because "the sky is an adventure." They jump in a puddle, launch a fleet of tiny sailboats, and rest quietly under a tree. Startled by a loud clap of thunder, they take shelter indoors until the storm gives way to a rainbow-filled sky.

To find a book like this one, look for the following:

- Texts where words are used in unique and interesting ways
- Language that children can borrow for their own writing

### Comprehension Conversation

#### Before Reading

#### Notice the Cover Illustration

**Learning Targets:**

- I notice how authors use unique and interesting words.
- I try to use unique and interesting words when I'm writing.

Look at the girl and the dog. Can you tell how they feel about the rain? Do you like going outside in the rain? Why or why not? Chris Turnham used digital tools to create the colorful illustrations in this book. If you were going to use one word to describe this book cover, which word would you choose? [In the hardcover version, notice that the paper book jacket is different than the book casing underneath.]

**Set a Purpose:** I can't wait to read you this book. It is written in such a unique way. Tune in to the words Kyo Maclear uses to vividly describe this rainy-day adventure. Grab your umbrella! Let's go out and play in the rain.

### During Reading

- *Old raincoat, rubber boots, big umbrella, best umbrella* page: What are some reasons the girl might like that particular umbrella the best? Notice where the author and illustrator placed the color words on this page. Why do you think they put them around the umbrella? Is that something you could do in one of your books?

- *Deluge, downpour, sprinkle, storm, a drizzle, a mizzle* page: All the words in the raindrop are synonyms for rain. Are there any words that are new to you? [Define any unfamiliar words.] At first, I didn't think *mizzle* was a real word, so I looked it up in the dictionary. *Mizzle* is a real word! It means a light rain, like the word *drizzle*. Which synonym is your favorite to say?

- *In a quiet spot, a single drop of rain touches five times* page: Can you picture the drop of rain touching all of these places on its way to the ground? See the ellipsis; what do you predict is going to happen next?

- *The ground is glistening green* page: Notice the illustration on this page. It's shown from the perspective of a bird's eye view. Why do you suppose it is called a bird's eye view?

- *Hello, sparrows with your bright sparrow voices* page: Which word is repeated over and over on this page? [Hello.] Remember the title of this book is *Hello, Rain!* Why do you suppose the author chose to repeat the word *hello* here?

### After Reading

- What did you notice about the words Kyo Maclear chose to use? Did you have a favorite part or page that you want me to revisit?

- Did this book make you feel differently about rain?

## Extend the Experience

- Which is your favorite kind of weather? Draw a picture. Then, add interesting words that describe what this weather looks like and sounds like.

- Be an Observer! Weather Watchers: To learn more about your favorite kinds of weather, I've gathered books and other resources. I've also placed a blank calendar nearby so that you can track and record the daily weather for the next week or so. I look forward to hearing what you discover about weather.

### Key Vocabulary and Kid-Friendly Definitions:

- *bursting*: suddenly popping open or breaking out

- *crouch*: to bend your legs and lower your body close to the ground

- *launch*: to put in the water

View the author reading *Soaked* at resources.corwin.com/shakeupsharedreading

........................................................................

### Similar Titles

 ***DROP: An Adventure Through the Water Cycle*** (Moon, 2021)

**About the Book:** I've read a lot of books about the water cycle, but this one floats above the rest. It is told from the expressive point of view of a personified drop of water who has been around for 4.5 billion years and experienced every aspect of the water cycle. Front and back endpapers present infographics about the states of water and the water cycle, respectively. [See Book Experiences on pages 186–189.]

 ***Soaked*** (Cushman, 2020)

**About the Book:** It's raining and none of the woodland animals are happy about it. Especially not Bear, the narrator. When the animals go inside Bear's cave for shelter, they find that Moose's hula hooping makes it a bit crowded. Once back outside, Bear interrupts his wallowing to retrieve Moose's hula hoop from a tree and decides to try it out. Splashy puddle fun follows. Abi Cushman's debut picture book is filled with humorous visual details and a lot of onomatopoeia.

## Short Bursts of Shared Reading: *Hello, Rain!*

### Focus 1—Wonder About Words: Onomatopoeia

**Before Reading**

**Set the Stage:** Writers use different kinds of words to add pizzazz to their writing. Adding onomatopoeia helps readers imagine the sounds.

**During Reading**

**Investigate Key Pages**

**My Turn**

*The air is full of waiting* page: As I read the onomatopoeias "Rumble, rumble," I can imagine how thunder sounds when it is far away.

**Our Turn**

*Plink, plunk, plonk on the rooftop* page: Wow, there are a lot of onomatopoeia on this two-page spread. Let's reread these pages together to listen to how the words sound.

**Your Turn**

*I wonder how it decides when to plonk . . .* page: Reread this page. Talk to a friend about the onomatopoeia. Let's compare it to the *Plink, plunk, plonk on the rooftop* page. How are the words the same? How are they different? What is Kyo Maclear showing us here?

**After Reading**

**Nudge Toward Independence**

Once you're on the lookout for onomatopoeia, I bet you'll notice them in a lot of the books you're reading. [Invite students to record their favorite onomatopoetic words on a class chart or in their notebooks.]

> **Innovate on Text:** The title of this book is *Hello, Rain!* If you were going to a write a book about weather, which type of weather would you choose? I'm going to write my book about snow. The title of my book is *Hello, Snow!* Then, on each page I'll say hello to something that I do when it snows. Here's my book!

*Hello, Snow! Demonstration Text*

## Focus 2—Notice Writer's Craft Moves: Using Figurative Language

### Before Reading

**Set the Stage:** To make stories memorable, authors use words or phrases creatively. One way to do this is by using figurative language. Figurative language means using words in an imaginative way. Let's explore what figurative language looks like and sounds like in *Hello, Rain!*

### During Reading

#### Investigate Key Pages

#### My Turn

*Every rainfall plays a different tune* page: I'm thinking to myself, "Does rain play an instrument?" No, the author is using figurative language so that I can imagine the sounds I hear when it rains. The sound rain makes when it is sprinkling is much different than a downpour. That's what I'm inferring the author means by "every rainfall plays a different tune." So instead of writing "every rainfall sounds different," she compares rain to music.

#### Our Turn

*On the streets, umbrellas bloom* page: Kyo Maclear uses figurative language again here. Do umbrellas really bloom? What blooms? Can you picture what she is trying to show you by using the words *umbrellas bloom*? Do you think it is more interesting to write "umbrellas bloom" than simply writing "people put their umbrellas up"?

#### Your Turn

*Hyacinth, foxglove, poppy, yarrow* page: Can you find the figurative language on this page? [Discuss the phrase "thirsty roots are drinking."]

### After Reading

#### Nudge Toward Independence

Understanding and using figurative language adds to your word power! As a writer, try describing things to your readers by comparing them to other objects readers might know.

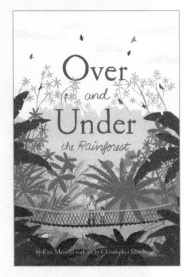

## Read-Aloud Experience: Spot Sensory Language

**Book Title:** *Over and Under the Rainforest* (Messner, 2020b)

**About the Book:** Put on your hiking boots to join a young girl as she treks through the rainforest with her caregiver, Tito. Together, they climb across footbridges and spy on the animals in the canopy or on the rainforest floor.

To find a book like this one, look for the following:

- Narrative nonfiction written in first-person point of view
- Events that are described using sensory language
- Main characters who are curious and explore nature

### Comprehension Conversation

#### Before Reading

#### Notice the Cover Illustration

Compare the size of the two people on the cover to the rainforest around them. What do you notice? Have you ever been hiking in a rainforest? If not, would you like to go hiking through a rainforest someday?

**Set a Purpose:** As we're hiking through the rainforest, let's think about how the author, Kate Messner, uses words to help us experience what the girl is seeing, hearing, and feeling. We can jot down the words she uses that connect to our senses. Words and phrases that connect to our senses are called *sensory language*.

#### During Reading

- *Into the rainforest we hike, through slivers of sunlight and dripping-wet leaves* page: Think about the words on this page. What senses might you use to imagine what the girl is experiencing?
- *Up in the trees, there's a symphony of sound!* page: Isn't this illustration amazing? It feels as if we are down on the ground looking up. What sense are you using to experience the rainforest on this page?
- *Our hanging bridge teeters and tips with every wobbly step* page: Stand up. Pretend you are on the wobbly hanging bridge. Show us what that might look like. How would you feel if you were on this bridge?
- *The afternoon rain begins with a patter—a pitter-soft drumming on the leaves up above* page: Close your eyes. Listen as I reread the first paragraph. Talk with your friend about what you hear.
- *There's a sudden, sharp s n a p—and I freeze in my tracks* page: How would you react if you heard a snap in the dark rainforest?

#### After Reading

- How did Kate Messner's use of sensory language help you imagine yourself on a rainforest hike?
- Why do you think Kate Messner chose to write this book from the girl's point of view?

**Learning Targets:**

- I notice sensory words or phrases in books.
- I think about how to use sensory words or phrases in my writing.

**Extend the Experience**

- Reread the sensory language we found in this book. What do you notice?

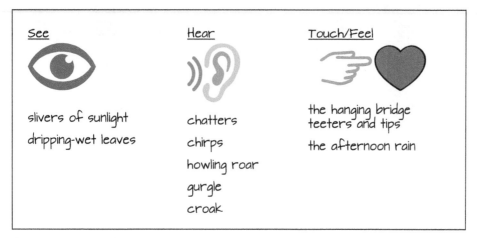

| See | Hear | Touch/Feel |
|---|---|---|
| slivers of sunlight<br>dripping-wet leaves | chatters<br>chirps<br>howling roar<br>gurgle<br>croak | the hanging bridge teeters and tips<br>the afternoon rain |

*Sensory Language Chart*

- In this book, we learned about two of the layers of the rainforest, the canopy and forest floor. There are two other layers. Learn about them by singing the "Rainforest Layers" song. (See "Rainforest Layers" Reproducible Song Page found on the companion website [resources.corwin.com/shakeupsharedreading.])

**Rainforest Layers**

Written by: Maria Walther
Tune: "My Bonnie Lies Over the Ocean"

Rainforests have four different layers.
From the sky to the ground you can see.
Each layer has its special creatures.
Let's start at the top of the trees.

Emergent, Canopy, Understory, and Floor,
you'll see . . .
Emergent, Canopy, Understory, and Floor.

At the top, you'll see harpy eagles.
Below them, the monkeys and vines.
The understory's home to the boas.
Poison dart frogs think the floor's just fine!

Emergent, Canopy, Understory, and Floor,
you'll see . . .
Emergent, Canopy, Understory, and Floor

iStock.com/Oceloti

*"Rainforest Layers" Reproducible Song Page*

**Key Vocabulary and Kid-Friendly Definitions:**

- *bask*: to lie in a warm, quiet place
- *feast*: to eat or drink a large amount
- *teeters*: moves back and forth; wobbles

online resources

View the author reading *Over and Under the Rainforest* at resources.corwin.com/shakeupsharedreading

| |
|---|
| Meet the Creator! |
| Book Creator Study: Kate Messner |
| Website: https://katemessner.com/ |
| **Did you know?** |
| • Kate was once a television news reporter and a middle school English teacher. |
| • She lives on Lake Champlain. |
| **A Few of Her Books:** |
| • *Dr. Fauci: How a Boy From Brooklyn Became America's Doctor* (Author, 2021) [Biography] |
| • *Fergus and Zeke* (Author, 2017) [Easy-Read Series] |
| • *How to Write a Story* (Author, 2020) [How-to Book] |
| • *Over and Under the Canyon* (Author, 2021) [Over and Under Series] |

## Similar Titles

 *Over and Under the Pond* (Messner, 2017b)

About the Book: In the third book of the Over and Under series, a mother and her son are out paddling around the pond when, like in the other books, the secret world hiding under the water is illuminated. In the Author's Note, Kate Messner briefly describes how, in the book, she's shown the interactions among the organisms that thrive in a mountain pond ecosystem and invites readers to return to the text to look for such interactions.

 *Up in the Garden and Down in the Dirt* (Messner, 2015)

About the Book: A girl and her grandmother plant, care for, and harvest their garden while readers learn about what is happening under the ground. Read this book in the spring, during a science unit on plants, or to inspire writers to use sensory language. You can also help listeners notice the repetitive see-saw structure "Up in the garden/Down in the dirt" that they could borrow in their own writing. [See read-aloud experience on page 120 in *The Ramped-Up Read Aloud*.]

My Favorite Texts and Resources for Inspiring Writers

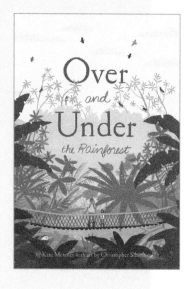

## Short Bursts of Shared Reading: *Over and Under the Rainforest*

### Focus 1–Wonder About Words: Prepositions

#### Before Reading

**Set the Stage:** The words *over* and *under* in the title of this book are *prepositions*. Prepositions tell where something is located in comparison to something else. On the cover, the bridge is *over* the rainforest floor and the people are *under* the rainforest canopy. I wonder if we can find other prepositions in the book.

#### During Reading

#### Investigate Key Pages

#### My Turn

*Up in the trees is a whole hidden world . . .* page: There are three prepositions on this page: *up, in,* and *under.* I'll record them on the preposition chart.

#### Our Turn

*On to the footbridge we climb . . .* page: Can you find any prepositions on this page? [*On, to, up, over, below, in.*] Use a preposition to describe where the ceiling is in this room. Where is the door? How about the floor? I'll add these prepositions to the chart.

#### Your Turn

*Deep in the forest, the rain lets up* page: Work with a friend to reread this page and find as many prepositions as you can. Write them on your whiteboard. [*In, over, up, around.*] Let's add them to the chart.

| Prepositions We Found in *Over and Under the Rainforest* (in order of appearance): | | |
|---|---|---|
| into | through | up |
| in | under | down |
| along | on | to |
| over | below | here |
| above | around | at |

#### After Reading

#### Nudge Toward Independence

When you're reading, prepositions help you imagine the location of people, places, or things. When you're talking or writing, you use prepositions to describe objects or people to others.

## Focus 2–Reread to Boost Comprehension: Read Backmatter to Learn Even More

### Before Reading

**Set the Stage:** Writers add backmatter to texts for many reasons. Information found in the backmatter might give you more background information, expand on the facts in the book, and/or explain more about how the writer or illustrator completed the book. In this book, Kate Messner includes an Author's Note that contains information about each of the animals pictured in the book.

### During Reading

### Investigate Key Pages

### My Turn

*About the Animals* page: There are many animals in this book that are unfamiliar to me. I want to learn more! In the back matter, Kate Messner has listed the animals in the order in which they appear in the book. I'm going to learn more about the long-nosed proboscis bats, so I'll read the paragraph next to their picture.

### Our Turn

Which animal do you want to learn more about? Pick one and we'll learn about it. [Continue in this same fashion with a few more animals.]

### Your Turn

[To provide access for all of your learners to the rest of the information about the rainforest animals, consider audio or video recording yourself reading it aloud. Then, place in an area where students can listen and learn more.] I'm going to put this book in the classroom library so you can learn more about the rainforest animals on your own or with friends.

### After Reading

### Nudge Toward Independence

The purpose of the backmatter in *Over and Under the Rainforest* is to teach you more about the animals pictured in the book. Notice backmatter in other books that you're reading. Think about the author's purpose for adding it. Is there something you would like to add to the back of a book you're writing? If so, try it out. We'd love to see what you added.

**Innovate on Text:** Pick a rainforest animal from the book that you want to learn more about. Read about the animal in the "About the Animals" section. Write the two most interesting facts you learned.

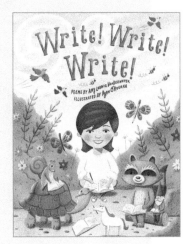

## Read-Aloud Experience: Learn From Poets

**Book Title:** *Write! Write! Write!* (VanDerwater, 2020)

**About the Book:** In this collection of 22 poems about the joys and challenges of writing, seasoned poetry writer and classroom teacher Amy Ludwig VanDerwater offers insights and inspiration for budding poets. For additional resources and writing ideas, check out Amy's website link listed on the Learning Target Chart on the companion website (resources.corwin.com/shakeupsharedreading).

To find a book like this one, look for the following:

- Poems about familiar topics
- Poems that use various poetic devices

## Comprehension Conversation

### Before Reading

#### Notice the Cover Illustration

What are the characters on the cover of this book doing? [Writing.] That makes sense since the title of this book is *Write! Write! Write!* What do you suppose Amy Ludwig VanDerwater wants you to do after reading this book?

**Set a Purpose:** Notice that the cover reads "Poems by Amy Ludwig VanDerwater." This book is a poetry anthology. An anthology is a collection of poems. There is even a poem called "One Wish" on the back cover! We're going to read like a poet to learn from Amy about poetry and writing.

### During Reading

[Below I share some different options for reading this book. I suggest only reading three to five poems in one read-aloud experience. Follow each poem with a conversation sparked by questions like these: "What did you notice Amy Ludwig VanDerwater did as a poet? How could you use that idea, structure, or technique in your own poems?"]

- Option 1: [Preselect poems that you think will resonate with your learners.] There are 22 poems in this book. I've picked the ones I think you will really like. I can't wait to share them with you.
- Option 2: Let's look at the table of contents. I'm going to read the name of the first few poems. [Read aloud the titles of the first five poems.] Which poem sounds interesting to you? [Continue in the same fashion until students' interest and engagement wane.]
- Option 3: This book has 32 pages of poems about writing. Pick a number between six and 32. We'll read the poem on that page. [Continue in the same fashion until students' interest and engagement wane.]

**Learning Targets:**

- I notice the techniques poets use.
- I use what I learn about poetry to write my own poems.

## After Reading

- Which was your favorite poem? What did you enjoy about that poem? What did it make you think about? How did it make you feel?

- Which poem would you like to study and learn from when you're writing poetry?

### Extend the Experience

- What did you notice as we were reading the poems? Let's make a list of the different techniques Amy Ludwig VanDerwater used.

- She wrote all of the poems in this anthology about one topic—writing. If you were going to make a book about poems about one topic, which topic would you choose?

**Key Vocabulary and Kid-Friendly Definitions:**

- Will vary based on which poems you choose to read aloud.

## Similar Titles

 ***Bookjoy Wordjoy* (P. Mora, 2018b)**

About the Book: In Pat Mora's words, she wrote this book to share "the pleasure of wordjoy, of discovering new words, of listening to words, of hearing them rhyme, of braiding English and Spanish or other languages into a poem, of shaping words on a page" (Note to Educators and Families). Read the poem "Collecting Words" to launch a yearlong quest to discover interesting words.

 ***Read! Read! Read!* (VanDerwater, 2017)**

About the Book: From cereal boxes to comic strips, the poems in this anthology celebrate reading in all of its forms. "Reading Time" on page 10 would be ideal to share before launching supported independent reading time, and read "Word Collection" on page 14 to spark word wonder.

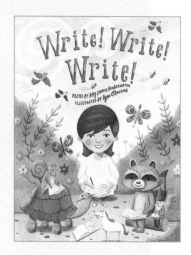

## Short Bursts of Shared Reading: *Write! Write! Write!*

### Focus 1—Reread for Fluency: Reader's Theater

#### Before Reading

**Set the Stage:** We are going to practice and perform one of Amy Ludwig VanDerwater's poems for people in our school community. [Invite another class, office staff, or any other members of your school community who would enjoy a poetry performance. Consider recording the short performance to send home to families.]

#### During Reading

#### Investigate Key Pages

#### My Turn

*"Thank You Notes"* page: This poem is perfect for reader's theater because there are four stanzas. We are going to practice and perform the first stanza together. Then, we'll divide into three groups and each practice our small-group stanza. At the end, we'll all say the last two words, "Love, Me," together. To start, I'm going to perform the whole poem aloud while you follow along. Listen to the way I read each stanza.

#### Our Turn

[Divide the class into three groups, and give each child in the group a copy of one stanza that begins with "Dear" from the poem "Thank You Notes."] Let's do some echo reading. I'll read a line, and then you'll echo the line back. Now it's your turn. Practice reading your stanza of the poem chorally. Your goal is to read your stanza together smoothly and with expression. [Provide practice time and offer support as needed.]

#### Your Turn

Get ready to perform. Remember to speak loudly so that your audience can hear. When you're performing, don't worry about small mistakes. Just ignore them and keep going. That's what actors do!

#### After Reading

#### Nudge Toward Independence

How did practicing and performing this poem help you as a reader? Did you notice your fluency improving the more you practiced? Now think about the poem from a writer's point of view. Amy Ludwig VanDerwater wrote three of the stanzas as if they were thank-you notes. That's an interesting way to structure a poem. You might want to try it out! If you were writing a thank-you poem, who would you thank?

**Innovate on Text:** Borrow Amy Ludwig VanDerwater's idea from her list poem "Revision Is . . ." to write your own poem about a topic of your choice. "Revision Is . . ." has a rhyming pattern, but your poem does not have to rhyme. You could write about a season, a sport, a family member, or even school. I wrote my poem about swimming.

## Focus 2—Notice Writer's Craft Moves: List Poems

**Before Reading**

**Set the Stage:** As poets, it's helpful to read and study poetry in order to learn techniques that we can use when we're writing our own poems. Reading other writers' poetry can spark ideas about possible topics, show us imaginative word choices, teach us different ways to structure a poem, and much more.

**During Reading**

**Investigate Key Pages**

**My Turn**

"Revision Is . . . ," page 23: I'll start by rereading the poem to see what I notice. I notice that it is organized like a list. Each line (except the last one) begins with the same phrase, "a little bit," and ends with a word to describe revision.

**Our Turn**

"Revision Is . . . ," page 23: Join in with me as we reread it again. Talk with your friend about what you notice. [Listeners will probably notice the rhyming pattern and the use of opposites.]

**Your Turn**

"Revision Is . . . ," page 23: This time, reread the poem to yourself. Then, talk with a friend about ideas, words, or structures you notice or would like to try when you're writing.

**After Reading**

**Nudge Toward Independence**

Did you enjoy this poem? What did you learn from studying this poem that you might use when you're writing? Was it helpful to reread it a few times?

Swimming is...

a little bit calm
a little bit splash
a little bit float
a little bit glide
a little bit wet
a little bit dry
and then...
     you're done.

*List Poem Demonstration Text*

## Read-Aloud Experience: Try Out Techniques

**Book Title:** *The Last Straw: Kids vs. Plastics* (Hood, 2021)

**About the Book:** Poets pen verses for a variety of reasons. In this case, Susan Hood aims to share the truth about plastic. She begins with the poem "Fantastic Plastic" detailing the many uses of plastic and then moves on to poems about the consequences of our overreliance on plastic products. To provide hope and inspiration, she writes about young activists working to find solutions. This multigenre, multilevel text offers poems, tidbits of information, and robust backmatter. In addition, Susan Hood includes "Poetry Notes" explaining the techniques and formats she's used for each poem. It's a scientific delight for both the eyes and ears.

To find a book like this one, look for the following:

- Poems about interesting topics
- Poems that use various poetic techniques and devices

## Comprehension Conversation

### Before Reading

#### Notice the Cover Illustration

**Learning Targets:**

- I ponder the purposes for writing poetry.
- I notice the techniques poets use.
- I use what I learn about poetry to write my own poems.

Talk with a neighbor about what the kids on the cover are doing. Look carefully at the trash they are picking up. What do you notice?

**Set a Purpose:** The title of this poetry anthology is *The Last Straw.* Have you heard that idiom before? An idiom is a saying that means something different than its literal meaning. [Discuss the meaning of the idiom *the last straw.*] The subtitle is *Kids vs. Plastics.* Let's read a few of the poems in the book to ponder Susan Hood's purpose for writing this book. Along the way, we'll learn more about being a poet.

### During Reading

- *"Fantastic Plastic,"* page 6: What was Susan Hood's purpose for writing this poem? If I read the paragraph of facts below the poem, it will give us a bit more insight.
- *"A Sea Change,"* page 10: How does this poem make you feel? Who are the "wisest of mammals"?
- *"From Bottles to Buddies,"* page 22: Here's a poem about a child who is an activist. That means she saw a problem and took action to make a change. What was the problem? How did she solve it?
- *"Join the Crew,"* page 34: What is this poem asking you to do?

### After Reading

- What was Susan Hood's purpose for writing this book?
- What did you learn about plastic that you didn't know before?

## Extend the Experience

- What will you do differently after reading this book? Write or draw to tell us your plan.

- *"The Road Back,"* page 20: [To prepare for this extension, collect some environmental print like food packages, images of road signs, or picture book covers. Provide kids with sticky note strips or something similar to cover up the words they don't want to use. Classroom newspapers also work well for this extension.] We're going to create some found poetry like the one on this page. To create a found poem, you gather text from your environment like signs, food packages, or picture book titles. Then, you cover up [or cross out] the words you don't want in your poem. Work with a partner to create a found poem.

## Key Vocabulary and Kid-Friendly Definitions:

- Will vary based on which poems you choose to read aloud.

## Similar Titles

### The Dirt Book: Poems About Animals That Live Beneath Our Feet (Harrison, 2021)

About the Book: A collection of poems about the fascinating underground world. Ideal for units about bugs and underground creatures. Notice the vertical orientation of each two-page spread highlighting the world that exists above and below the ground.

### Just Like Me (Brantley-Newton, 2020)

About the Book: In this anthology of girl-power poetry, the poems and vibrant illustrations celebrate girls who appreciate themselves, flaws and all. Don't miss the poem "Feelings," where the similes pop off the page, or "Explorer," which can lead to conversations about curiosity.

View the author reading *The Last Straw* at resources.corwin.com/shakeupsharedreading

# Short Bursts of Shared Reading:
## *The Last Straw: Kids vs. Plastics*

### Focus 1—Reread for Fluency: Reader's Theater

#### Before Reading

**Set the Stage:** We are going to practice and perform one of Susan Hood's poems to convince the people in our school community to stop using plastic bags. [Invite another class, office staff, or any other members of your school community who would enjoy a poetry performance. Consider recording the short performance to send home to families.]

#### During Reading

#### Investigate Key Pages

#### My Turn

*"Ban the Bag,"* page 16: This poem is perfect for reader's theater because there are ten stanzas. In small groups, you are going to practice and perform a stanza together. Before we break into groups, I'm going to perform the whole poem aloud while you follow along. Listen to the way I read each stanza.

#### Our Turn

[Divide the class into ten groups, and give each child in the group a copy of one stanza from the poem "Ban the Bag."] Let's do some echo reading. I'll read a line, and then you'll echo the line back. Now it's your turn. Practice reading your stanza of the poem chorally. Your goal is to read your stanza together smoothly and with expression. [Provide practice time and offer support as needed.]

#### Your Turn

Get ready to perform! Remember to speak loudly so that your audience can hear. When you're performing, don't worry about small mistakes. Just ignore them and keep going. That's what actors do!

#### After Reading

#### Nudge Toward Independence

How did practicing and performing this poem help you as a reader? Did you notice your fluency improving the more you practiced? Now think about the poem from a writer's point of view. Susan Hood wrote this poem to persuade readers to stop using plastic bags. What reasons did she give? Did this poem convince you? Do you think we convinced our audience to ban the bag? If you were going to write a persuasive poem, what topic would you choose?

## Focus 2—Notice Writer's Craft Moves: Concrete or Shape Poems

### Before Reading

**Set the Stage:** Susan Hood uses many types of poems in this book. We can learn more about the techniques she uses in the "Poetry Notes" found on pages 46–47. The format we are going to revisit today is called a *concrete or shape poem.* The words in a concrete or shape poem are arranged on the page so that they form a picture of the topic of the poem.

### During Reading

### Investigate Key Pages

### My Turn

*"The Great Pacific Garbage Patch,"* page 14: When I first looked at this page, it was a little confusing to me. I had to figure out how to read this concrete or shape poem. I saw that Susan Hood gave me a signal with the bold capital H. I'll read it aloud.

### Our Turn

*"The Great Pacific Garbage Patch,"* page 14: Before we reread this shape poem together, there are a few words that might help you better understand the meaning. The first is *vortex.* A vortex is like a whirlpool; it happens when liquid or air whirls around and makes a vacuum in the center that can suck things into it. When you flush the toilet, it makes a vortex. A *gyre* is the circular pattern of currents in the ocean. Let's reread "The Great Pacific Garbage Patch" and ponder why Susan Hood chose this particular shape.

### Your Turn

*"Stand Up. Speak Up,"* page 32. Here is another shape poem. What shape did Susan Hood choose for this poem? What do you notice about every phrase in this poem? [They end with the word *up*.] Stand up and reread this poem as if it is coming out of a megaphone.

### After Reading

### Nudge Toward Independence

As we reread the shape poems in the book, we noticed how the shape Susan Hood chose enhanced the meaning of her words. Concrete or shape poems are unique. If you're interested in writing a concrete poem, start by choosing a topic that's important to you. Then, think about the shape that best represents your idea. Once you have the shape in mind, you can brainstorm the words that you might use to describe the topic. Then the fun begins—play with the words until they sound like a poem. Finally, sketch your shape and place your words in and around it in a way that will make sense to your readers.

**Innovate on Text:** Select a topic for your own shape or concrete poem. To begin, write your poem. Then, draw a pencil outline of the shape of the topic or object. Write the words along the edge of your pencil line. If you find you have too few words, try repeating a word or line. If you find you have too many words, add some details to your shape and put the words there.

# References

## Professional Bibliography

Adams, M. (1990). *Beginning to read: Thinking and learning about print.* MIT Press.

Allington, R. L. (2009). *What really matters in fluency: Research-based practices across the curriculum.* Pearson.

Britton, J. (1983). Writing and the story of the world. In B. M. Kroll & C. G. Wells (Eds.), *Explorations in the development of writing: Theory, research, and practice* (pp. 3–30). Wiley.

Burkins, J., & Yaris, K. (2016). *Who's doing the work?* Stenhouse.

Burkins, J., & Yates, K. (2021). *Shifting the balance: 6 ways to bring the science of reading into the balanced literacy classroom.* Stenhouse.

Cobb, C., & Blachowicz, C. (2014). *No more "look up the list" vocabulary instruction.* Heinemann.

Cunningham, P. M. (2013). *Phonics they use: Words for reading and writing* (6th ed.). Pearson.

Cunningham, P. M. (2017). *Phonics they use: Words for reading and writing* (7th ed.). Pearson.

España, C., & Herrera, L. Y. (2020). *En comunidad: Lessons for centering the voices and experiences of bilingual Latinx students.* Heinemann.

Fisher, B., & Medvic, E. F. (2000). *Perspectives on shared reading: Planning and practice.* Heinemann.

Fisher, D., Frey, N., & Hattie, J. (2021). *The distance learning playbook: Teaching for engagement and impact in any setting.* Corwin.

Hammond, Z. (2015). *Culturally responsive teaching and the brain: Promoting authentic engagement and rigor among culturally and linguistically diverse students.* Corwin.

Hiebert, E. H., & Raphael, T. E. (1998). *Early literacy instruction.* Harcourt.

Holdaway, D. (1982). Shared book experience: Teaching reading using favorite books. *Theory Into Practice, 21*(4), 293–300.

Hoyt, L. (1999). *Revisit, reflect, retell: Strategies for improving reading comprehension.* Heinemann.

Hoyt, L. (2002). *Make it real: Strategies for success with informational texts.* Heinemann.

Johnston, P., Champeau, K., Hartwig, A., Helmer, S., Komar, M., Krueger, T., & McCarthy, L. (2020). *Engaging literate minds: Developing children's social, emotional, and intellectual lives, K–3.* Stenhouse.

Mesmer, H. A. (2019). *Letter lessons and first words: Phonics foundations that work.* Heinemann.

Parkes, B. (2000). *Read it again! Revisiting shared reading.* Stenhouse.

Pearson, P. D., & Gallagher, M. D. (1983). The instruction of reading comprehension. *Contemporary Educational Psychology, 63*(5), 317–344.

Pinnell, G. S., & Fountas, I. C. (1998). *Word matters: Teaching phonics and spelling in the reading/writing classroom.* Heinemann.

Rasinski, T., & Smith, M. C. (2018). *The megabook of fluency: Strategies and texts to engage all readers.* Scholastic.

Rawlins, A., & Invernizzi, M. (2019). Reconceptualizing sight words: Building an early reading vocabulary. *The Reading Teacher, 72*(6), 711–719.

Routman, R. (2018). *Literacy essentials: Engagement, excellence, and equity for all learners.* Stenhouse.

Souto-Manning, M., Llerena, C. L., Martell, J., Maguire, A. S., & Arce-Boardman, A. (2018). *No more culturally irrelevant teaching.* Heinemann.

Walther, M. (1998). *First grade teachers blending phonics and whole language: Two case studies.* Northern Illinois University.

Walther, M. (2019). *The ramped-up read aloud: What to notice as you turn the page.* Corwin.

Walther, M., & Biggs-Tucker, K. (2020). *The literacy workshop: Where reading and writing converge.* Stenhouse.

Weakland, M. (2021). *How to prevent reading difficulties: Proactive practices for teaching young children to read.* Corwin.

Zygouris-Coe, V., Wiggins, M. B., & Smith, L. H. (2004/2005). Engaging students with text: The 3-2-1 strategy. *The Reading Teacher, 58*(4), 381–384.

## Children's Literature Bibliography

Abe, M. (2020). *Avocado asks: What am I?* Doubleday.

Allen, T. (2020). *Sometimes people march.* HarperCollins.

Archer, M. (2021). *Wonder walkers.* Nancy Paulsen.

Archer, P. (2018). *A hippy-hoppy toad* (A. Wilsdorf, Illus.). Schwartz & Wade.

Ardagh, P. (2019). *Bunnies on the bus* (B. Mantle, Illus.). Candlewick.

Arnold, A. (2020). *What's the matter, Marlo?* Roaring Brook.

Ashman, L. (2013). *Rain!* (C. Robinson, Illus.). Houghton Mifflin Harcourt.

Atinuke. (2020). *Catch that chicken!* (A. Brooksbank, Illus.). Candlewick.

Bailey, J. (2019). *A friend for Henry* (M. Song, Illus.). Chronicle.

Barnett, M. (2020). *A polar bear in the snow* (S. Harris, Illus.). Candlewick.

Becker, A. (2013). *Journey.* Candlewick.

Bernstein, A. (2021). *We love fishing!* (M. Rosenthal, Illus.). Simon & Schuster.

Bernstrom, D. (2020). *Big Papa and the time machine* (S. W. Evans, Illus.). HarperCollins.

Betts, B. (2020). *My first book of planets: All about the solar system for kids.* Rockridge Press.

Bigwood, K. (2021). *Secret, secret agent guy* (C. Krampien, Illus.). Atheneum.

Boelts, M. (2020a). *Kaia and the bees* (A. Dominguez, Illus.). Candlewick.

Boelts, M. (2020b). *The purple puffy coat* (D. Duncan, Illus.). Candlewick.

Bogan, C. (2017). *Where's Rodney?* (F. Cooper, Illus.). Yosemite Conservancy.

Brantley-Newton, V. (2020). *Just like me.* Knopf.

Brewer, H. D. (2020). *Love is powerful* (L. Pham, Illus.). Candlewick.

Brown, P. (2021). *Fred gets dressed.* Little Brown.

Bryon, N. (2019). *Rocket says look up!* (D. Adeola, Illus.). Random House.

Bryon, N. (2020). *Rocket says clean up!* (D. Adeola, Illus.). Random House.

Camper, C. (2020). *Ten ways to hear snow* (K. Pak, Illus.). Kokila/Penguin.

Canty, J. (2019). *Heads and tails: Underwater.* Candlewick.

Carr, J. (2021). *Star of the party: The solar system celebrates* (J. Medina, Illus.). Crown.

Cherry, M. A. (2019). *Hair love* (V. Harrison, Illus.). Kokila/Penguin.

Chin, J. (2014). *Gravity.* Roaring Brook.

Condon, J. (2020). *The pirates are coming!* (M. Hunt, Illus.). Nosy Crow/Candlewick.

Copp, M. W. (2020). *Wherever I go* (M. D. Mohammed, Illus.). Atheneum.

Cordell, M. (2019). *Explorers.* Feiwel and Friends.

Cornwall, G. (2017). *Jabari jumps.* Candlewick.

Cornwall, G. (2020). *Jabari tries.* Candlewick.

Curry, P., & Curry, J. (2019). *Parker looks up: An extraordinary moment* (B. Jackson, Illus.). Aladdin.

Cushman, A. (2020). *Soaked!* Viking.

Cusolito, M. (2018). *Flying deep: Climb inside deep-sea submersible ALVIN* (N. Wong, Illus.). Charlesbridge.

Czajak, P. (2018). *The book tree* (R. Kheiriyeh, Illus.). Barefoot Books.

de la Peña, M. (2015). *Last stop on Market Street* (C. Robinson, Illus.). Putnam.

de la Peña, M. (2018). *Carmela full of wishes* (C. Robinson, Illus.). Putnam.

de la Peña, M. (2021). *Milo imagines the world* (C. Robinson, Illus.). Putnam.

Deenihan, J. L. B. (2019). *When Grandma gives you a lemon tree* (L. Rocha, Illus.). Sterling.

Deenihan, J. L. B. (2020). *When Grandpa gives you a toolbox* (L. Rocha, Illus.). Sterling.

Detlefsen, L. H. (2020). *On the go awesome* (R. Neubecker, Illus.). Knopf.

Diaz, L. (2021). *Paletero man* (M. Player, Illus.). HarperCollins.

DiPucchio, K. (2019). *Grace goes to Washington* (L. Pham, Illus.). Disney/Hyperion.

DiPucchio, K. (2021). *Oona* (R. Figueroa, Illus.). HarperCollins.

Dorléans, M. (2020). *The night walk.* Floris.

Drago, F. Z. (2020). *Gustavo the shy ghost.* Candlewick.

Duffield, K. S. (2020). *Crossings: Extraordinary structures for extraordinary creatures* (M. Orodán, Illus.). Beach Lane.

Elliott, D. (2012). *In the sea* (H. Meade, Illus.). Candlewick.

Elliott, Z. (2020). *A place inside of me: A poem to heal the heart* (N. Denmon, Illus.). Farrar Straus Giroux.

Elya, S. M. (2017). *La princesa and the pea* (J. Martinez-Neal, Illus.). Putnam.

Evans, S. W. (2012). *We march.* Roaring Brook.

Ferry, B. (2020). *Swashby and the sea* (J. Martinez-Neal, Illus.). Houghton Mifflin Harcourt.

Fisher, V. (2019). *Now you know what you eat: Pictures and answers for the curious mind.* Scholastic.

Fleming, C. (2020). *Honeybee: The busy life of Apis Mellifera* (E. Rohmann, Illus.). Holiday House.

Floca, B. (2021). *Keeping the city going.* Atheneum.

Flood, N. B. (2020). *I will dance* (J. Swaney, Illus.). Atheneum.

Florian, D. (2012). *UnBEElievables: Honeybee poems and paintings.* Beach Lane.

Florian, D. (2007). *Comets, stars, the moon, and Mars: Space poems and paintings.* Harcourt.

Fogliano, J. (2020). *My best friend* (J. Tamaki, Illus.). Atheneum.

Franklin, A. (2019). *Not quite Snow White* (E. Glenn, Illus.). HarperCollins.

Gravel, E. (2021). *The bug club.* Drawn & Quarterly.

Griffin, M. B. (2021). *Ten beautiful things* (M. Lechuga, Illus.). Charlesbridge.

Grimes, N. (2020). *Southwest sunrise* (W. Minor, Illus.). Bloomsbury.

Hale, S., & Hale, D. (2014). *The princess in black* (L. Pham, Illus.). Candlewick.

Hall, M. (2011). *Perfect square.* Greenwillow.

Hare, J. (2020). *Field trip to the ocean deep.* Holiday House.

Harrison, D. L. (2021). *The dirt book: Poems about animals that live beneath our feet* (K. Cosgrove, Illus.). Holiday House.

Haughton, C. (2019). *Don't worry, Little Crab.* Candlewick.

Haworth-Booth, E. (2020). *The last tree.* Pavilion.

Heard, G. (2021). *My thoughts are clouds: Poems for mindfulness* (I. Roxas, Illus.). Roaring Brook.

Heavenrich, S. (2021). *13 ways to eat a fly* (D. Clark, Illus.). Charlesbridge.

Higgins, R. T. (2015). *Mother Bruce.* Disney/Hyperion.

Hill, S. L. (2020). *Mars' first friends: Come on over, Rovers!* (E. Paganelli, Illus.). Sourcebooks.

Hillery, T. (2020). *Harlem grown: How one big idea transformed a neighborhood* (J. Hartland, Illus.). Simon & Schuster.

Himmelman, J. (2010). *Pigs to the rescue.* Henry Holt.

Ho, J. (2021). *Eyes that kiss in the corners* (D. Ho, Illus.). HarperCollins.

Ho, R. (2019). *Red rover: Curiosity on Mars* (K. Roy, Illus.). Roaring Brook.

Hoang, Z. G. (2020). *A new kind of wild.* Dial.

Hoffman, M. (1991). *Amazing grace* (C. Binch, Illus.). Dial.

Hoffman, M. (2020). *Dirt cheap.* Knopf.

Hood, S. (2021). *The last straw: Kids vs. plastics* (C. Engel, Illus.). HarperCollins.

Hudson, N. (2021). *Turtle in a tree.* Dial.

Hughes, C. D. (2012). *National Geographic Kids first big book of space.* National Geographic.

Hughes, C. D. (2013). *National Geographic Kids first big book of the ocean.* National Geographic.

Hurley, J. (2020). *Beehive.* Paula Wiseman/Simon & Schuster.

Ismail, Y. (2020). *Joy* (J. Desmond, Illus.). Candlewick.

James, L. (2020). *I promise* (N. Mata, Illus.). HarperCollins.

James, S. (2017). *Frog and beaver.* Candlewick.

Jenkins, S. (2003). *What do you do with a tail like this?* (R. Page, Illus.). Houghton Mifflin.

Jenkins, S. (2014). *Eye to eye: How animals see the world.* Houghton Mifflin Harcourt.

Jenkins, S. (2016). *Animals by the numbers: A book of animal infographics.* Houghton Mifflin Harcourt.

Jenkins, S., & Page, R. (2017). *Who am I? An animal guessing game* (S. Jenkins, Illus.). Houghton Mifflin Harcourt.

Jin, B. (2019). *Two wool gloves* (L. Li, Illus.). Reycraft.

John, J. (2021). *Something's wrong! A bear, a hare, and some underwear* (E. Kraan, Illus.). Farrar Straus Giroux.

Jonker, T. (2021). *Blue floats away* (G. Snider, Illus.). Abrams.

Joseph, D. (2020). *I want to ride the tap tap* (O. Ganthier, Illus.). Farrar Straus Giroux.

Joyner, A. (2020). *Stand up! Speak up! A story inspired by the climate change revolution.* Schwartz & Wade.

Judge, L. (2020). *Play in the wild: How baby animals like to have fun.* Roaring Brooks.

Kerascoët. (2018). *I walk with Vanessa: A story about a simple act of kindness*. Schwartz & Wade.

Khalil, A. (2020). *The Arabic quilt: An immigrant story* (A. Semirdzhyan, Illus.). Tilbury House.

Kousky, V. (2018). *Harold loves his woolly hat*. Schwartz & Wade.

Ku Rhee, H. (2020). *The paper kingdom* (P. Campion, Illus.). Random House.

Larios, J. (2021). *Delicious! Poems celebrating street food around the world*. Beach Lane/Simon & Schuster.

Larkin, S. (2019). *The thing about bees*. Readers to Eaters.

Layton, N. (2016). *The tree*. Candlewick.

Lê, M. (2018). *Drawn together* (D. Santat, Illus.). Disney/Hyperion.

Lê, M. (2020). *Lift* (D. Santat, Illus.). Disney/Hyperion.

Lendler, I. (2021). *Nia and the new free library* (M. Pett, Illus.). Chronicle.

Lindstrom, C. (2020). *We are water protectors* (M. Goade, Illus.). Roaring Brook.

Lobel, A. (1985). *Whiskers and rhymes*. Greenwillow.

Loney, A. J. (2019). *Double bass blues* (R. Gutierrez, Illus.). Knopf.

Ludwig, T. (2020). *The power of one: Every act of kindness counts* (M. Curato, Illus.). Knopf.

Maclear, K. (2021). *Hello, rain!* (C. Turnham, Illus.). Chronicle.

Maier, B. (2018). *The little red fort* (S. Sánchez, Illus.). Scholastic.

Maillard, K. N. (2019). *Fry bread: A Native American family story* (J. Martinez-Neal, Illus.). Roaring Brook.

Maizes, S. (2021). *Atticus Caticus* (K. Kramer, Illus.). Candlewick.

Mann, J. K. (2020). *The camping trip*. Candlewick.

Marcero, D. (2020). *In a jar*. Putnam.

Martinez-Neal, J. (2018). *Alma and how she got her name*. Candlewick.

Martinez-Neal, J. (2021). *Zonia's rain forest*. Candlewick.

Mattick, L. (2015). *Finding Winnie: The true story of the world's most famous bear* (S. Blackwell, Illus.). Little, Brown.

Maynor, M. (2021). *A house for every bird* (K. Juanita, Illus.). Knopf.

McAnulty, S. (2021a). *A small kindness* (W. Leach, Illus.). Running Press Kids.

McAnulty, S. (2021b). *Mars! Earthlings welcome* (S. Lewis, Illus.). Henry Holt.

McCardie, A. (2021). *Let's play! A book about making friends* (C. Larmour, Illus.). Candlewick.

McClure, W. (2021). *A garden to save the birds* (B. Mayumi, Illus.). Albert Whitman.

McGinty, A. B., & Havis, A. B. (2020). *The sea knows* (S. Laberis, Illus.). Simon & Schuster.

McKinlay, M. (2021). *How to make a bird* (M. Ottley, Illus.). Candlewick.

Méndez, Y. S. (2019). *Where are you from?* (J. Kim, Illus.). HarperCollins.

Messner, K. (2015). *Up in the garden and down in the dirt* (C. S. Neal, Illus.). Chronicle.

Messner, K. (2017a). *Fergus and Zeke* (H. Ross, Illus.). Candlewick.

Messner, K. (2017b). *Over and under the pond* (C. S. Neal, Illus.). Chronicle.

Messner, K. (2020a). *How to write a story* (M. Siegel, Illus.). Chronicle.

Messner, K. (2020b). *Over and under the rainforest*. Chronicle.

Messner, K. (2021a). *Dr. Fauci: How a boy from Brooklyn became America's doctor* (A. Bye, Illus.). Simon & Schuster.

Messner, K. (2021b). *Over and under the canyon* (C. S. Neal, Illus.). Chronicle.

Metcalf, L. H., Dawson, K. V., & Bradley, J. (2020). *No voice too small: Fourteen young Americans making history* (J. Bradley, Illus.). Charlesbridge.

Miller, P. Z. (2019). *Remarkably you* (P. Barton, Illus.). HarperCollins.

Milner, C. (2018). *The bee book*. Dorling Kindersley.

Moon, E. K. (2021). *DROP: An adventure through the water cycle*. Dial.

Moore, J. (2007). *Freckleface Strawberry* (L. Pham, Illus.). Bloomsbury.

Mora, O. (2018). *Thank you, Omu!* Little, Brown.

Mora, P. (2018). *Bookjoy wordjoy* (R. Colón, Illus.). Lee & Low.

Morris, R. T. (2019). *Bear came along* (L. Pham, Illus.). Little Brown.

Mosco, R. (2021). *Butterflies are pretty gross!* (J. Souva, Illus.). Tundra.

Mosco, R. (2022). *Flowers are pretty weird!* (J. Souva, Illus.). Tundra.

Muhammad, I., & Ali, S. K. (2019). *The proudest blue: A story of hijab and family* (H. Aly, Illus.). Little, Brown.

Murrow, E., & Murrow, V. (2020). *Zero local: Next stop: Kindness*. Candlewick.

Newman, M. (2011). *Polar bears*. Henry Holt.

O'Leary, S. (2020). *Maud and Grand-Maud* (K. Pak, Illus.). Random House.

Olson, J. G. (2020). *A little space for me*. Roaring Brook.

Page, R. (2021). *The beak book*. Beach Lane.

Pak, K. (2016). *Goodbye summer, hello autumn*. Henry Holt.

Park, L. S. (2010). *A long walk to water*. Clarion.

Park, L. S. (2019). *Nya's long walk to water* (B. Pinkney, Illus.). Clarion.

Penfold, A. (2018). *Food truck fest!* (M. Dutton, Illus.). Farrar Straus Giroux.

Penfold, A. (2021). *Big feelings* (S. Kaufman, Illus.). Knopf.

Pham, L. (2016). *The bear who wasn't there*. Roaring Brook.

Pham, L. (2021). *Outside, inside*. Roaring Brook.

Portis, A. (2020). *A new green day*. Holiday House.

Prasadam-Halls, S. (2020). *I'm sticking with you* (S. Small, Illus.). Henry Holt.

Pumphrey, J. (2020). *The old truck* (J. Pumphrey, Illus.). W. W. Norton.

Quintero, I. (2019). *My papi has a motorcycle* (Z. Peña, Illus.). Kokila/Penguin.

Read, K. (2019). *One fox: A counting book thriller*. Peachtree.

Rex, A. (2016). *School's first day of school* (C. Robinson, Illus.). Roaring Brook.

Reynolds, E. (2021). *Amara and the bats*. Atheneum.

Richards, D. (2021). *Watch me* (J. Cepeda, Illus.). Feiwel and Friends.

Roberts, J. (2014). *The smallest girl in the smallest grade* (C. Robinson, Illus.). Putnam.

Robinson, C. (2019). *Another*. Atheneum.

Robinson, C. (2020). *You matter*. Atheneum.

Rocco, J. (2011). *Blackout*. Disney/Hyperion.

Rockliff, M. (2021). *Try it! How Frieda Caplan changed the way we eat*. Beach Lane.

Rockwell, L. (2020). *The all-together quilt*. Knopf.

Rosenstock, B. (2018). *Otis and Will discover the deep: The record-setting dive of the Bathysphere*. Little, Brown.

Rosenthal, A. K. (2009). *Yes day!* (T. Lichtenheld, Illus.). HarperCollins.

Saeed, A. (2019). *Bilal cooks daal* (A. Syed, Illus.). Simon & Schuster.

Salas, L. P. (2019). *Lion of the sky: Haiku for all seasons* (M. López, Illus.). Millbrook.

Sayre, A. P. (2013). *Eat like a bear* (S. Jenkins, Illus.). Henry Holt.

Scanlon, L. G. (2018). *Kate, who tamed the wind* (L. White, Illus.). Schwartz & Wade.

Scheele, K. (2021). *A pizza with everything on it* (A. J. Pizza (Miller), Illus.). Chronicle.

Scott, J. (2020). *I talk like a river* (S. Smith, Illus.). Neal Porter/Holiday House.

Sheppard, M. (2020). *My rainy day rocket ship* (C. Palmer, Illus.). Simon & Schuster.

Shiraishi, A. (2020). *How to solve a problem: The rise (and falls) of a rock-climbing champion* (Y. Xiao, Illus.). Make Me a World/Random House.

Singer, M. (2021). *Best day ever!* (L. Nixon, Illus.). Clarion.

Singh, S. J. (2020). *Fauja Singh keeps going: The true story of the oldest person to ever run a marathon* (B. Kaur, Illus.). Kokila/Penguin Random House.

Smith, H. (2019). *A plan for Pops* (B. Kerrigan, Illus.). Orca.

Smith, M. G. (2020). *When we are kind* (N. Neidhardt, Illus.). Orca.

Snyder, G. (2021). *Listen* (S. Graegin, Illus.). Simon & Schuster.

Soontornvat, C. (2020). *Simon at the art museum* (C. Davenier, Illus.). Antheneum.

Soontornvat, C. (2021). *Ramble shamble children* (L. Castillo, Illus.). Nancy Paulsen.

Spencer, S., & McNamara, M. (2020). *The bug girl (a true story)* (Kerascoët, Illus.). Schwartz & Wade.

Spires, A. (2019). *Fairy science*. Crown Books.

Spires, A. (2020). *Fairy science: Solid, liquid, gassy*. Crown Books.

Springstubb, T. (2020). *Khalil and Mr. Hagerty and the backyard treasures* (E. Taherian, Illus.). Candlewick.

Steele, K.-F. (2019). *A normal pig*. HarperCollins.

Sterling, M. (2021). *When Lola visits* (A. Asis, Illus.). Katherine Tegen/HarperCollins.

Stewart, M. (2014). *Feathers: Not just for flying* (S. S. Brannen, Illus.). Charlesbridge.

Stewart, M. (2017). *Can an aardvark bark?* (S. Jenkins, Illus.). Beach Lane.

Stewart, M. (2018). *Pipsqueaks, slowpokes, and stinkers: Celebrating animal underdogs* (S. Laberis, Illus.). Peachtree.

Subisak, T. (2021). *Jenny Mei is sad*. Little, Brown.

Swanson, M. (2020). *Sunrise summer* (R. Behr, Illus.). Imprint.

Tariq, A. (2021). *Fatima's great outdoors* (S. D. Lewis, Illus.). Kokila.

Tekiela, S. (2021). *Whose house is that?* Adventure.

Tey, P. (2018). *In-between things*. Candlewick.

Trevino, C. (2021). *Seaside stroll* (M. Lechuga, Illus.). Charlesbridge.

Trius, M. (2020). *Me and the world: An infographic exploration* (J. Casals, Illus.). Chronicle.

Underwood, D. (2019a). *Ogilvy* (T. L. McBeth, Illus.). Henry Holt.

Underwood, D. (2019b). *Reading beauty* (M. Hunt, Illus.). Chronicle.

Underwood, D. (2020). *Outside in* (C. Derby, Illus.). Houghton Mifflin Harcourt.

VanDerwater, A. L. (2017). *Read! Read! Read!* (R. O'Rourke, Illus.). Wordsong.

VanDerwater, A. L. (2020). *Write! Write! Write!* (R. O'Rourke, Illus.). Wordsong.

Velasquez, E. (2019). *Octopus stew*. Holiday House.

Walker, T. (2020). *Nana Akua goes to school* (A. Harrison, Illus.). Schwartz & Wade.

Wang, A. (2021). *Watercress* (J. Chin, Illus.). Neal Porter/Holiday House.

Ward, C. (1988). *Cookie's week* (T. de Paola, Illus.). Putnam.

Ward, J. (2017). *What will grow?* (S. Ghahremani, Illus.). Bloomsbury.

Ward, J. (2020). *How to find a bird* (D. Sudyka, Illus.). Beach Lane.

Watson, S. (2018). *Best friends in the universe* (L. Pham, Illus.). Scholastic.

Williams, L. (2017). *If sharks disappeared*. Roaring Brook.

Williams, L. (2018). *If polar bears disappeared*. Roaring Brook.

Williams, L. (2019). *If elephants disappeared*. Roaring Brook.

Williams, L. (2021). *If bees disappeared*. Roaring Brook.

Wolff, A. (2021). *How to help a pumpkin grow*. Beach Lane.

Woodson, J. (2018). *The day you begin* (R. López, Illus.). Penguin.

Yang, K. K. (2019). *A map into the world* (S. Kim, Illus.). Carolrhoda.

# Index

Actions, 96–97, 102–103, 126–130
Active participation, 7
Adams, M., 17
Adjectives, 82
    Omu chart, 124
    trio poem work sample, 87
    word wonder, 124
*A Friend for Henry* (Bailey), 79
*A House for Every Bird* (Maynor), 135
Ali, S. K., 89
Allen, T., 190–193
Alliteration, 18
*The All-Together Quilt* (Rockwell), 196
*Amazing Grace* (Hoffman), 47
*A Normal Pig* (Steele), 34–37
*Another* (Robinson), 119
*A Plan for Pops* (Smith), 71
*The Arabic Quilt: An Immigrant Story* (Khalil), 88–91
Archer, M., 205
Ardagh, P., 225
Arnold, A., 74–77
Atinuke, 96–101
Authors' craft moves, 21
    backmatter, 181, 235, 245
    character's inner thoughts, 137
    comparisons, 161, 215
    concrete/shaping poems, 253
    diagrams, 185
    dialogue, 69, 117, 219
    fiction and nonfiction, 105
    figurative language, 239
    graphic format illustrations, 121
    inner thinking, 69, 117
    personification, 173
    poems, 249
    point of view, 81
    problem solving, 61
    repeated phrase, 53
    repetition, 133, 153
    see-saw pattern, 199
    speeding up time, 207
    times of day, 169
    transition words and phrases, 37, 91
    unique poetry techniques, 165
*Avocado Asks: What Am I?* (Abe), 35

Backmatter, 181, 235, 245
Bailey, J., 79
*The Beak Book* (Page), 174–177
Becker, A., 119
Bernstein, A., 142–145
Bernstrom, D., 150–152
*Best Day Ever!* (Singer), 143
*Big Feelings* (Penfold), 23, 51
*Big Papa and the Time Machine* (Bernstrom), 150–152

*Blue Floats Away* (Jonker), 187
Boelts, M., 106–109
Bogan, C., 147
Book experiences, 31
*Bookjoy Wordjoy* (P. Mora), 247
*The Book Tree* (Czajak), 31
Brantley-Newton, V., 251
Brewer, H. D., 191
*The Bug Club* (Gravel), 233
*The Bug Girl (A True Story)* (Spencer & McNamara), 47
*Bunnies on the Bus* (Ardagh), 225
Burr, A., 8
*Butterflies Are Pretty Gross!* (Mosco), 233

Camper, C., 209
*The Camping Trip* (Mann), 213
*Can an Aardvark Bark?* (Stewart), 221
*Catch That Chicken!* (Atinuke), 96–101
Character, Problem, And Solution Reproducible Response Page, 107
Characters
    actions, 102–103
    decisions, 50–53
    describing and understanding, 97–106
    developing self-awareness, 34–39
    dialogue, 138–140
    feelings and emotions of, 42–45, 46–49
    inner thoughts, 137
    opinions, 142–145
    reactions, 54–57
Characters Change Reproducible Response Page, 85
Character-Trait-Clues Reproducible Response Page, 67, 103
Character Trait Tree Reproducible Response Page, 97
Cherry, M. A., 131
Child-friendly definitions. *See* Kid-friendly definitions, vocabulary
Choral reading, 10
Clapping syllables, 36
Co-created class promise, 39
    *See also* Self-promises
Collaborative for Academic, Social, and Emotional Learning (CASEL), 4
Collaboratively negotiating meaning, 4
Commas in series, 52
Community event, 1
Comparisons, 161, 215
Compound words, 56
Comprehension conversation, 14–15, 88–89
    actions, 96–97, 102
    author's purpose, 190–191
    characters feelings and emotions, 42, 46
    decisions, 50, 62
    dialogue, 138

explaining how, 228
exploring with illustrations, 170–171
facts, sharing, 232
historical events, 194–195
ideas/memories, 204–205
illustrations study, 114–115
imagination, 118–119, 134–135
informational text, 174–175
kindness/comfort, 74–75
learning from illustrations, 166–167
learning life lessons, 150–151
make-believe stories, 216–217
narrative nonfiction, 178–179
observations, 208–209
opinions, 142
patterns, 224–225
persistence and ingenuity, 66, 70
picture clue prediction, 122
playful language, 236–237
poems, 246–247
poetic techniques, 250
predictions, 126–127
problem solving, 58, 70
question-answer structure, 158–159, 182–183, 186–187
reactions, characters', 54
real-life story, 212–213
relationship development, 84–85, 88–89
riddles, 220
self-awareness, 34–35
sensory language, 130–131, 240
story elements, 106–107, 110–111
understand others, 78
unique structures, 162–163
Comprehension strategies. *See* Rereading comprehension strategies
Condon, J., 110–113
Contractions, word, 144
Conversations, 12
    language-expanding, 8, 9
    rereading, 6
    *See also* Comprehension conversation
Copp, M. W., 98
Cordell, M., 115
Cornwall, G., 59, 70–73
COVID-19 pandemic, read-aloud experience, 13
*Crossings: Extraordinary Structures for Extraordinary Animals* (Duffield), 175
Curry, J., 115
Curry, P., 115
Cushman, A., 237
Cusolito, M., 166–169
Czajak, P., 31

*The Day You Begin* (Woodson), 89
Decision-making process

characters and, 50-53
consequences, 62
problem solving, 63
Deenihan, J. L. B., 54-57
Deep thinking books, 24
De la Peña, M., 134-137
Diagrams, 185
Dialogic engagement, 12
Dialogue
characters, 138-140
inner thinking and, 69, 117
DiPucchio, K., 66-69
*The Dirt Book: Poems About Animals That Live Beneath Our Feet* (Harrison), 163, 251
*Dirt Cheap* (Hoffman), 58-61
Dorléans, M., 205
*Drawn Together* (Lê), 55
*DROP: An Adventure Through the Water Cycle* (Moon), 186-189, 237
Duffield, K. S., 175

EARS (expression, automatic word recognition, rhythm and phrasing, smoothness), 20-21
Echo reading, 10
Elliott, Z., 24
Ellipses, 64. *See* Punctuation
Elya, S. M., 111
Empathize
kindness/comfort, 74-77
point of view, 81
understand others, 78-82
Evans, S. W., 191
*Explorers* (Cordell), 115
Expository nonfiction books, 174-181
Expressive words
fluency in reading, 73
word wonder, 48
*Eyes that Kiss in the Corners* (Ho), 131

*Fairy Science: Solid, Liquid, Gassy* (Spires), 187
*Fatima's Great Outdoors* (Tariq), 213
*Fauja Singh Keeps Going: The True Story of the Oldest Person to Ever Run a Marathon* (Singh), 43
Ferry, B., 84-87
Fiction books
actions, 96-97, 102-103
illustrations, 117-122
learning life lessons, 150-152
and nonfiction, 105
picture clue prediction, 122-129
point of view, 139-146
story elements, 105-106, 110
structure of story, 106-113
visualizing, 130-137
Figurative language, 239
Fill in the blank, fluency-building method, 10
Floca, B., 196
Flood, N. B., 79
Fluency in reading, 5, 9-10

bold print, 128
excitement, 101
expressive words, 73
italicized words, 141, 211
joining repeated parts, 113
punctuation, 145
reader's theater, 248, 252
repeated phrase, 45
speech bubbles, 76
tag-team reading, 223
*Flying Deep: Climb Inside Deep-Sea Submersible ALVIN* (Cusolito), 166-169
Formative assessment sources, 17
Fountas, I., 11-12
Franklin, A., 46
*Fred Gets Dressed* (Brown), 35
*Frog and Beaver* (James), 107

*A Garden to Save the Birds* (McClure), 51
Give-and-take relationship, reader and text, 11
Gravel, E., 233
Griffin, M. B., 208-211
Grimes, N., 147

*Hair Love* (Cherry), 131
*Harlem Grown: How One Big Idea Transformed a Neighborhood* (Hillery), 50-53
*Harold Loves His Woolly Hat* (Kousky), 126-129
Harrison, D. L., 163, 251
Havis, A. B., 167
Haworth-Booth, E., 62-65
Heard, G., 162-165
Heavenrich, S., 232-235
*Hello, Rain!* (Maclear), 236-239
High-frequency words, 20, 192
number words, 210
question words, 180
word hunt, 230
Hillery, G., 50
Hill, S. L., 171
*Hippy-Hoppy Toad* (Archer), 22
Hoang, Z. G., 75
Hoffman, M., 47, 58-61
Ho, J., 131
Hood, S., 250-253
Ho, R., 170-173
Hort burst planning, 25-27
*How to Find a Bird* (Ward), 228-231
*How to Make a Bird* (McKinlay), 229
*How to Solve a Problem: The Rise (and Falls) of a Rock-Climbing Champion* (Shiraishi), 229
Hudson, N., 143

Illustrations
book selection and, 14, 21-22
characters' decisions, 50
characters' feelings and, 42, 46
characters' reactions, 54
decisions and consequences, 62

exploring with, 170-173
graphic format, 121
to infer ideas, 149
learning from, 166-169
persistence, 66
picture clue prediction, 122
problem solving, 58, 70
relationship development, 84
rereading comprehension strategies, 116
self-awareness, 38
study, 114-121
Imagination, 134-137
Imaginative texts, 118-121
*I'm Sticking With You* (Prasadam-Halls), 138-141
*In a Jar* (Marcero), 204-207
*In-Between Things* (Tey), 209
Infographic learning process, 177, 189
Informational text and images
exploring with illustrations, 170-173
infographic learning, 177
learning from illustrations, 166-169
Inquiry-based learning, 11
Inspiration
facts, 232-235
patterns, 220-227
playful language, 236-239
poems, 246-253
riddles, 220-223
sensory language, 240-245
stories, 212-219
text structure, 229-235
uncover ideas, 204-211
word collection, 236-245
Instructional context, 11
Interjections, 188
Invitation Reproducible Response Page, 181
*I Promise* (James), 38-41
Irresistible texts selection, 22-25
deep thinking, 24
interesting topics, 24
memorable language, 23
repeated words/phrases, 23
rhythmic books, 22-23
vocabulary, 23
Ismail, Y., 7
Italicized words, 21, 141
*I Talk Like a River* (Scott), 78-82
*I Want to Ride the Tap Tap* (Joseph), 224-227
*I Will Dance* (Flood), 79

*Jabari Tries* (Cornwall), 59, 70-73
James, L., 38-41
James, S., 107
John, J., 107
Johnston, P., 12
Jonker, T., 187
Joseph, D., 224-227
*Journey* (Becker), 119
Joyner, A., 103
Judge, L., 175
*Just Like Me* (Brantley-Newton), 251

*Kate, Who Tamed the Wind* (Scanlon), 63
*Keeping the City Going* (Floca), 196
*Khalil and Mr. Hagerty and the Backyard Treasures* (Springstubb), 85
Kid-friendly definitions, vocabulary, 13
Kindness/comfort chart, 74–75
Kousky, V., 126–129
Ku Rhee, H., 217

Language
    descriptive, 168
    figurative, 239
    playful, 236–239
    sensory, 130–131, 240–245
Language-expanding conversations, 8–9
*La Princesa and the Pea* (Elya), 111
*Last Stop on Market Street* (de la Peña), 135
*The Last Straw: Kids vs. Plastics* (Hood), 250–253
*The Last Tree* (Haworth-Booth), 62–65
Layton, N., 63
Learning life lessons, 150–152
Learning process, 8
    illustrations and, 166–169
    infographic, 177
    poems, 146–153
    See also Reading process
Lê, M., 55
Lendler, I., 71
*Let's Play! A Book About Making Friends* (McCardie), 75
*Lift* (Lê), 21, 118–121
Lindstrom, C., 103
*Lion of the Sky: Haiku for All Seasons* (Salas), 221
Listening sounds, 17–18
    See also Phonological awareness
Literacy development, 1
Literacy skill/strategies, 16–22
    authors' craft moves, 21
    comprehension, 21
    high-frequency words, 20
    letters to sounds (phonics), 19
    phonological awareness, 17–18
    punctuation, 20
    reread for fluency, 20–21
    word wonder, 21
*The Little Red Fort* (Maier), 59
Looking at Art Reproducible Response Page, 115
*Love Is Powerful* (Brewer), 191

Maclear, K., 236–239
Maier, B., 59
Make-believe stories, 216–219
Mann, J. K., 213
*Map Into the World* (Yang), 85
Marcero, D., 204–207
*Mars! Earthlings Welcome* (McAnulty), 171
*Mars' First Friends: Come on Over, Rovers!* (Hill), 171

*Maud and Grand-Maud* (O'Leary), 151
Maynor, M., 135
McAnulty, S., 171
McCardie, A., 75
McClure, W., 51
McGinty, A. B., 167
McKinlay, M., 229
McNamara, M., 47
Memorable language books, 23
Memories, 204–212
Messner, K., 240–245
Metcalf, L. H., 163
Miller, P. Z., 39
*Milo Imagines the World* (de la Peña), 134–137
Moon, E. K., 186–189, 237
Mora, O., 122–126
Mora, P., 247
Mosco, R., 233
Muhammad, I., 89
Multilingual learners, 11
My Inner Weather Report Reproducible Response Page, 163
*My Papi Has a Motorcycle* (Quintero), 130–133
*My Rainy Day Rocket Ship* (Sheppard), 22
*My Thoughts Are Clouds: Poems for Mindfulness* (Heard), 162–165

*Nana Akua Goes to School* (Walker), 151
Narrative nonfiction books, 178–181
*A New Green Day* (Portis), 220–223
*A New Kind of Wild* (Hoang), 75
*Nia and the New Free Library* (Lendler), 71
*The Night Walk* (Dorléans), 205
Nonfiction books
    author's purpose, 191–196, 199
    comparisons, 161
    historical events, 194–199
    informational text, 174–179
    learning from illustrations, 166–173
    narrative, 178–181
    questions, 182–189
    text structure/pattern, 159–166
    topics and details, 174–181
    unique structures, 162–166
*Not Quite Snow White* (Franklin), 46–49
*No Voice Too Small: Fourteen Young Americans Making History* (Metcalf), 163
*Nya's Long Walk to Water: A Step at a Time* (Park), 43

Observer center, 115, 171
*Octopus Stew* (Velasquez), 216–219
*The Old Truck* (Pumphrey), 225
O'Leary, S., 151
Onomatopoeia, 18, 132, 218, 238
*On the Go Awesome* (Detlefsen), 23
*Oona* (DiPucchio), 66–69
Opinions, 142–145
Oral language development, 8

*Otis and Will Discover the Deep: The Record-Setting Dive of the Bathysphere* (Rosenstock), 167
*Outside In* (Underwood), 146–149
*Outside, Inside* (Pham), 194–199
Outside-inside chart, 147
*Over and Under the Pond* (Messner), 242
*Over and Under the Rainforest* (Messner), 240–245

Page, R., 174–177
*The Paper Kingdom* (Ku Rhee), 217
Parentheses, 68
*Parker Looks Up: An Extraordinary Moment* (Curry & Curry), 115
Park, L. S., 43
Patterns, 224–227
Penfold, A., 51
Personification, 173
Pham, L., 21, 194–199
Phonemes, 17
Phonics, 19
    chunks in big words, 86
    -ed ending, 234
    short-i word families, 112
    word families, 44, 226
Phonological awareness, 17–18
    alliteration, 100
    clapping syllables, 36
    rhyming words, 40, 140
Phrases, 18, 23, 37, 53, 91, 136
Picture clue prediction, 122–129
Pinnell, G. S., 11–12
*The Pirates Are Coming!* (Condon), 110–113
*A Pizza With Everything on It* (Scheele), 217
*A Place Inside of Me* (Elliott), 24
Playful language, 236–239
*Play in the Wild: How Baby Animals Like to Have Fun* (Judge), 175
Poems
    learning from, 246–249
    techniques and devices, 250–253
Poetry techniques, 165
Portis, A., 220–223
*The Power of One: Every Act of Kindness Counts* (Ludwig), 24
Prasadam-Halls, S., 138–141
Prediction using evidence, 122–129
Prepositions, 244
Problem solving, 58–61, 70–73
    cause and effect, 65
    decisions and consequences, 63
    tips for, 71
*The Proudest Blue: The Story of Hijab and Family* (Muhammad & Ali), 89
Pumphrey, J., 225
Punctuation, 20
    commas in series, 52, 206
    creative conventions, 164
    ellipses, 64
    exclamation marks, 104
    parentheses, 68

quotation marks, 222
riddles, 160
sentences, 193
*The Purple Puffy Coat* (Boelts), 106–109

Questions
answer structure, 158–161
high-frequency words, 180
Quintero, I., 133
Quotation marks, 222

"Rainforest Layers" Reproducible
Song Page, 241
*Ramble Scramble Children* (Soontornvat), 23
*The Ramped-Up Read Aloud* (Walther), 13
Rasinski, T., 20
Read-aloud experience, 1, 2, 14–15
conversation, 12
COVID-19 pandemic, 13
extension of, 13
kid-friendly definitions, vocabulary, 13
relationship-building practice of, 13
and shared reading interactions, 11–15
student response options, 12
Reader's theater, 248, 252
*Reading Beauty* (Underwood), 111
Reading process
demonstration of, 10–11
inner workings of, 11–12
*See also* Fluency in reading
Read, K., 9
*Read! Read! Read!* (VanDerwater), 247
Real-life stories, 212–215
Real objects and make-believe chart, 120
*Red Rover: Curiosity on Mars* (Ho), 170–173
Relationship skills, 5
*Remarkably You* (Miller), 39
Reproducible
Character, Problem, and Solution
Response Page, 107
Characters Change Response Page, 85
Character's Feelings Response Page, 43
Character-Trait-Clues Response
Page, 67, 103
Character Trait Tree Response Page, 97
Invitation Response Page, 181
Looking at Art Response Page, 115
My Inner Weather Report Response
Page, 163
"Rainforest Layers" Song Page, 241
Rereading Song, 6
three3-2-1 Response Page, 233
Retelling Story Response Page, 111
Retell/Recount Response Page, 179
Riddle Response Page, 221
Time Capsule Response Page, 195–196
Where Does Your Door Lead?
Response Page, 119
Reread for fluency, 20–21
Rereading, 2, 6–7
Rereading comprehension strategies, 21
backmatter, 214, 245

cause-and-effect relationships, 65, 184
characters' feelings, change in, 49, 77
detail detectives, 57
identifying character traits, 129
infographics, 177, 189
investigation process, 60
labels, 231
picture clue prediction, 125
point of view, 152, 172
problem solving, 72
reactions of characters', 65, 184
real objects and imaginary, 120
turning point in story, 109
words and illustrations, 116, 149
Responsible decision making, 5
Retell/Recount Reproducible
Response Page, 179
Retell the Story Reproducible
Response Page, 111
Rhyming words, 18, 22–23, 40
Rhythmic books, 22–23
Richards, D., 42, 98
Riddle Reproducible Response Page, 221
Riddles, 160, 220–223
Robinson, C., 119
Rockwell, L., 196
Rosenstock, B., 167
Routman, R., 1

Salas, L. P., 221
Scanlon, L. G., 63
Scheele, K., 217
Scott, J., 78–82
*The Sea Knows* (McGinty & Havis), 167
*Seaside Stroll* (Trevino), 23
Self-awareness, 5, 34–35, 37, 39
Self-promises, 38–39
Sensory language, 130–133
Sentence creation, 193
Shared reading interactions, 1
active participation, 7
benefits, 1
benefits of short bursts, 2
camaraderie, 3
fluency-focused methods, 9–10
irresistible texts selection, 22–25
language-expanding
conversations, 8–9
learners engagement, 7–8
literacy skill/strategies, 16–22
multilingual learners, 11
oral language development, 8
read-aloud experiences and, 11–15
reading process demonstration, 10–11
reasons to shake up, 3–11
rereading, 6–7
short burst planning, 25–27
story sense, 9
teachers as planners, 16
virtual, 16
Sheppard, M., 22
Shiraishi, A., 229

Short bursts
planning, 25–27
of shared reading, 2
Similes, word wonder, 80
*Simon at the Art Museum* (Soontornvat), 114–117
Singer, M., 143
Singh, S. J., 43
*Small Kindness* (McAnulty), 24
Smith, H., 71
Smith, M. C., 20
Smith, M. G., 39
*Soaked* (Cushman), 237
Social awareness, 5
Social-emotional learning (SEL), 4
competencies, 4–5
*Something's Wrong! A Bear, A Hare, and
Some Underwear* (John), 107
*Sometimes People March* (Allen), 190–193
Soontornvat, C., 23, 114–117
Sounds (phonics)
letters to, 19
listening, 17–18
*See also* Phonics
*Southwest Sunrise* (Grimes), 147
Speech bubbles, 76
Spencer, S., 47
Spires, A., 187
Springstubb, T., 85
*Stand Up, Speak Up* (Joyner), 103
*Star of the Party: The Solar System
Celebrates!* (Carr), 178–181
Steele, K.-F., 34
Sterling, M., 23
Stewart, M., 221
Stories
make-believe, 216–219
real-life, 212–215
Story elements
identifying, 106–107
to predict and retell, 110–111
Story schema, 9
*Sunrise Summer* (Swanson), 212–215
Swanson, M., 212–215
*Swashby and the Sea* (Ferry), 84–87
Syllable clapping, 36
Synonyms, 124

Tag-team reading, 10
Tariq, A., 213
Teachers as planners, 16
Techniques in poems, 250–253
Tekiela, S., 158–161
*Ten Beautiful Things* (Griffin), 208–211
*Ten Ways to Hear Snow* (Camper), 209
Tey, P., 209
*Thank You, Omu!* (O. Mora), 122–126
Thinking flexibly, 51–53, 55, 57
*13 Ways to Eat a Fly* (Heavenrich), 232–235
3-2-1 Reproducible Response Page, 233
Time Capsule Reproducible Response Page,
195–196
Transition tool, 11–12

Transition words and phrases, 37
*The Tree* (Layton), 63
Trevino, C., 23
Turning point of story, 109
*Turtle in a Tree* (Hudson), 143

Uncover ideas
    ideas/memories, 204–207
    observations, 208–211
Underwood, D., 111, 146–149
*Up in the Garden and Down
    in the Dirt* (Messner), 242

VanDerwater, A. L., 246–249
Velasquez, E., 216–219
Verbs, 82, 176
Virtual shared reading interactions, 16
Visualization, 130–138
Vocabulary
    kid-friendly definitions, 13
    knowledge, 23

Walker, T., 151
Ward, J., 228–231
*Watch Me* (Richards), 42–45, 98
*We Are Water Protectors* (Lindstrom), 103
*We Love Fishing!* (Bernstein), 142–145
*We March* (Evans), 191
*What's the Matter, Marlo?* (Arnold), 74–77
*When Grandma Gives You a Lemon Tree*
    (Deenihan), 55
*When Grandpa Gives You a Toolbox*
    (Deenihan), 54–57
*When Lola Visits* (Sterling), 23
*When We Are Kind* (Smith), 39
*Where Are You From?* (Méndez), 4
Where Does Your Door Lead? Reproducible
    Response Page, 119
*Where's Rodney* (Bogan), 147
*Wherever I Go* (Copp), 98
*Whose House Is That?* (Tekiela), 158–161
*Wonder Walkers* (Archer), 205
Woodson, J., 89

Word family chart, 45
Word hunt, 230
Word play, 18
Words/phrases, 23, 37
Word wonder, 21
    adjectives, 87, 108
    compound words, 56, 148, 198
    contractions, 144
    descriptive language, 168
    expressive words, 48
    interjections, 188
    onomatopoeia, 132, 218, 238
    prepositions, 244
    said, 90
    sensory words and phrases, 136
    similes, 80
    synonyms, 124
    verbs, 176
*Write! Write! Write!* (VanDerwater), 246–249

Yang, K. K., 85

A SAGE Publishing Company

**CORWIN HAS ONE MISSION:** to enhance education through intentional professional learning.

We build long-term relationships with our authors, educators, clients, and associations who partner with us to develop and continuously improve the best evidence-based practices that establish and support lifelong learning.

# Because...

## ALL TEACHERS ARE LEADERS

**DOMINIQUE SMITH,
DOUGLAS FISHER, NANCY FREY**

Take an active approach toward disrupting the negative effects of labels and assumptions that interfere with student learning.

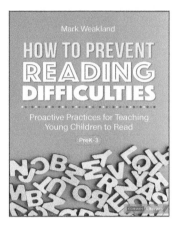

**MARK WEAKLAND**

Build on decades of evidence and years of experience to understand how the brain learns to read and how to apply that understanding to Tier 1 instruction.

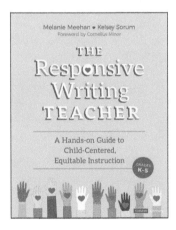

**MELANIE MEEHAN, KELSEY SORUM**

Learn how to adapt curriculum to meet the needs of the whole child. Each chapter offers intentional steps for responsive instruction across four domains: academic, linguistic, cultural, and social-emotional.

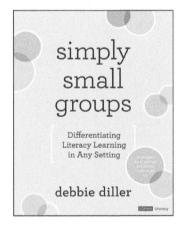

**DEBBIE DILLER**

Discover concrete guidance for tailoring the small-group experience to literacy instruction in order to give every reader a pathway to success.

**To order your copies, visit corwin.com/literacy**

At Corwin Literacy we have put together a collection of just-in-time, classroom-tested, practical resources from trusted experts that allow you to quickly find the information you need when you need it.

**DOUGLAS FISHER, NANCY FREY, NICOLE LAW**

Using a structured, three-pronged approach—skill, will, and thrill—students experience reading as a purposeful act with this new comprehensive model of reading instruction.

**PAM KOUTRAKOS**

Packed with ready-to-go lessons and tools, this user-friendly resource provides ways to weave together different aspects of literacy using one mentor text.

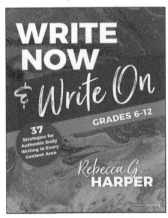

**REBECCA G. HARPER**

Customizable strategies turn students' informal writing into a springboard for daily writing practice in every content area—with a focus on academic vocabulary, summarizing, and using textual evidence.

**MELANIE MEEHAN, CHRISTINA NOSEK, MATTHEW JOHNSON, DAVE STUART JR., MATTHEW R. KAY**

This series offers actionable answers to your most pressing questions about teaching reading, writing, and ELA.

**CORWIN**